WITHDRAWN

Pitt Latin American Series

Pitt Series in Policy and Institutional Studies

POLITICS
WITHIN
THE STATE

ELITE BUREAUCRATS AND INDUSTRIAL POLICY IN AUTHORITARIAN BRAZIL

BEN ROSS SCHNEIDER

University of Pittsburgh Press

Published by the
University of Pittsburgh Press,
Pittsburgh, Pa. 15260
Copyright © 1991, the
University of Pittsburgh Press
All rights reserved
Eurospan, London
Manufactured in the United States of America

Library of Congress Cataloging–in–Publication Data

Schneider, Ben Ross.
    Politics within the state : elite bureaucrats and industrial
policy in authoritarian Brazil / Ben Ross Schneider.
        p.   cm. — (Pitt Latin American series)
    Includes bibliographical references and index.
    ISBN 0-8229-3689-5
    1. Government executives—Brazil.   2.   Bureaucracy—Brazil
3.   Industry and state—Brazil.   4.   Government business enterprises—
Brazil—Case studies.   I.   Title   II.   Series
JL2449.E9S36   1991
654.81′01—dc20   91-9333
                                                                          CIP

A CIP catalogue record for this book is available from the British Library.

To my parents

Mackay McCord Schneider
Ben R. Schneider, Jr.

CONTENTS

Tables and Illustrations

Tables

Figures

Maps

Glossary

abertura   The political "opening" of the authoritarian regime. *Abertura* was a gradual process of liberalization begun in 1974 and completed with the transition to civilian rule in 1985.

anfíbio   "Amphibian," a military officer who enters electoral or party politics and who is equally at home in political and military environments.

autarquia   "Autarchy," a semi-independent government organ.

classe política   The political class of Brazil is made up of elected and party officials. At times it may also include politically active generals and bureaucrats, as well as powerful individuals who may temporarily be without formal positions.

confidence position   This term is a translation of the Portuguese, *cargo de confiança*, which denotes positions that can be filled by personal appointment and where appointers usually seek subordinates they can trust and confide in. The usual equivalent in the United States is political appointment. A confidence appointee is one who fills such a confidence position.

estatização   "Statization," the process of increasing state control over the economy, especially the expansion and diversification of state enterprises.

grandeza   "Grandeur," a (largely military) vision of Brazil's future superpower status.

mineiro   A native or resident of the state of Minas Gerais.

panelinha   "Small pot," an informal, personalized power group or clique.

Abbreviations

ABDIB Associação Brasileira para o Desenvolvimento das Indústrias de Base (Brazilian Association for the Development of Basic Industries)

Acesita Companhia Aços Especiais Itabira (Itabira Specialty Steel Company)

Açominas Aço Minas Gerais S.A. (Minas Gerais Steel)

Albrás Alumínio Brasileiro S.A.

Alunorte Alumina Norte do Brasil S.A.

Amza Amazônia Mineração (Amazon Mining)

Arena Aliança Renovadora Nacional (National Renewal Alliance)

BAHINT Booz, Allen, and Hamilton International

BNDE Banco Nacional de Desenvolvimento Econômico. After May 1982, **BNDES**—Banco Nacional de Desenvolvimento Econômico e Social (National Bank for Economic and Social Development)

Cacex Carteira de Comércio Exterior of the Banco do Brasil (International Trade Bureau)

CBA Companhia Brasileira de Alumínio

CDE Conselho de Desenvolvimento Econômico (Economic Development Council)

CDI Conselho de Desenvolvimento Industrial (Industrial Development Council)

CIP Conselho Interministerial de Preços (Interministerial Price Council)

CIPGC Conselho Interministerial do Programa Grande Carajás (Interministerial Council for the Greater Carajás Program)

CMN Conselho Monetário Nacional (National Monetary Council)

CNI Confederação Nacional de Indústria

Cofavi Companhia Ferro e Aço de Vitória

CONSIDER Conselho Nacional da Indústria Siderúrgica. After 1974, Conselho Nacional de Não-Ferrosos e de Siderurgia (National Council for Non-Ferrous Metals and Steel)

Cosipa Companhia Siderúrgica Paulista (Paulista Steel Company)

CPA Conselho de Política Aduaneira (Customs Policy Council)

xv

CPRM Companhia de Pesquisa de Recursos Minerais (Mineral Resources Research Company)

CSN Companhia Siderúrgica Nacional (National Steel Company)

CST Companhia Siderúrgica de Tubarão (Tubarão Steel Company)

CVRD Companhia Vale do Rio Doce

DOCEGEO Rio Doce Geologia e Mineração

DOCENAVE Vale do Rio Doce Navegação

DNPM Departamento Nacional de Produção Mineral (National Department of Mineral Production

Eletrobrás Centrais Elétricas Brasileiras

Eletronorte Centrais Elétricas do Norte do Brasil

Finame Agência Especial de Financiamento Industrial (Special Agency for Industrial Finance)

GCIS Grupo Consultativo da Indústria Siderúrgica (Consultative Group for the Steel Industry)

IBA International Bauxite Association

IBS Instituto Brasileiro de Siderurgia (Brazilian Steel Institute)

ISI Import-substituting industrialization

IUPERJ Instituto Universitário de Pesquisa do Rio de Janeiro (University Research Institute of Rio de Janeiro)

LMSA Light Metal Smelters Association

MDB Movimento Democrático Brasileiro

MIC Ministério da Indústria e do Comércio

MME Ministério das Minas e Energia

MNC Multinational corporation

MRN Mineração Rio do Norte

Nalco Nippon Amazon Aluminum Company

PDS Partido Democrático Social (Democratic Social party)

Petrobrás Petróleo Brasileiro

Petroquisa Petrobrás Química (Petrobrás Chemicals)

PFL Partido da Frente Liberal (Liberal Front party)

PMDB Partido do Movimento Democrático Brasileiro (party of the Brazilian Democratic Movement)

PND II Plano Nacional de Desenvolvimento II

PSN Plano Siderúrgico Nacional (National Steel Plan)

RDEP Rio Doce Engenharia e Planejamento

Seplan Secretaria de Planejamento (Secretary of Planning)

SEST Secretaria de Controle das Empresas Estatais (Secretariat for the Control of State Enterprises)

Siderbrás Siderurgia Brasileira S.A.
SIMESP Sindicato da Indústria de Máquinas do Estado de São Paulo
SNI Servico Nacional de Informações
Sudene Superintendência do Desenvolvimento do Nordeste
USIBA Usina Siderúrgica da Bahia
Usiminas Usinas Siderúrgicas de Minas Gerais

Preface

> When people ask me why I keep
> wanting to go to Brazil, part of the
> answer is that it's because the country
> is so vast and so raw and sometimes so
> monstrously beautiful; but it's mostly
> because I find it easy to get along with
> the people.
>
> —John Dos Passos, 1963

STUDYING BRAZIL from a comparative perspective is full of surprises, frustrations, and rewards (in this sequence for the fortunate researcher). What makes for surprise is that social and political actors keep acting out of character. Social classes, parties, military officers, races, interest groups, and the state and its officials continually defy expectations derived from standard social science. Many conceptual labels apply in their most general sense, but researchers who use them rigidly do so at their peril.

The limited utility of traditional concepts became quite clear in my analysis of bureaucratic behavior. Little in organization theory or public administration helped to explain the behaviors observed in the Brazilian state. This discrepancy was surprising; it quickly became frustrating. The reward comes in that the patterns of bureaucratic behavior that predominate in Brazil exist in less extreme form in most other countries, which opens up new avenues for comparative research.

For instance, appointments proved to be the key to power relations in the bureaucracy. Appointments of course influence politics in all countries, but this mechanism, which distributes a sizable chunk of power, is one of the more neglected topics in political science. The evidence from Brazil may help, then, to develop a more general understanding of the recondite relationships that appointments create. Similarly, bureaucratic circulation is higher in Brazil than in most industrial democracies . This high circulation weakens formal organization and hence reduces the utility of concepts developed to explain bureaucratic behavior in the First World. However, understanding the effects of circulation in Brazil allows one to return to comparative study with a powerful new factor for explaining variations in patterns of bureaucratic politics.

This study does of course engage the prevailing theoretical and conceptual debate on bureaucratic politics and addresses a wide range of sub-literatures including those on elite administrators, public policy, state enterprise, state-led industrialization, bureaucratic authoritarianism, public administration, and the state. From a distance these sub-literatures appear to focus on pretty much the same thing—the executive bureaucracy. What is surprising though is the lack of integration among these subfields. Besides contributing to each, I hope this study facilitates an overdue dialogue among them.

The attempt to address these literatures exacerbates centrifugal tendencies in the book. I was initially often tempted to divide the research into two separate monographs: one on bureaucratic careers and politics (part I) and the other on case studies in industrial policy (part II). In some ways this separation would have fitted better conventional subfields, classifications, and cataloguing systems. Yet it was precisely this artificial separation between public administration and politics, between elite studies and industrial policy, that I wanted from the outset to overcome.

Attempting the synthesis made it clearer why the divisions existed before. Uniting the two parts was harder than imagined and the result is two interrelated yet fairly independent analyses. The case studies in part II do not attempt a full empirical test of the propositions advanced in part I. Nor is all of the argument in part I necessary to explain the outcomes in Part II. Nonetheless, the linkage between the two still goes further than previous attempts, and the whole is greater than the sum of the parts. Moreover, since neither half depends fully on the other, and readers with particular interests in bureaucratic politics and elites can focus primarily on part I and those more interested in Brazilian industrial policy can skim through to part II.

At the end of his study of modernization in the 1960s in Brazil, Philippe Schmitter noted that for all the changes brought on by rapid industrialization, there was still an enduring, underlying, informal system. *O sistema* was only dimly perceptible, but it guided elite behavior and explained many discrepancies between the formal and informal, public and private, apparent and real. Twenty years later the system was still there. It was much changed, but still powerful and still arcane. What for Schmitter was epilogue was for me a point of departure and in the end the body of this work. Partly because *o sistema* lacks organization charts, by-laws, committee minutes, and annual reports, I ended up extending my field work well beyond the year initially allotted. In the process I incurred many debts.

The Inter-American Foundation funded my field work in Brazil from December 1983 to October 1985 (it is of course not responsible for the views expressed here). IUPERJ, the Instituto Universitário de Pesquisa do Rio de Janeiro, provided me with an office and administrative support. Tema Pechman's research assistance was indispensable. She was very efficient and creative in tracking down articles, data, and lost technocrats who, as I discuss at length, were always on the move.

I asked a great deal of the Brazilian state, and the parts I contacted were remarkably forthcoming and willing to give of their time and information. I thank the hundreds of government officials who met with me or answered my calls and letters. In return I can only try to render their views as faithfully as possible.

One of my earliest debts is to one generation of the Berkeley mafia. When we shared an office in Berkeley in 1980, Andrea Calabi, Paolo Zaghen, Jerry Reiss, and Edson Nunes helped my research along even before I had a question. Later, Barry Ames, Leslie Armijo, Nancy Bermeo, Luiz Carlos Bresser Pereira, Stephen Bunker, Forrest Colburn, David Collier, Frank Dobbin, Albert Fishlow, Élio Gaspari, Maria D'Alva Kinzo, Atul Kohli, David Leonard, Raymundo Machado, Joel Rennó, Gesner Oliveira, Paul Sigmund, Helen Shapiro, John Waterbury, Eliza Willis, and John Zysman read all or parts of earlier drafts. I am grateful for their comments. My deepest gratitude goes to my closest critic, Kathleen Thelen, who improved this project at every stage.

Several institutions and individuals assisted with the final revisions. The Program in Latin American Studies at Princeton University funded brief visits to Brazil in 1988 and 1989. In 1990, CEBRAP, the Centro Brasileiro de Análise e Planejamento, and the Instituto de Economia do Setor Público provided office space and logistical assistance, and Kristin Johnson and Marcos Moraes helped in my research.

Berlin, April 1991

Part I

The Argument

1

Studying the Brazilian State

Providence has not created mankind
entirely dependent or entirely free. It
is true that around every man a fatal
circle is traced beyond which he cannot pass; but within the wide verge of
that circle he is powerful and free.

—Alexis de Tocqueville[1]

IN 1974, THE YEAR OF Brazil's worst trade deficit ever, imports of
aluminum jumped to nearly four times their level of 1970 and
nearly exceeded domestic production for the first time in decades. Some months later, Fernando Roquette Reis, Eduardo
Carvalho, and other managers from the Companhia Vale do
Rio Doce (CVRD), one of Brazil's largest state enterprises, were
sitting across the table from the representatives of a Japanese
aluminum consortium.[2] The negotiations over the timetable
for constructing a giant joint venture in aluminum were detailed, time consuming, and often exasperating. In one of the
many lulls when the Brazilian team waited for a response or a
translation, Reis jotted something down on a scrap of paper and
slid it over to Carvalho. "Edu," it said, "why don't we build our
own smelter in Rio now and start producing our own aluminum?" Carvalho initialed it "OK" and passed it on to two other
directors, who also agreed.

However, the project quickly ran into stiff opposition. Managers of the state electricity companies did not want to guarantee cheap, plentiful energy. Private aluminum producers did
not want another competitor. Officials in the state development
bank refused to finance it. And President Geisel would not approve it without a private partner.

Undaunted, Reis and especially Carvalho persevered and
wove together a coalition with contacts in the state government

3

of Rio de Janeiro and in other planning agencies. They even managed to get a loan from the World Bank and a minority private partner. In 1978, after three years of planning and politicking, they started constructing an 80,000 ton (per year) plant. In 1982, Valesul, a CVRD aluminum subsidiary, started smelting four years ahead of the joint venture with the Japanese group, and Brazil became self-sufficient in aluminum. By 1987, Brazil was the world's fourth largest exporter of the metal.

Those who analyze strategies of state-led development are really writing about a composite of thousands of decisions and political battles such as Valesul made by thousands of officials such as Carvalho and Reis. However, some of the most neglected subjects of comparative research are the mechanisms that motivate, coordinate, and facilitate these myriad decisions and the factors that determine who wins in the bureaucratic politics of making industrial policy.

Brazil was one of the most successful examples in the postwar period of state-led industrialization, at least until the debt debacle of the 1980s, and offers a promising starting point for filling these empirical and analytic gaps. Brazil grew at a remarkable 7 percent per year from 1945 to 1980, and moved up from around the fortieth largest capitalist economy to the eighth. Many factors contributed to this growth. Brazil has extraordinary natural resources. An inviting climate, fertile soil (much of it still untilled), abundant mineral deposits, and vast river potential eased many development constraints. Brazil's industrial regions boast an entrepreneurial drive and growth mania rivaled by few countries in history. In politics, Brazil has not been prone to stability, but it has a relatively cohesive political culture that has attenuated the crippling class, racial, and ideological polarizations that accompanied and at times stalled industrialization elsewhere. Until the 1980s the international economy was very accommodating for an industrializing country hungry for capital, imports, and export markets.

All these factors facilitated and conditioned industrialization, but they did not lead and orchestrate the process. The ubiquitous and highly visible hand of the state did. Abundant resources, entrepreneurial spirit, and international capital would

Map 1. Brazil: Major States and Cities

probably have shaped some form of industrialization, but
Brazilian industry today is much more the consequence of

conscious and deliberate state intervention. The questions of how, why, and toward what ends the state managed this intervention first inspired this research.

Previous studies have analyzed the developmentalism that inspired political leaders, both civilian and military, and the political coalitions that favored state-led industrialization. What is less understood is how top-level directives to industrialize got transformed into industry, which is only partially and secondarily a question of implementation. Preponderant political will at the top is a necessary condition for industrialization, but so too is commensurate will and capability of officials at the second and third levels of the bureaucracy who decide how much of what industries to build.

In Brazil the puzzle is that the state should hardly work, let alone promote rapid economic transformation.[3] The extreme fragmentation of the bureaucracy would appear to thwart even minimal policy coordination and coherence.[4] In 1985 the new Ministry of Debureaucratization (*sic*) and the Secretariat of Planning (Seplan) conducted censuses of all central government agencies, "councils, commissions, departments, superintendencies, institutes, and *autarquias*." Seplan officials counted about 20,000 agencies, which they estimated to cover only about a third of the state. They identified 553 different agencies in health, 339 in education, 282 in industry and commerce, and 897 agencies just to coordinate other agencies (*Veja*, 30 October 1985). Moreover, policy makers often lack training for their jobs and move from job to job so quickly that their familiarity with the agencies they run is at best fleeting. In addition, the president of Brazil has the power to appoint over fifty thousand officials, tens of thousands more than most national leaders (the Japanese prime minister appoints a few dozen, and the U.S. president appoints several thousand). Fifty thousand personal political appointments in Brazil open up an equal number of opportunities for nepotism, patronage, corruption, and simple incompetence.

Most theories of organization and public administration can explain why a bureaucracy afflicted by personalism, fragmentation, and "adhocracy" should not work. But not only does the

Brazilian bureaucracy often work, but it has also led industrialization. A closer examination of circulation, careers, and appointments reveals why.

The argument, in abbreviated form, is as follows: Rapid bureaucratic circulation weakens organizational loyalties and increases reliance on personal ties, a factor that in turn further undermines formal organization (chapter 2). High mobility allows officials to formulate and coordinate policy in spite of the organizational fragmentation, because they care less about their agencies and because the stronger personal ties provide alternative channels of communication. Personalism can in fact enhance bureaucratic performance. And, since officials' preferences do not necessarily coincide with those of the agency in which they happen to work, traditional perspectives in bureaucratic politics (based on organizational interests and procedures) are of limited use.

If officials are not tied to their agencies and do not defend them in bureaucratic conflicts, what, then, are the bases for their preferences? Officials are not primarily motivated by immediate material interests, organizational goals, or ideology. They pursue careers (chapter 3). Where officials stand on a particular policy depends less on where they sit than on where they have been and where they are going. Careers shape preferences in two ways. First, personality and early socialization affect a bureaucrat's initial choice of career, and through on-the-job socialization officials further internalize the values of their career. Second, officials learn early on what types of behavior will earn them promotions in their careers. Careers condition preferences internally (through socialization) and externally (through the signals superiors send to those who want to advance).

In Brazil distinct groups of officials or social types follow four basic career tracks (politician, military officer, *técnico*,[5] or political técnico) and develop distinctive outlooks on industrial policy (chapter 3). Politicians accept executive appointments as a temporary stage in their careers. They promote policies that help them electorally, that are useful in forming coalitions, and that will give them national visibility. Military officers generally favor policies that respond to their national security concerns.

Técnicos adhere tenaciously to efficiency analysis. Political técnicos combine characteristics and preferences of both politicians and técnicos, and fulfill the roles of broker and intermediary. In sum, politicians and officers tend to bring political influences to policy making, técnicos push technical rationality, and political técnicos may favor one or the other (or a mix) depending on the situation.

All policy positions in Brazil are appointive. Hierarchy depends on appointments, not formal procedure (and appointment power may or may not conform to the organization chart). Political appointments during the military regime distributed social types within the state and structured the informal coalitions that determined specific policy outcomes (chapter 4). Appointments, more than organizations, structure power and incentives within the state. Since appointments are the only means of rising to the top of the bureaucracy, they communicate clearly the types of behaviors that will earn promotions. Over time appointers can use their powers to elicit effective behavior and policy. The key to industrialization under state auspices is to find a way to link bureaucratic careers to industrial promotion. In the non-institutionalized Brazilian state, leaders forged this link through appointments.

The Approach

What do officials want from their jobs: income, security, budgets, promotion, prestige, or ideological satisfaction? In the abstract we can conceive of individuals as primarily motivated by either direct material interest, organizational goals, ideologies, or career advancement. Each motivation would yield different policy preferences and policy dynamics and require a different conceptual and empirical approach to policy analysis. Which approach gives us the most realistic bureaucrat's-eye view of the world?

Arguing that officials pursue careers hardly seems controversial, until it forces a rejection of conventional approaches and reorients research agendas. If the bases for divergent policy preferences are primarily material, then policy should be viewed as the outcome of competition for booty among rival personal factions. Research would concentrate on the intrastate distributional consequences of policy options. If the bases for policy preferences are mostly organizational, then researchers should dedicate themselves to understanding the structure, evolution, and goals of the agencies involved, as well as their relative formal power within the bureaucracy. If policy preferences derive from ideologies, then we should study ideological currents, the ways in which different policy participants internalize them, and how strongly attached they are to them. Lastly, if policy makers are primarily pursing careers, then their understanding of appropriate behavior for promotion will inform the preferences they bring to policy politics and indicate how strongly they push them. This career perspective has the greatest analytic power in the study of Brazilian policy making.

Material, organizational, and ideological preferences (and their associated research methodologies) are secondary, and relevant insofar as they affect careers (such as when careers are tied to single organizations). In this sense the concept of a career can also be more composite, a framework in which individuals balance the goals they pursue and make satisficing trade-offs. It is simplistic to argue that officials single-mindedly pursue budgets, income, prestige, organizational discretion, or ideological goals. Like most mortals, they desire all of these things and pursue them as they can, when they can. They cannot have it all, so they make short-term sacrifices to achieve longer-term results. These trade-offs constitute the career calculus. The quest for one fundamental interest, the essential drive, is doomed to explain only part of the variance, even if it is a large part. Rather than seek a single core interest, we need to find concepts, such as careers, that organize the various interests bureaucrats pursue and that orient their pursuit over time and across issues.

Arguing that bureaucrats pursue careers does not mean they are all obsessed workaholics. On the one hand, people pursue careers with greater or lesser intensity, and most sacrifice some career opportunities for family, leisure, or scruple. The point is: they almost always recognize that they are making a career sacrifice. On the other hand, few careers demand complete devotion. When it comes to the myriad daily trade-offs required to pursue a career, most people do what they must to advance. Most policies have little or no bearing on their noncareer objectives. Thus policy options are likely to be reviewed first in terms of their possible impact on one's career.

What career analysis may lack in theoretical parsimony and elegance it makes up for in approximating more closely real-world bureaucracies. It does not reduce bureaucrats to automatons confined within rigid structures (prisoners of either their own indifference curves or institutional bounds). Nor does a career approach allow for complete voluntarism, where bureaucrats are free to pursue whatever ideal ends they may have. The career approach places voluntarism within constraints and opportunities within structures.

Career analysis has been around for a long time and crops up in many disparate studies, though not as centrally as I advocate. Weber carefully defined the distinctive elements of bureaucratic organization (and legal-rational authority) in terms of careers: entrance by examination, lifelong tenure, fixed money salaries, and identifiable promotion paths within the bureaucratic structure (Gerth and Mills 1946, 199–203). Promotion depends on impersonal evaluations by hierarchical superiors. Careers are bound to offices, which tie loyalties to these offices (not to other officials) and channel bureaucratic relations through them. Weber's pure bureaucracy is of course an ideal type, but many bureaucracies approximate it closely enough to make it a useful analytic framework. However, when the career patterns are fundamentally different, as in Brazil, and offices no longer channel loyalties and relations, then its application is less appropriate. Nonetheless, Weber's ideal type helps single out the critical element—careers—in bureaucratic politics.

More recently other scholars have studied careers in a wide variety of contexts. For example, Stepan (1971) examines the training and careers of Brazilian officers prior to 1964 to explain why they took power and why they pursued the policies they did. Johnson (1982) seeks the sources of the policies of the Ministry of International Trade and Industry (and its successes in promoting Japanese industrialization) in the careers of its top officials. In a very different context, Sabel (1982) explains industrial conflict in Europe by analyzing the different concepts of career that workers bring to the workplace. White (1978) argues that revolutionary leaders in Shanghai induced changes in the general population by manipulating career incentives. Leonard (1977) found that agricultural extension services in Kenya suffered because promotion procedures penalized those doing effective hands-on work in rural areas. Each of these scholars, independently of the others, selected an outcome that ranged from the coup in Brazil to strikes in Italy, to the failure of Kenyan agricultural extension and then analyzed careers to explain the outcome.[6] However, none of these authors pushed the general methodological or conceptual ramifications of this career approach as far as they could have.

Perrow in his classic survey of the literature in *Complex Organizations* writes in the introduction that "it is a tenet of the bureaucratic model of organizations that an employee is expected to pursue a 'career' *in the organization*" (1986, 9, emphasis added). What if employees do not? If they do not, how should we reevaluate our approach to the study of bureaucratic politics? It was the lack of institutionalization in the Brazilian bureaucracy that first forced a rejection of normal approaches to bureaucratic politics. In fact, most studies of *organizations* quickly come to the conclusion that policy and power do not really follow the organization chart. Yet policy studies, especially analyses of industrialization in Latin America, return again and again to formal structure and procedure.[7] Sometimes this kind of policy analysis works, sometimes not. In both instances the career approach can identify when. If organizational explanations are weak, careers probably are not tied to organizations. If organizational analysis does seem to work, it is usually because careers follow institutionalized channels through impersonal promotions within a single organization. Individuals act as "organization men," but the prior explanation lies in their careers.

The goal here is to demonstrate a methodology for studying careers that would be broadly useful for comparative analysis. Bureaucratic careers vary extensively from country to country along dimensions that range from recruiting patterns and entrance examinations to type of regime and cultural norms.

The empirical beauty of the career approach developed here is that it helps researchers identify types of career track using a relatively small number of variables such as entrance (what is the social base for recruiting elite bureaucrats?), circulation (how closely are careers tied to particular agencies?), promotion (procedural or political), and exit (where do officials go when they leave?).[8] Individual careers may seem idiosyncratic, but most bureaucracies manifest identifiable clusters of careers. The level of aggregation desired in defining a career track depends on the thing to be explained. It may be enough for certain analyses to specify differences between doctors and lawyers; others may require delving into differences between tax lawyers and public defenders.

Extensive empirical work has generated vast information on top officials around the world, but, of the great number of studies of bureaucratic elites, only a few relate their findings more than obliquely to concrete policies (Smith 1979: 13). Bureaucrats occupy increasingly central positions in nearly all polities, so it is important to know where they come from, what education they received, how they advanced in their careers, and how long they stayed in top positions. But it is frustrating to be left hanging when it comes time to assess the impact of these variables on policy outputs. One of the most thorough empirical studies is by Aberbach, Putnam, and Rockman (1981); it is also a fine example of the limits of this sort of study. The authors provide exhaustive information on social background, education, careers, and attitudes, and regress everything in interesting ways, but they can demonstrate no concrete impact on policy.

Of course, making the link is complicated by mismatches in the levels of analysis; the characteristics of the bureaucracy or bureaucrats in general are little help in explaining day-to-day policy in specific areas. However, this study explores a promising middle ground—the interrelation of types of careers and types of policy outputs. In Brazil politicians, técnicos, military officers, and political técnicos bring different perspectives to decision making, and policies will have different balances of political and technical rationalities depending on the career composition of the coalition that makes the policy.

Economists and others labor tirelessly to understand the link between policy outputs (what the government does) and policy outcomes (how the economy in fact responds). It was the outcome, Brazilian industrialization, that inspired this study. However, this causal link is not the core empirical concern of this book. Each of the case study chapters (discussed below) presents a rough evaluation of the contribution of the policy to overall industrialization. However, the small number of cases and the summary economic analysis make modest conclusions advisable. The primary focus is on those factors and conditions—circulation, careers, and appointments (independent variables)—that promote positive policy outputs (intermediate variables), which in turn foster industrialization (dependent variable).[9] The case studies serve better to illuminate policy making in Brazil and to identify the conditions under which policy improved than to prove that the state was primarily responsible for Brazil's industrial success. Despite these restrictions, this research still goes farther than previous studies in demonstrating empirically the effect of bureaucratic elites and politics on industrial development.

My approach brings politics back into the bureaucracy, both as an inherent part of policy making and as an element that can improve policy outputs. The normative and analytical distinction between politics and administration is at least implicitly very much with us and can have a distorting influence on interpretations of bureaucratic politics and policy making.[10] An offshoot of this distinction is a widespread and enduring assumption that politics distorts and worsens the more technical policies that governments are increasingly called on to adopt (see, for example, Sloan 1982; 1984).

The conventional wisdom is that policy success in authoritarian Brazil resulted from technocratic or legal-rational policy making. Most observers agree that no elected government could have implemented the fiscal, monetary, and wage reforms undertaken by the Castelo Branco government. Early supporters of, and participants in, the military regime made this claim explicitly. Roberto Campos and Mário Henrique Simonsen both faulted pre-1964 governments for politicizing economic policy and argued that their policies were free of politics and therefore superior (see Alves 1985, 108). In surveying much of the accumulated wisdom on industrial policy, Stepan concludes that "a persistent stream of the development literature calls attention to the technocratic advantages of apolitical management" (Stepan 1989, xi).

My research takes issue with the technocratic argument on two counts. First, policy making in Brazil was usually politicized (especially after 1967) despite protests to the contrary by the actual participants. Second, successful policy usually resulted from a balance of technical and political rationales, manifested in informal coalitions of social types brokered by political técnicos. Politics can improve policy. Policy failure normally came from over attention to either politics or engineering, excessive centralization (to which a non-institutionalized bureaucracy is particularly vulnerable), and/or the breakdown of informal channels and the consequent resurgence of organizational fragmentation.

In Brazil certain kinds of political influence made for better policies than those technocrats would have adopted on their own. What is commonly disparaged as outside political "meddling" or "interference" can sometimes improve policy directly. Or it can intensify the policy dispute and thereby force more rigorous technical debate. Furthermore, the notions of meddling and interference give the mistaken impression that politics are external to the bureaucracy and obscure the inherently political preferences and behavior of bureaucrats themselves.

The analysis does not draw heavily on perspectives in rational or public choice, but it does find resonance in the recent trend of seeking individual or micro-level explanations for macro phenomena. The core of the approach is to assess how and why the careers, the individual pursuits, interact with macro constraints and opportunities in economic and political structures to produce a macro-level outcome such as industrialization. Like much recent choice-theoretic work, the argument centers on the incentives that individual decision makers face. However, the career approach improves on many choice theories in that it is more inductive, it assesses long- and short-term incentives, and it anchors preferences in a historical context.

This micro-political approach is less a methodological manifesto than most choice-theoretic studies and more a statement about where we need to go empirically in the study of the Brazilian political economy: open the black box of the state. In the major enduring theories on the Brazilian political economy, such as dependent development, bureaucratic authoritarianism, and patrimonialism (or other cultural variants), the state— and bureaucratic officials—are major protagonists.[11] We know a lot about military officers, clientelistic politicians, and multinational corporations, yet few previous studies provide more than a cursory empirical glimpse of the bureaucracy. Who are the officials who mediate the relations of dependency? What incentives do they have to distribute patronage? And what mechanisms shield technically minded officials from clientelistic pressures? Empirical answers to these questions are essential to confirming theories of dependency, bureaucratic authoritarianism, and patrimonialism, but the major works in these approaches have yet to furnish them.

This research does not necessarily challenge these macro analyses of Brazilian industrialization, but it does provide a necessary and overdue complement to them. Brazil is a late, capitalist, dependent industrializer. The nature of industrialization in the late twentieth century and Brazil's particular pattern of insertion into the international economy close off certain development options. Previous research (cited in note 11) has spelled out fairly clearly what the structures and constraints are. What is less well known, and where this research fits, is what goes on within these constraints. The following analysis of policy makers and their preferences may sometimes give a mistaken impression of a very voluntarist state deciding freely what to do. The point is not to counter structural analyses, but rather to complement them by analyzing what officials do with what discretion they have.

This study fills another gap in the literature on Brazil by analyzing the mature military regime. A flurry of books in the 1970s examined the first decade of military rule (Stepan 1971; 1973; Schneider 1971; Flynn 1978; O'Donnell 1973; Collier 1979). By the 1980s attention had turned to democratization, and political evolution in the 1970s was viewed less as the maturing of an authoritarian regime and more as a prelude to the transition to civilian rule in 1985. In some respects, Stepan's two edited volumes, *Authoritarian Brazil* (1973) and *Democratizing Brazil* (1989), illustrate the shift in the prevailing focus of research from authoritarianism to democratization. This study takes the 1970s more at face value (as does Skidmore 1988). The regime was an authoritarian one that had stabilized the economy and was now trying to implement its development strategy and maintain political support. It is important, now that the record of the military's twenty-one-year rule is far better known, to take stock of that regime, to consider its characteristics over the full period, and to revise initial interpretations of Brazilian authoritarianism.

State Enterprise and Development by Project

To get beyond the many studies of bureaucracy that stop before relating their conclusions to policy outputs, this research sought to relate the general findings on the bureaucracy to concrete decisions in large projects run by state enterprises. The focus on development projects serves several purposes. First, the economic and political programs of military governments after 1970 revolved around these projects. Many analyses of the economic strategies of the authoritarian regime focus on the institutional reforms and stabilization policies of the 1960s. What is less well understood is what successive governments did once these programs were complete. Second, these projects represent the deepest and most direct form of state intervention and reveal most clearly the impact of careers and appointments on industrialization. Lastly, because they are so visible and costly, they excite a lot of interest and bring politics into higher relief, which facilitates research in a relatively closed and "apolitical" regime.

Brazil has a long history of huge development projects, beginning in the 1940s with the first integrated industrial project, when the state built Brazil's first large-scale steel mill. In the 1950s the major projects were the first huge hydroelectric dams and the construction of a new capital in Brasília. The first two military governments shied away from new development cathedrals, but the last three made development-by-project central to both their economic and their political strategies. Médici channeled the energies and resources of his government into several major projects such as the Rio-Niteroi bridge, the construction of a petrochemical pole in the northeast, and the Transamazon highway. Geisel picked up projects planned in the Médici government and added several of his own: Itaipú (the largest dam in the world), the Ferrovia de Aço (the Steel Railroad), Tucuruí (the fourth largest dam in the world), the Açominas steel plant, the nuclear program, and lesser projects in other sectors. The debt crisis and subsequent austerity measures deprived Figueiredo of his share of new projects, though he was able to christen many begun by Geisel.

State enterprises were the natural tools for implementing these projects, many of which prompted the creation of new firms. For these and other enterprises, project management was synonymous with running the firm. In some ways this perhaps distorts "normal" state enterprise behavior. But to the extent that almost all governments expect more of their firms than simple production, project implementation becomes the more relevant side of state enterprise behavior. Political leaders and central planners in developing countries are more interested in how well they can use state enterprises as policy instruments than in how efficient they are at performing assigned routines.

In aggregate these projects decisively affected sectoral and even macro economic performance in the 1970s and 1980s. The Instituto Brasileiro de Análises Sociais e Econômicas identified 33 major projects (due to cost $1 billion or more), begun or authorized before the debt crisis, in industry, mining, agriculture, energy, housing, steel, petrochemicals, aluminum, transport, and communications (IBASE 1983, 13–32). The institute calculated that these 33 projects would absorb $229 billion in investment, require an additional $88 billion in foreign debt, employ 1.5 million people, and add another $47 billion to annual output. That is, these 33 projects would invest the equivalent of Brazil's entire gross domestic product [GDP] and require more than doubling Brazil's foreign debt to jack up GDP by 20 percent over a dozen or so years. The figures are clearly fantastic, even spread out over a decade and a half of projected implementation, but they convey well the "projectitis" that came to afflict the economic bureaucracy and state enterprises in the 1970s.

The debt crisis of the 1980s forced planners to choose among these projects. They shelved some sine die, slowed others, and scaled down many of the rest. Data on the actual amounts invested figure in the tens of billions: Itaipú $15.3 billion; Tucuruí $5.4 billion; Açominas $6 billion; Carajás $2.9 billion; nuclear reactors $5.4 billion; cst $3.4 billion; and the alcohol program $10.5 billion.[12] The magnitudes were in any case large enough to affect total investment, production, debt, imports (and eventually exports), government spending, and industrialization.

Beyond their economic significance these projects had a profound political impact. They mobilized groups, pro and con. Suppliers and contractors scrambled to participate. Regional elites rushed to Brasília to attempt to influence the location and amounts invested. And ecologists and opponents of the regime mobilized to criticize, stop, or revise them. For a regime that staked its legitimacy on its ability to industrialize the country, these projects became visible indicators of how they were doing.

In the early 1970s these outsized projects fitted the developmental euphoria of the "economic miracle" and seemed to redound to the popularity of the military, the self-appointed leaders of Brazil's sprint to greatness. However, by the late 1970s and into the 1980s, these projects became synonymous with all that was wrong with military rule. When growth lagged and the majority of the population continued barely to scrape by, despite the miracle, the great projects came to symbolize military hubris and neglect of social development. The recently unfettered press dubbed the projects "Pharaonic" and the project mentality "megalomaniacal." The reference to the Pharaohs and pyramids questioned simultaneously the productive value of these projects and the scale of human suffering required to build them.

The projects warrant examination because they highlight planning politics in a developmental state. This window may give a somewhat distorted view of policy politics (precisely because they are manifest and inflamed), but these projects con stitute critical cases because they exemplify the goal orientation of a developmental state. In Hirschman's terms, "development projects . . . are the privileged particles of the development process" (1967, 1).

Windows and Vistas

The research on development projects covers four cases during the period 1967–85: the creation of a holding company in steel (Siderbrás), the construction of an integrated steel mill (Açominas), the opening of an iron mine in the Amazon (Carajás), and CVRD's aluminum ventures.[13] The choice of these cases addressed several methodological concerns. The first was to study the largest projects with the greatest impact on their respective sectors. Siderbrás was the most significant organizational change in steel; Açominas was the largest new steel mill; Carajás is the largest iron-ore mine in Brazil (and should become the largest mining complex in the world); and Mineração Rio do Norte (MRN), Albrás, and Valesul were the largest new undertakings in aluminum. Were the projects not representative of policy making more generally, they would at least cover some of the major projects of the military regime.

The universe comprised about twenty cases of major industrial projects directed by state enterprises. The cases are quite disparate and include projects in petrochemicals, dam building, nuclear energy, alcohol production, computers, and of course steel, mining, and aluminum. Several criteria informed the selection of these cases. The selection permits a comparison of more and less successful projects in order to evaluate the hypothesis that effective policy depends on a balance of political and technical rationales as pursued by different social types. It also kept the range of variation on other variables within manageable bounds. Though it was impossible to choose cases randomly for a representative sample, the selection excluded the extreme outliers. So, for example, I rejected cases such as the nuclear program, which was an intense national security concern of the military. The cases selected may not be representative in a statistical sense, but neither are they atypical.

The cases chosen also allow for assessing alternative hypotheses on bureaucratic preferences and processes (chapter 9). In particular, I wanted to be able to control for organization and sector by selecting two of four cases in the same firm, and two of four projects in the same industrial sector. Were organization the major determinant of bureaucratic politics, then they would be similar in the two cases under CVRD's guidance and fundamentally different from those in steel. If the major determinants were sectoral, or market in the case of state enterprises, then the two projects in steel should be similar and far different from those in aluminum and iron ore. Organization and industrial sector did have some impact, but it was residual and narrow (e.g., the location of the mine) compared to the force of circulation, careers, and appointments.

The four cases provide detailed illustrations of the arguments in a variety of different situations. Each study highlights some concepts, but together they provide concrete examples of nearly all the general arguments in part I. The case studies are first and foremost an attempt to open windows onto the mysterious and opaque inner workings of the state. We know a lot about what the state-as-monolith does in late industrialization, but we know very little about what those inside the state think and do.

The primary empirical sources are nearly one hundred one- to two-hour interviews with government officials ranging from mid-level engineers to presidents of state enterprises and ministers (see the chronologies of cases in appendix B for the names of many of the officials interviewed). Each interview probed the official's participation in, and interpretation of, particular decisions affecting one or more of the four projects examined. The interviews were unstructured, and the questions depended on the positions the interviewee had occupied.[14]

The original evidence to support the arguments on circulation and career types comes from biographical data on 281 officials who served in top positions in the economic bureaucracy from 1964 to 1985 (see appendix A for a further discussion of the career survey). Biographical information on about 200 officials came from published sources and a mail questionnaire. Data for the remaining officials came from personal interviews. Interviews with dozens of officials in the top ranks of the bureaucracy also provided the evidence for the arguments on appointment relations.

The case studies provide four of many possible windows, and much of the state is as opaque as ever. However, the cases do provide somewhat broader vistas than they might appear to. The term *case* here is misleading: each case is the sum of thousands of decisions. In big investment projects a decision is never final; it becomes the proposal for the next round of decision making. All four projects took over a decade from first proposal to completed construction and covered several governments and several groups of officials. Moreover, a decision to build a dam or petrochemical plant immediately breaks down into hundreds of subdecisions on where, when, and how to build it. Hence each single case study covers many component decisions. Furthermore, each project at some point, and sometimes repeatedly, came across the desks of ministers and presidents. The way they acted in the case studies is probably similar to the way they acted in hundreds of other decisions they made during their tenure. In sum, the N of subdecisions is much larger than four, and generalizing is facilitated by the fact that the same officials were protagonists in other policies.

These factors encourage broader conclusions about decision making in development projects, but the argument may extend less well to other types of policy making. Macro policy confronts economic actors with a different logic in collective action. Varying the money supply affects all economic agents, but few have incentive to mobilize to try to influence the policy (unlike those who stand to gain or lose in development projects). Moreover, organizational goals loom larger. For instance, officials in the agencies that manage government debt have to balance government books and have to view policy options in terms of their immediate institutional responsibility. Of course, much of fiscal, credit, and exchange policy in Brazil is handled in very discretionary fashion in the form of tax exemptions, credit subsidies, or tariff exemptions, and in these policies the politics are likely to resemble those in development projects.

Social policy also differs from development projects in that it usually requires the delivery of goods and services to large dispersed target groups such as sick children, illiterate adolescents, or landless peasants. To reach these groups requires strong institutions or, if they do not exist, institution building, and policy politics involve large numbers of people. In contrast, development projects often bypass institutions, and the politics are usually restricted to a small elite. Though the framework developed here may be less applicable to social and macro policy, my central interest was in explaining the impact of the Brazilian state on industrialization, and development projects (and industrial policy more generally) had a more direct and profound impact on industry than did macro or social policy.

Mobile Bureaucrats and Weak Institutions

> I cannot but believe that more is lost by the long continuation of men in office than is generally to be gained by their experience. . . . I submit therefore to your consideration whether the efficiency of the Government would not be promoted and officials' industry and integrity better secured by the general extension of the law which limits appointments to four years. . . .
>
> The proposed limitation would destroy the idea of property now so generally connected with official station, and although individual stress may sometimes be produced, it would . . . give healthful action to the system.
>
> —Andrew Jackson[1]

Non-Institutionalized Policy Making

IN THE CASE STUDIES in part II, the institutions or formal organizations of the economic bureaucracy often did not channel power or formulate policy. Time and again circuitous, personalized politics supplanted the formal institutional process. In few instances did the idea and first initiative arise in the proper forum, was the decision made in the appointed arena, or was the policy executed as commanded from above. Officials' preferences often differed from those to be expected from their positions, powerful participants entered from outside the organizational sphere, and personal ties, more than a convergence of organizational interests, were usually the basis for coalition building. Both procedures and organizations lacked institutionalization.

For Polsby an institutionalized organization: 1) is "well-bounded, . . . it is relatively difficult to become a member, and its leaders are recruited principally from within the organization"; 2) is internally complex and has a regular division of labor; and 3) uses "universalistic rather than particularistic criteria, and automatic rather than discretionary methods."[2] Few of the agencies I studied scored high on Polsby's indicators, especially at top levels of the bureaucratic "hierarchy." In contrast, in Brazil at the top three or four hierarchical levels: (1) organizations are extremely porous, and top officials are recruited principally from outside the organization (though it is still quite difficult to become a member of the bureaucratic elite); (2) the bureaucracy is exceedingly complex, but the division of labor is fluid; and (3) the methods employed are highly discretionary and usually particularistic.

This non-institutionalized view is a common refrain in analyses of the Brazilian public administration.[3] The terms used to describe this personalized administration vary from evocative Brazilian terms such as *estado cartorial* (sinecure state), *panelinha* (discussed below), and *jeito* or *jeitinho*[4] to standard categories of corruption, clientelism, patronage, and patrimonialism. Most of these analyses find the sources of personalism in nineteenth- and twentieth-century traditions and the clientelistic parties that invaded the bureaucracy after 1945. But, as I argue in the next section, high mobility provides a more immediate and rational motivation to circumvent formal organization.

These studies and early theories of bureaucratic authoritarianism would lead us to expect greater institutionalization under military rule.[5] The military itself is the exception that scores high on Polsby's indicators and usually acts as an institution (though the rigors of rule exacerbated internal divisions). The coup conspirators were publicly outraged at the corruption, clientelism, and personalism of the democracy they overthrew. The military also presented its mission as modernizing: to root out inefficient and dysfunctional traditional behavior.

However, the lack of institutionalization continued into the second decade of military rule.[6] The military attempted unsuccessfully to institutionalize their rule and mold a new democracy to succeed them. They wrote a new constitution, reformed the party system, and held regular elections. They even arranged for private consulting in the early 1970s by one of the strongest advocates of institutions, Samuel Huntington (Skidmore 1988, 165, 167, 170). But none of these reforms stuck, because the military kept tinkering with the rules to achieve short-term goals, thereby undermining the "institutions" they had created. They sacrificed procedure to outcome. This characteristic inability of authoritarian rulers to institutionalize their power is perhaps the most effective pathogen in raising the fortunately high rate of mortality of their regimes.

The military's record in institutionalizing the bureaucracy was little better. The new military rulers went after the bureaucracy immediately after the coup. Among other things, Institutional Act no. 1 suspended job security in the civil service, and the Castelo Branco government purged 1,408 officials in its first year (see Skidmore 1988, 20; Alves 1985, 41). The new economic team of Planning Minister Campos and Finance Minister Bulhões was most intent on administrative reform. Campos was a champion of technocracy, meritocracy, and administrative efficiency. He and others in the new government were most successful in creating new policy instruments and revamping financial agencies, but they had little impact on existing personnel and personnel practices (see chapter 10).

Most of the newly rationalized agencies survived, but subsequent governments buffeted them about so much that they never became strong institutions. The history of the National Monetary Council (CMN), one of the most important financial reforms of the Castelo Branco government, is particularly illustrative (see Vianna 1987; Guimarães and Vianna 1987). Campos and Bulhões modeled the CMN after the U.S. Federal Reserve Board. It was to have statutory autonomy, and appointees were to serve staggered terms that spanned governments to ensure the council's political independence. But one of the first things Finance Minister Delfim Netto did upon arriving in 1967 was to take away its autonomy and pack its voting membership. Delfim used the CMN as a personal vehicle for centralizing most aspects (not just monetary) of macroeconomic policy. After

1974, Geisel's Economic Development Council (CDE) eclipsed the CMN. The CMN never achieved a stable, institutionalized position in monetary policy.

After 1967 military presidents and their economic ministers were more concerned with policy outcomes than procedures. Subsequent governments also abandoned the quest for administrative rationality and created hundreds of new, often redundant, agencies and enterprises. This gives the military regime one of its curious qualities: a highly institutionalized force ruling over an ad hoc civilian bureaucracy. The military could not remake the civilian bureaucracy in its own image. Institutionalization requires more than administrative tinkering; it must be accompanied by measures that commit bureaucrats and others to the new organizations and procedures.

Bureaucratic Circulation

What the military left out of their reforms (and what Polsby left out of his definition) were provisions that would commit people to the new, rationalized procedures and organizations. Strong institutions exist only when those who deal with them, bureaucrats and outsiders, are committed to the procedures by which they operate. In Huntington's definition, "institutions are stable, valued, recurring patterns of behavior."[7]

The first problem with the military's political and administrative reforms was instability. Officials are not going to commit themselves to procedures that they expect not to recur. This lack of commitment was particularly evident in Congress, parties, and elections, where the military made it clear that they would change any rule to achieve the desired, short-term result. Similar instability afflicted most of the new agencies and policy-making procedures.

More generally, a variety of mechanisms such as ideology, leadership, or charisma can bind people to organizations, but the surest and most lasting bonding mechanism is to restrict careers to a single organization. If careers are tied to one organization, officials' commitment will naturally transfer to that agency. As Kaufman concludes in his study of the forest rangers, whose careers are tied exclusively to the Forest Service, "as they become part of the organization, the organization becomes part of them" (1960, 179). If officials move from agency to agency, the identification of career with organization is missing. Alvin Toffler was one of the first to recognize these linkages.[8] One of the "future shocks" we are suffering is "adhocracy," which comes about in part because mobility is so high in business that managers have no long-term interest in the companies through which they pass.

Much of Brazil's public "adhocracy" owes its condition to similarly high levels of circulation. A typical high-level official in the economic bureaucracy worked, over the course of a nineteen-year career in the state, for four different state agencies and changed agencies every five years ($N=281$). Changing agencies does not mean moving between different departments within a firm, for example, but rather between firms, between ministries, or between other nonhierarchically related agencies.[9] If we add movement into and out of the private sector, the rates of circulation are even higher: in a full twenty-six-year career, officials work for almost six organizations (public and private) and change agencies every four years. These high rates of circulation show up in officials' perceptions of career opportunities. In 1976, nine in ten top officials ($N=107$) in state enterprises or government thought that they had a medium or good chance of moving to a comparable or better position in either the government, state firms, or private Brazilian firms (they were less optimistic about multinational corporations [MNCs] [calculated from L. Martins 1985, 220]).

These levels of circulation have been quite stable over time; whether you graduated in 1930 or 1960, you could expect to change agencies in the public sector every five years. The rates are fairly stable across agencies as well, ranging from 5.7 years between changes for Siderbrás ($N=66$) to 3.6 years in money ministries ($N=38$). Officials on the fast track move more often: ministers moved every 4 years on the way up (and afterward) whereas those who rose only to the level of director of a minor state enterprise changed jobs once every 8 years (see table 3).

These aggregate averages still mask significant differences within the civil service. Table 1 offers another measure of state manager circulation. In terms of organizational commitment, only 20 percent of officials spend their careers in only one or two organizations, one of which is likely to become part of them as they become more permanent parts of it. For them the convergence of organizational interests and their preferences is likely to be high. At the other extreme, one-third of all officials moved through seven or more agencies (public and private).

These rates of circulation are high compared to those in industrial countries, though they may not stand out in the developing world.[10] Elite Japanese bureaucrats typically spend their public careers in a single ministry (Johnson 1982). In the United States, "only a rare 'successful' higher civil servant makes more than one interdepartmental or interagency move in a lifetime of public service and . . . this move is most likely to occur early in a . . . career."[11] In industrial countries generally, Aberbach, Putnam, and Rockman found few elite bureaucrats who had worked for more than one ministry: 51 percent in Britain ($N=92$); 31 percent in West Germany ($N=90$); 18 percent in Italy ($N=84$); 22 percent of U.S. Civil servants ($N=64$); and 18 percent of U.S. political executives ($N=61$) (1981, 71). The figure for Brazil would be about 75 percent, though the data are not strictly comparable (see Schneider, 1989). Brazilian circulation is high compared to that in the in-

Table 1
Number of Agencies Officials Have Worked for per Career (percentage)

	Number of Agencies					
	1–2	3–4	5–6	7+	Total[a]	Number[b]
Public agencies	32	31	22	15	100	281
Public and private agencies	20	24	25	32	101	268

a. Does not sum to 100 because of rounding.
b. The sample is the same, but data are lacking on private sector movement for 13 officials.

stitutionalized agencies of the industrialized world, and hence high in comparison to the cases that have served as the bases for most general theorizing about public administration and bureaucratic politics.

High circulation in Brazil reduces parochialism and inoculates against strong organizational loyalties. Mobility breeds indifference to the agency that currently employs you. Some officials did not even remember all the jobs they had held and could not have developed much attachment to the offices through which they dashed. If you know your next career step is likely to take you to another organization or state enterprise, you are less likely to fight to preserve bureaucratic turf in the name of the organization. Bureaucratic wanderlust enables officials to delink their policy preferences from the organization. The more peripatetic interviewees often described their careers in terms of the issues on which they had worked or people with whom they had collaborated rather than the organizations that had employed them. One official who had circulated a great deal told me to forget about the *organograma* (organization chart) of the government and to use, as he did, a *humanograma* (human chart) (interview with José Knaack de Souza, 14 July 1985).

The patterns of circulation that emerged more or less spontaneously in Brazil are deliberate procedure in other governments and organizations. The goal is usually to shift loyalty from the immediate place of work to an overarching organization, especially in geographically dispersed agencies. For instance, the foreign services of most countries move their employees regularly to break potential local ties. The typical forest ranger moves every few years and "never has time to sink roots in the communities in which he sojourns to briefly" (Kaufman 1960, 178). The circulation ultimately helps to build strong loyalty to the Forest Service overall, but the first function is to break local ties. In the Brazilian bureaucracy, circulation does not bind officials to some overarching entity, but it does prevent them from sinking roots into the agencies in which they sojourn so briefly.

The less the organization figures in one's future career, the more one's personal contacts count in promotion. Moreover, after a few interagency shifts, any individual bureaucrat belongs to a web of former co-workers, now distributed throughout the state apparatus, that they can call on for information and support. Hence circulation creates not only the desire but also the opportunity for personal politics.

For officials in the appointed bureaucracy, the turnover following presidential succession presents enormous opportunity and great uncertainty. Over the five successions from 1967 to 1985, nearly all bureaucrats left their jobs at the end of the term. However, each incoming government offered thousands of new opportunities, and most would get a job in the new government. On average,and not discounting for natural retirement, almost one-half of top appointees served in high positions in two consecutive governments, though almost always in different agencies (see table 2 and appendix A). Officials could get burned if they were associated too closely with one patron, who might not be appointed to the next government (one of the clearest manifestations was the mass exodus of *Delfim boys* in the succession from Médici to Geisel). Hence officials are hesitant to enter into binding groups, or *panelinhas,* and they seek weaker, personal ties to a wide range of other bureaucrats, because one never knows (see chapter 4). This accounts for the amorphous quality of personalism. Uncertainty discourages the formation of cliques and encourages extensive personal ties and exchange, which in turn open more channels for communication and coordination.

High mobility across agencies and sectors decreases the levels of job-specific bureaucratic skills and project-specific technical skills. In the 1970s and 1980s one finds, for example, a financial economist planning aluminum plants, an aeronautical engineer running an oil company, and an electrical engineer at the head of a steel company. However, the final effect of this mismatch of expertise depends on the person and the position. Some officials outside their area of expertise used their extensive appointment powers to surround themselves with the best-qualified staff. Also, many positions such as that of president of a state enterprise require managerial and political skills more than technical expertise.

Table 2
Presidential Succession and Continuity in the Economic
Bureaucracy, 1970–1986

	Officials Who Went On to Serve in Next Government (%)	Officials Who Served in Previous Government (%)	Number
Médici	66	50	87
Geisel	66	49	118
Figueiredo	50	53	148
Sarney	—	60	125

Note: Officials appointed to top, confidence positions, including, ministry depart-ment head or director of second-level state enterprise and higher. Also included are a few secretaries in the governments of the largest states and Arena congressmen.

Circulation can improve policy coordination by giving state managers easy informal access to, and understanding of, a wide range of agencies through which they move. Coordination is doubly important in Brazil, where the bureaucracy is so frag-mented. Moreover, to the extent that officials need the cooper-ation of those in other agencies, personal contacts become more important and bureaucratic turf less so.

Career uncertainty can improve bureaucratic performance. Knowing that personal ties might not ensure advancement and could, if too close, hurt them, officials tried to enhance their visibility and reputation as effective bureaucrats.[12] For most of the postwar period, it was clear that presidents sought support and legitimacy through industrialization, and that they would therefore want to appoint effective officials. Uncertainty en-couraged officials to cultivate many semiclose personal rela-tions and to demonstrate bureaucratic, technical, and political skill; it was best to know many upwardly mobile bureaucrats, have a visible worth beyond loyalty, and show a willingness to enter into personal exchange.[13]

High circulation promoted the midstream modification of long-term policies and projects. One team of officials could be-gin a policy, only to be replaced by another group with different

preferences. Whether or not these influences improved or
worsened policy depended on the nature of policy and the types
of changes introduced. Some claim that policy flip-flop and unnecessary haste (encouraged by high turnover) ruined rational
long-term development. But the evidence in part II suggests
that periodic reevaluation through a new optic can make for
better and more flexible policy, and that working with all due
bureaucratic haste can very well speed industrialization.

Of course, state managers often do take up their agency's col-
ors to go into bureaucratic battle. They are just far more likely
to drop them when faced with a conflicting interest on the part
of one of their (informal) superiors or when the organization's
interests obstruct a policy. Getting things done will get one a
promotion sooner than defending the institution will. As in
Chalmers's (1977) politicized state, substance prevails over
rules, ends over means. Officials are more interested in having
the state apparatus function effectively than in setting or defending rules for that functioning.

All organizations depend on personal contacts to sidestep excess formalism and the remaining faults in administrative engineering. In other countries circulation is often rapid and
sometimes even deliberate. However, few countries have such
high levels of mobility and personalism, and it is therefore rea-
sonable to use the organizational shorthand to analyze economic policy in most countries. This is not the case in Brazil,
where personal politics consistently overwhelms formal organization. Institutionalization can be conceived as a continuum.
Different organizations or bureaucracies have different degrees
of institution. The midpoint marks a divide: on one side, organizations prevail over individuals; on the other, organizations
behave more in accordance with the particular incumbents who
run them. The Brazilian bureaucracy as a whole falls on the latter side of the continuum.

The Institutional Fallacy

If the institutional perspective is suspect, then many previous
policy studies are on unsure footing. Examinations of diverse
policy areas such as alcohol production (Barzelay 1986), import

licensing (Abranches 1978), development banking (L. Martins 1985), and land settlement in the Amazon (Bunker 1983), as well as nearly all works on Brazilian state enterprise, take this institutional approach (see also Daland 1981; Sloan 1984). Some studies adopt, at least implicitly, an Allisonian model of bureaucratic politics, where standard operating procedures and interagency conflict determine policy outcomes. Other studies, especially of state enterprise, follow a state capitalist or state bourgeoisie approach, where state managers pursue their own material interests by promoting those of their firms.

Allison's model of bureaucratic politics is based on institutionalized patterns of administrative behavior. Officials adopt organizational interests—"where you stand depends on where you sit" (Allison 1969, 711). Allison derives a bureaucrat's politicking from: the "obligations" and the "advantages and handicaps" of a particular job; "organizational parochialism"; and the fact that "positions define what players both may and must do" (1969, 709). Individual behavior is "framed" by organization. More recently, Nordlinger posits similar bases for bureaucratic politics: officials share institutional interests (most importantly budgets and agency authority) and "these institutional interests sharply impinge upon the relative attractiveness of policy alternatives" (1981, 32–33).

Brazilian policy studies in this Allisonian tradition rely on the concepts of fragmentation, segmentation, balkanization, and feudalization to explain policy failures or paralysis. Myriad redundant entities make parts of one policy and inhibit a global, integrated approach to planning.[14] The common view is that agencies and their technocrats pursue their interests single-mindedly and fiercely guard their prerogatives. Fragmentation therefore supposedly explains policy failures, such as those in steel planning (Abranches 1978) and pre-1979 Pró-álcool (Barzelay 1986), and the long list of complaints against state enterprises.[15]

What this fragmentation thesis cannot explain is the emergence over time of relatively coherent and coordinated policy from unreformed administrative chaos. In general, the quality of policy and of coordination varies greatly in the absence of organizational change.[16] Policy change usually follows changes in top personnel, with or without changes in the task environment or the organizational universe. New officials bring new policy orientations and new intrastate networks that enable them to forge new policy coalitions.

The second, state capitalist approach trusts too much in the explanatory power of the material interests of organizations and their occupants.[17] In this perspective the basis for organizational conflict is the pursuit and accumulation of resources. To be sure, officials will resist short-term encroachments on their budgets and policy discretion (unless they are about to move out and up). It is, however, over the medium and long run that the material argument falls apart. The vast majority of officials cannot take great self-interest in long-term investment, accumulation, or policy because they know that they will be in another agency well before the policy or investment bears fruit.

This approach also fails to explain why an organization, particularly a state enterprise, would change its policy preference without prior organizational change. Personalism, circulation, and the lack of strong organizational loyalties explain how policies and "institutions" can flip-flop from one moment or government to the next. However, when not faced with conflicting superior claims, state managers are wont to pursue agency and state enterprise interests with sometimes important second-order, and not necessarily negative, consequences.

To conclude, two lines of critique have evolved to explain bureaucratic pathology in Brazil. The first, covered in previous sections, focuses on dysfunctional behavior including personalism, clientelism, patronage, and patrimonialism. The remedy is legal-rational Weberian bureaucracy. The second concentrates on fragmentation, overlapping jurisdiction, and the unchecked pursuit of organizational self-interest. The solution lies in administrative rationalization. Schmitter sums up the impact of these twin evils: "The result of these processes of structural overbureaucratization and behavioral underbureaucratization has been still another bottleneck impeding development" (1971, 34). What is missing is an appreciation of the symbiosis of these "pathologies," an appreciation that would permit the critics to see why the bureaucracy in fact often functions.

Though personalism may once have had other sources, it is now made indispensable by bureaucratic fragmentation. Personalism (behavioral underbureaucratization) cuts through fragmentation (structural overbureaucratization) and permits coordination, while continued fragmentation enhances the need for personalism.

The BNDE: The Rise and Decline of an Institution

In general, high circulation weakens institutions in the economic bureaucracy. For specific agencies institutionalization is better viewed as a variable. This section considers the process of institutionalization over time in an extreme and illustrative case (see Selznick 1957). For almost three decades since its creation in 1952, the National Bank for Economic Development (BNDE) set new standards for institutionalization that had a broad impact on the economic bureaucracy and policy-making in general.[18] The bank set the standard for administrative professionalism, and its técnicos gained a reputation as among the most competent in Brazil. Managers codified bank procedures and defended them and the bank in intrastate politics. The BNDE also developed a distinctive mentality of nationalist developmentalism that informed its policies and policy battles. Many BNDE técnicos left the bank (they were often in great demand) and took its institutionalization, professionalism, and developmental nationalism to others parts of the bureaucracy (see Willis 1986, 101).

The quest for neutral professionalism began in the first years after the bank's establishment. In 1956 managers instituted an entrance examination, and over the years the BNDE established codified rules for merit-based promotion (which was also on the whole rapid).[19] The bank also instituted a range of technical courses, management training programs, and scholarships for outside study. In part because of the rigors of entry and advancement (and the reinforcing outside reputation the bank gained), BNDE técnicos quickly developed a strong esprit de corps, on which few observers or bank employees fail to comment. The bank's managers in 1972 further attempted to cement their institutional position within the state by adopting a resolution requiring that three of five directors come from within the bank (L. Martins 1985, 103).

BNDE's managers also attempted to institutionalize internal procedures. They tried to make decision making "automatic and universalistic" instead of "discretionary and particularistic" (Polsby 1968, 45). An indicator of their success was the consecration of the *opinião do técnico* (Willis 1986, 110–12). If low-level técnicos rejected or approved a loan on the basis of codified procedures and analyses, then higher-level managers almost always respected their opinion. Reversing the opinion was grounds for scandal and técnico resignations.[20]

The bank was one of the few agencies in the bureaucracy that managed to achieve a high degree of institutionalization. However, we should not confuse this institutionalization with a Weberian legal-rational bureaucracy. Luciano Martins in fact thinks the BNDE is less an institutionalized administrative organ than a highly developed political party that makes alliances, propagates ideology, maintains internal cohesion and commitment, and represents interests (1985, 93). That is, the bases for the esprit de corps, the defense of the BNDE as an institution, and its developmentalist mentality were political, and importantly, the bank relied on outside political support to maintain its institutional integrity.

The BNDE-as-party interpretation helps to explain its recent demise or deinstitutionalization in the 1980s (see Willis 1988). In the mid 1970s the bank's institutional power came under siege from within and without. Increasing fragmentation undermined internal cohesion. The bank assumed more disparate functions and hived many of them off in subsidiaries. The new functions and funding required new staff, which grew from six hundred in 1972 to fifteen hundred in 1975 (Willis 1986, 104). The influx greatly diluted the old sodality. The BNDE slipped farther from the center of planning. Its exile rendered it more a standard development bank and therefore less worthy of the fervent support of its internal and external defenders. The bank suffered its coup de grace within the state when Figueiredo banished it from the Ministry of Planning and subordinated it to a mere sectoral ministry, the Ministry of Industry and Commerce (MIC). In the early 1980s, Figueiredo's political appointees finished off one era of the BNDE by undermining internal procedure and personnel policies. Following the party analogy, the bank lost its cadres, its internal cohesion, some of its outside support, and its mission.

The BNDE offers a transparent case of the processes of institutionalization and deinstitutionalization in the politicized Brazilian bureaucracy. The process had internal and external dynamics. Internally, the small, early BNDE achieved "legal-rational" operation and attracted committed, elite técnicos. By the early 1980s it became a huge, diluted, fragmented bureaucracy, with little of its old spirit. Externally, the bank grew up as the darling of the development set. It found supporters in the bureaucracy, the military, the private sector, Congress, and public opinion generally. This support was critical in permitting the bank to insulate itself from other political forces and in giving it its substantial policy power. However, both BNDE's internal and external strength had political bases, and when these eroded, so too did the BNDE institution.

The rise of the BNDE and other similar professional, universalistic, merit-based agencies has often been heralded as the beginning of a piecemeal process of administrative modernization. The implication was that the bureaucracy would modernize through administrative demography; new generations of agencies would supplant traditional ones. Some evidence supports this hypothesis. And, in fact, the BNDE took on this modernizing role and fought traditionalism and personalism where it could. The bank's demise demonstrates, however, that this is hardly a unilinear process.

The Institutional Residual

Despite the lubricants of circulation and personalism, bureaucratic conflict and competition were still common in the military regime, though rarely paralyzing. Whether or not a particular policy battle was cast along organizational lines depended on the kinds of officials and agencies participating, the goals of extra-agency actors, and the general availability of resources.[21]

Técnicos (whose careers are closely tied to single agencies) and young officials are more likely to enter into organizationally based conflicts (though these officials are concentrated in low-level positions and are hence not prominent in major disputes). These bureaucrats circulate less, and their next move up will probably be in the same agency (see table 3). Also, the superiors who (or, in some cases of merit promotion, the rules that) control advancement are in the same agency, so the organization is more likely to inform the policy preferences of these officials. Hence the lower the actors are in the bureaucratic hierarchy, the more likely that conflict will be organizational.[22]

Agencies vary in their degree of institutionalization and hence in the extent to which bureaucrats will bring organizational interests to the policy process. Like the BNDE, state enterprises such as the Bank of Brazil, Petrobrás and CVRD score higher on Polsby's indicators than most other state enterprises and agencies. They are some of the oldest organizations (i.e., over thirty years old) in an economic bureaucracy whose age profile is remarkably skewed by a large infant population. They have set internal career paths, have had more insiders as presidents and directors,[23] enjoy greater respect, and have (or had) strong esprits de corps (i.e., employees value the organization).

Table 3
Circulation by Highest Job Attained

	Number of Agencies per Official	Years between Agency Moves	Number
Minister	5.0	3.7	42
General secretary (vice minister)	4.2	3.7	28
President of major state firm	4.5	4.5	32
President of minor firm	4.0	5.0	29
Head of a Ministry department	4.7	5.1	13
Director of major firm	3.5	5.7	82
Director of minor firm	2.6	7.6	40
All officials	3.9	5.0	281

Managers in CVRD and Petrobrás also tend to circulate less than officials in other firms and ministries (see Schneider 1987a, table 3.5).

Outside groups allied with different agencies can contribute to institutionalization. For instance, since Petrobrás's creation in 1950s, the military has defended it, attempted to institutionalize it, and protected it from outside meddling, thereby encouraging its managers to further the organization's interests (see G. Carvalho 1977). However, institutionalization is not permanent. As the BNDE's story illustrates, even relatively institutionalized agencies can be invaded by outsiders and woven into personal networks.

Lastly, scarcity of resources affects whether officials act organizationally. Informal coalitions work better as positive-sum games, whereas budget cuts ruffle organizational feathers. Bureaucratic logrolling is much simpler when officials can support the policies of their colleagues without jeopardizing their own projects.[24] Budget cuts threaten officials. When career advancement depends on performance and effectiveness, budget reductions can impede policy making and thereby thwart upward mobility. So threatened, bureaucrats are likely to throw up a first organizational line of defense. While they know that this Maginot Line is unlikely to hold and that they must patch together an informal defense alliance, they are likely to be uncongenial policy partners over the short term. The resource constraint is particularly evident in the politics of stabilization. The debt crisis of the early 1980s (and the austerity policies adopted to confront it) disarticulated many policies and policy coalitions. Although the disarticulation often appeared organizational, the major decisions (in part II) on allocating remaining resources still depended on informal coalitions.

Benign Bureaucratic Competition

Institutionalization and organizational conflict vary over time and across agencies. When high, and exacerbated by organizational fragmentation, they can paralyze policy. In moderate doses, contrary to the fragmentation thesis, they can be beneficial. Residual interbureaucratic conflict and competition often had the unintended consequence of producing technically sounder projects. For officials to shoot down someone else's project, they need a minimum technical argument against it (especially in the wake of the military's attempts to impose a "new" technical discourse within the state). A technically weaker project has less chance, unless backed by overwhelming political force, of surviving the crucible of bureaucratic infighting. More generally, bureaucratic competition can increase the quantity and quality of the policy debate. In other cases bureaucratic fragmentation and conflict promote reevaluation and modification that improve policy in midstream.[25]

In her study of the development of hydroelectric power in Brazil in the 1950s, Tendler goes farthest in identifying the beneficial aspects of competition. Before the centralization in the electricity sector in the 1960s, state-level and federal enterprises competed for financing for their dam projects. Tendler explicitly uses the term *competition* "to characterize such rivalry even though it occurred in a noncompetitive industry—in order to describe its efficiency-inducing aspects" (Tendler 1968, 146). These firms competed not for customers but for scarce government loans, but the competition still produced efficient, "private" behavior (Tendler 1968, 152). The rivalry first enhanced the technical debate. Técnicos carried on "perpetual campaigns" extolling their projects and poking technical holes in other proposals. That companies had to compete for financing throughout construction greatly improved performance in the most critical phases of implementation. The companies had constantly to prove that they were efficient builders.[26] In sum, piecemeal and partial financing (often considered a bane of Third World development projects) provoked organizational competition, which in turn made dam building efficient.

Tendler does not completely specify the bases of this competition, but they were not necessarily just organizational. The firms in question were quite new, and their organization and procedures could not be considered valued in themselves. The officials running them had not been there long, nor were their careers tied to them. The reputations that some técnicos (such as João Camilo Penna and Mário Bhering) gained in these firms later catapulted them into other major policy positions. Furthermore, rival regional groups supported and fueled the competition. Overall, competition may have been less between rival enterprises than between ambitious officials (tied to their projects) and their local backers.

In sum, I take issue with the fragmentation interpretation on two counts. First, because institutions are weak, fragmentation (and its deleterious policy consequences) is not the best way to characterize the Brazilian state overall or explain policy failure. Too many policies emerge that, while far from perfect, are effective and more or less coordinated. Second, when fragmentation and organizational infighting do emerge, their secondary policy impact is not necessarily all bad. In an environment where compromise and collaboration are common, residual bureaucratic competition can often improve policymaking. The goal is to account for variation and to paint a more nuanced picture of *where* organizational conflict is likely to arise and *when* it is likely to have a positive or negative effect.

Institutional and Non-Institutional Bases for Failure

Though institutionalization and organizational conflict are variable, a confluence of factors promoting this sort of strife can thwart policy making. For instance, some of the strong institutions might enter a conflict, they might find powerful backers to support their organizational claims, they might be able to mobilize their técnicos, and the policy issue and task environment might offer nothing but the option of major losses. In such cases, policy will suffer if not get trampled in a battle of organizational Titans. While such a confluence is rare, it is one source of policy failure.

An excess of deinstitutionalizing personalism is the other source of policy failure. Informal policy processes are highly vulnerable to over-centralization (largely through the informal appointment powers discussed in chapter 4).[27] The Geisel period was one of extreme centralization, and several projects from this period (Açominas, Ferrovia de Aço, and the nuclear program) were subject to little interbureaucratic conflict and less debate. With the benefit of hindsight, they are clearly among the most economically and technically questionable projects of the 1970s. Personalism allows the president and some ministers to pierce organizational boundaries and override opposition. Central decision makers simply do not have the capacity to make all policy. When they try, they can usually prevail over subordinate organizations, and some of their policies will fail.

It would seem the argument has come full circle: structural overbureaucratization and behavioral underbureaucratization can impede development. However, this chapter should have at least specified the fairly infrequent circumstances in which these factors impede. Institutional rigidity arises only in instances where other factors combine. The danger of personalism lies not in the perversion of legal-rational behavior—and to the extent it does so, it is often beneficial—but in its vulnerability to centralization.

Discretionary policy making in Brazil is a fluid, noninstitutionalized, and personalized process. More often than not, interbureaucratic politics in Brazil diverge from a classic Allisonian approach of battles between organizations. The central explanation resides in the high levels of mobility, which weaken organizational loyalties and strengthen attachment to personal ties. Personalism and circulation form a deinstitutionalizing circle: high circulation weakens organizations and makes officials seek out personal bonds, and these personal interagency ties in turn undermine formal organization and procedure.

In short, formal organization is a hypothesis, not an assumption. Overall, if we cannot assume that formal organizations determine officials' preferences and interaction, then we need to search farther for the sources of bureaucratic preferences and the informal bases of power. The next two chapters address these issues.

3

Careers in the State

AN EXAMINATION OF the economic bureaucracy in Brazil raises
the perennial questions about elite bureaucrats. What sort of
sociological formation do they constitute? Are there identifiable and relevant subtypes of officials? What preferences and
interests to they have? Where do these preferences come from:
social background, socialization, ideology, careers, or position in
the capitalist mode of production? This chapter offers preliminary answers. Brazilian officials do not form a separate state
bourgeoisie or technocracy, nor do they act as such. The best
way to understand their preferences is to look at the career patterns they follow. Career patterns allow us to identify the aspi-
rations officials have and the kinds of behavior they adopt to
advance in any one career.

The bulk of this chapter is devoted to analyzing the four major careers in the Brazilian bureaucracy: political, military, technical, and politico-technical. The officials who follow these
careers constitute social types, each of which brings different
preferences to policy politics. By understanding the interaction
of these preferences and their roots in careers, we can better explain policy outputs in Brazil. While careers offer a generally
promising subject of inquiry, the conclusions of the preceding
chapter make such an analysis essential. If we cannot assume
that officials adopt organizational interests, we have to find
other guides to bureaucratic behavior.

Men Behind Big Desks

The labels for top economic bureaucrats run from state bourgeoisie, technocracy, state entrepreneurs, *marajás*, state managers, technobureaucrats, state capitalists, técnicos, and economic
mandarins to a number of other more flowery or derogatory
terms. In Brazil they all refer to a small, homogeneous group of
men (there are virtually no women) who have university-level

43

technical training and who hold jobs that give them formal responsibility in economic decision making.[1] Before selecting appropriate labels, it is worth pausing to reject some terms currently in vogue for exceeding limits for theoretical baggage.

Terms that imply a ready-made cohesion or power are inappropriate. *State bourgeoisie, state capitalists,* and other class labels are the most problematic. They lead one to believe that this group, like the non-state variant, is a fairly coherent class and that its defining feature is its position as the appropriator of surplus value in a system of capitalist relations. Some authors use these terms precisely because they believe bureaucrats to constitute such a group. Bresser Pereira argues that Brazil has three classes: bourgeoisie, proletariat, and technobureaucracy (1978, 16). The technobureaucracy has class interests, a unifying ideology, and uses its control of large public and private bureaucracies to expropriate its share of surplus value (Bresser Pereira 1978, 15–21). While lacking Bresser Pereira's definitional clarity, Roett also considers elite bureaucrats a powerful "technocratic class" that pursues its independent interests (Roett 1978, 26). Conceptually these terms err by overstretching the reach of the original labels (Sartori 1970, 1034–35).

Bureaucrats' dependence on surplus value is very indirect, they have fairly disparate views of the world (and certainly nothing approaching a class consciousness), and they are incapable of mobilizing as a group to defend collectively their interests.[2] They do not accumulate as a bourgeoisie does; rather, they direct "the process of accumulation in the general interests of capital as a whole, and not in their own particular interests."[3] Block argues convincingly that state managers are capitalist and promote capitalist accumulation not because they share in surplus value or benefit directly from capitalist expansion, but rather because they stand to lose their jobs if the (capitalist) economy does not perform (1977, 15).

A corollary confusion arises from extending the power of an occupational category to a social group (see Zartman 1974, 471). At their desks bureaucrats individually may have wide discretion, but there is no reason to presume that, when they leave the office, they form part of a correspondingly powerful and cohesive sociopolitical group. If elite bureaucrats do manifest more coordinated group power and shared worldviews, it is usually, as in the French and Japanese cases, the result of training and socialization, which have little to do with the offices they occupy. Too often authors lump bureaucrats, state elites, or especially technocrats into various ruling coalitions. In the absence of detailed empirical support, most of these officials should be grouped together with the historically weaker, salaried middle class.

The empirical evidence in Brazil also stacks up against a class perspective. The economic crisis of the early 1980s demonstrated that Brazilian bureaucrats had no collective, organized voice to defend their immediate material interests, their salaries. Figueiredo's economic team imposed real salary cuts of 40–60 percent for the highest-paid state managers over the first four years of the government (*Senhor,* 14 December 1983). The most visible response was confined to exit, as some bureaucrats left to take jobs in the private sector.[4]

The terms *technocrat* and *technocracy* connote greater power than this group actually has.[5] It does not rule but is delegated power. The bureaucracy has continuous power; bureaucrats or technocrats do not. While the Brazilian bureaucracy has dominated civil society, the polity, and the economy, the power of individual officials has always depended on bureaucratic superiors—the president and his inner circle, and ultimately the military (see also Leff 1968, 151). Furthermore, while the bureaucracy as a whole decrees policy, individual bureaucrats often derive their power more from informal ties than the attributes of their position or expertise.

The alternative taxonomy in this book uses less laden terms such as *state managers, administrators, officials,* or *bureaucrats* to denote top civil servants. These terms define the group as officeholders in the state apparatus and as an elite grouping distinct from civil society. These terms are also close to the labels that these men prefer. In 1976, three quarters of 41 government officials chose the term *executive* and the other quarter opted for *high official (alto funcionário).* All but two of 66 managers in state firms preferred *executive* (L. Martins 1985, 209).

From Careers to Social Types

Elite bureaucrats are sociologically distinct from society but not completely homogeneous; the state harbors many subspecies. Others have attempted to differentiate the diverse types of people normally subsumed under the homogenizing label of bureaucrat. Allison classifies them by bureaucratic position: Chiefs (top bureaucrats), Staffers, Indians (department personnel), and Ad Hoc Players (outsiders) (1969, 709). Downs combines nine general psychological motivations to construct five types of officials, on the basis of their mix of motives: climbers, conservers, zealots, advocates, and statesmen (1967, 84–88). What type of official a person is depends on motivation, psychological predisposition, and the position occupied.[6] Kelly divides state enterprise managers into engineers and commissars depending on their careers and on when their career interests are likely to coincide with those of the firm. In simplified form, engineers are like managers in private firms and "generally see the firm's betterment in their own self-interest," while "the commissar's principal interest lies outside the firm." Moreover, "for the commissars, days spent in a state-owned company make up a season in a political career" (Kelly 1982, 107–08). This career approach is the most promising basis for the empirical classification of bureaucratic subtypes.

The neglect of careers in the literature on organizations and public administration is endemic.[7] Much of the literature on public administration takes static snapshots of bureaucrats in particular positions, and hence the emphasis is on how *positions* condition behavior. To outsiders organizations may be matrices of positions, structures, or functions, but insiders are watching a series of careers, especially their own; "indeed, organizations themselves are little more than interlocking sets of career paths" (Van Maanen 1977c, 165).

One of the things newcomers first learn—and one of the issues that generates the most general interest, speculation, and gossip—is why some people receive promotions and others do not. Most Brazilian officials can easily rattle off the complete curricula vitae of dozens of other officials. Smith noted the same phenomenon in Mexico (1979, 252). Bureaucrats monitor their careers carefully while keeping a watchful eye on their colleagues; "observations and speculations about who is moving where, when, and why are perhaps the most frequent and engrossing topics dealt with by people when 'talking shop.' "[8]

Career considerations are more important in big decisions and long-term policy than in day-to-day bureaucratic functioning. The latter may conform to organizational norms and the stuff of organization theory. Big decisions, and hence politics, are much more clearly tied to careers. Careers offer a better way to assess the fundamental interests people have. Most studies on the economic bases of political action focus on direct, immediate interests. Capitalists want profits, workers wages, and bureaucrats budgets.[9] Most of these analyses end up with a large unexplained residual, which can be chalked up to false consciousness or other perceptual ailments. The alternative hypothesis is that most people will relinquish short-term gain in favor of long-term interests such as careers.[10]

A career involves both internal and external bases for preferences and behavior. Careers encompass initial psychological predispositions, socialization, and a framework of incentives and sanctions for advancing in the chosen career. On the internal side people choose (to the extent they can) the priesthood, the military, or medicine because they identify with the values of that career. Presumably they enter the career already sharing some of its values and preferences.

Socialization in education and early career reinforce the initial internal predisposition. Socialization also serves to impose external norms of conduct. In particular, individuals learn the types of behaviors and preferences that are likely to earn them rapid promotion (Stinchcombe 1968, 110). These external career conditioners offer an important additional factor to studies of social roots and socialization of elite bureaucrats. Officials are not merely the sum of past experience. Their behavior is designed to get them somewhere. To rephrase Allison, where you stand on an issue depends less on where you sit than on where you are going.[11]

The argument has two parts. First, careers are paths that individuals follow. The individuals become social types: doctors, politicians, craftsmen, and so forth. Because of some mix of internal and external motivations, they act in more or less predictable ways. In early stages, psychological predisposition certainly affects behavior; however, by the last third of one's career (likely to correspond with promotion to policy positions), the career path is well defined and the bureaucrat knows well the behavior expected of him to continue advancing in his selected career path. Furthermore, by this point in one's life and career it is difficult to jump the tracks.

Second, identifiable career patterns, filled by social types, should give us a fairly good empirical map of bureaucratic behavior and politics. In policy analysis it is a fairly simple matter to identify the participants and their preferences on any given policy. From this analysis one can infer the general types of officials and explain that one policy outcome. One is left, however, with the questions: how did these officials develop their general policy orientations, and how did they achieve their positions of power. Analysis of career patterns allows one to tag bureaucratic types before analyzing their impact on policy and to predict the preferences they will bring to the policy.

The career approach is not without its problems. Some criticize these social types because in any one decision the participants are likely to be mixed types and will often act out of type; analytic distinctions break down too quickly as they approach the analysis of concrete cases (see, for example, Raw 1983). Kelly recognizes this pitfall:

> Engineers and commissars do not represent the children of light and the children of darkness. . . . Nor can an individual claim to be purely one or the other. At any time, however, a given [state-owned enterprise] will be directed by some relatively fixed mixture of engineers and commissars. The point is that *the two groups, and the balance between them, provide the dynamics of goal conflict within the firm.*[12]

My general argument also adopts this rationale to depersonalize or disembody the social types in order to understand bureaucratic politics in terms of the mix of, and conflict between, these behaviors.[13] At an abstract level, bureaucratic politics in Brazil are most intelligible as the outcome of conflict and co-operation between social types (with varying power resources).

Nonetheless, empirical warts and all, careers are an improvement over organizational and material interests as a basis for understanding bureaucratic politics. Career analysis provides concrete data about the people who work for the state. It is empirically simpler to identify a social type than, say, Downsian personality types. Career interest captures more of the diversity of individuals in organizational settings than two-dimensional organization men seeking immediate material gratification. Knowing an official's social type is still the best, albeit imprecise, basis for predicting probable behavior.

Using careers, we can first of all establish the existence of a state elite that depends on whether Brazilian bureaucrats make their careers primarily within the state (Nordlinger 1981, 31–32). On average, officials in the economic bureaucracy spent about one-quarter of their twenty-six-year careers in the private sector, and the mean number of moves between the public and private sectors is 1.5 ($N=281$). A full third of officials never work for anyone but the state, and another 23 percent make one move.[14] The 20 percent who move twice sometimes work briefly in the private sector at the beginning and end of their careers, or sometimes for political reasons they sit out one government in the private sector. A last 24 percent move three or more times and seem to have fairly free transit. Sometimes these are top political appointees who move in step with political cycles; sometimes they have skills in equal demand in both sectors and merely accept the best offer of the moment. Overall, though, most officials spend most of their working lives in the bureaucracy, and a core state elite of over half moves only once or not at all. Moreover, these proportions are stable over the postwar period. At least one-half of each cohort (classified by decade of graduation from university) from the 1930s through the 1960s moved at most once to or from the private sector (see Schneider 1987a, table 4.1).

Four subtypes of official were most common in the sectors I studied: military, political, técnico, and political técnico. This classification covers most of the economic bureaucracy, though other types may be prevalent in other parts of the state. Within each type there are significant differences, explored in the following sections. For the most part, though, this classification captures sufficiently distinct categories within which the range of variation is not too great.[15]

The Military

Direct military influence on policy has often been exaggerated, and the military participated less directly in discretionary industrial policy than their counterparts in other military regimes such as those in Peru, Chile, and Argentina. The military's greatest impact came indirectly though profoundly in macroeconomic policy; the authoritarian order it installed allowed civilian policy makers to serve up draconian stabilization measures and impose severe sacrifices. Although they did not militarize the economic bureaucracy, they did affect industrial policy through three mechanisms: the small number of officers who held civilian posts in the economic bureaucracy; the highly militarized presidency; and a latent impact where civilian policy makers sometimes designed projects to meet military approval.[16] Military influence in industrial policy varied according to where the particular sector fitted in the military's broad conception of national security, and in priority sectors their involvement came through all three channels.

The military brought a strategic, long-range vision of Brazil to policy. The vision is that of an industrial, geopolitical superpower, self-sufficient in the increasingly sophisticated means of war. Not only should Brazil be self-sufficient, but Brazilians should also control production and technology.[17] The typical preference of the military policy maker is pro-industry (especially heavy industry), pro–import substitution, pro-national, and all in favor of the latest technologies. The military influence is political in that it is willing to sacrifice technical rationales in order to nationalize technology or substitute for imports (but on other occasions it will defend technical criteria against clientelistic claims).

The traditional military career is one of the most closed and standardized occupations, which engenders one of the strongest social types.[18] Early socialization is particularly forceful.

Officer cadets often come from military families and attend military high schools before entering the officer academy. Nearly all of the postwar generation of officers "entered the military academic system around the age of twelve," and the proportion of cadets from military families increased to 35 percent by the 1960s (Stepan 1971, 40–41).

Subsequent social and geographic isolation reinforces the social distinctness of the military and probably contributes to a more uniform set of preferences. Lacking combat criteria, promotion in the officer corps depends increasingly on "academic" performance, which further strengthens the common socialization. Before advancing to the next rank, officers return to the classroom for several years of study (Stepan 1971, 50). Lastly, colonels and junior generals are likely to spend a year at the military think-tank, the Superior War college, which has been a central institution in disseminating, among other things, a national security approach to industrialization and development (see Stepan 1971, 51; and chapter 8).

A number of other modified career tracks are open to a minority of junior officers, especially those who end up in the economic bureaucracy. In terms of the internal and external aspects of careers, officers share a strong early socialization (internal) but may experience different incentive structures in their subsequent careers (external). Divergent mid-careers promote subtypes within the military social type, as the following examples illustrate.[19] By 1975, four ex–army officers had reached top management positions in electricity and steel firms. Alfredo Américo da Silva was the president of Siderbrás, José Costa Cavalcanti headed the company created to build the Itaipú dam, César Cals was a director of Eletrobrás, and Odyr Pontes Vieira was director for raw materials with the National Steel Company (CSN).

Twelve years earlier, a year before the coup, their different paths to the top were already taking shape. Américo was working his way up the hierarchy in the Army Arsenal and Department of Production. When he came to the end of his forty-year career in the army, his reward was a golden parachute into a state enterprise. By 1963, Costa Cavalcanti had already shifted to a political career by winning election to the

Federal Chamber of Deputies, thereby becoming an *anfíbio*—
an amphibian who can thrive in both military and political environments. He was an important liaison between Congress and
the first military government and served as minister to the next
two presidents before Geisel appointed him to head Itaipú. He
continued there through the end of the Figueiredo administration, when he launched a short-lived and unsuccessful campaign for president.

In 1963, Vieira was already working in the raw materials department of CSN. He worked his way up the company ladder to
director, before dropping to a staff position, where he stayed
straight through 1985 into the civilian government. César Cals
had also already begun work as an electrical engineer in the
early 1960s. He went on to be appointed governor of his home
state, Ceará, in 1970, after which Geisel invited him to direct
Eletrobrás. Cals went on to become Figueiredo's minister of
mines and energy before returning to his seat in the Senate.

For the few officers who embark on extramural careers, these
are four typical routes to the top positions in state enterprises,
ministries, and state governments. Some of these routes have
been common throughout this century, whereas others became
more so under military rule.[20]

The bureaucracy did not suffer the blanket invasion that
many expected. At the cabinet level the calculations of the proportion of military officers in civilian ministries range from 11
to 25 percent.[21] Below the cabinet level, Barros found military
participation to vary greatly across ministry and sector, to conform by and large to pre-1964 penetration, and to be fairly low
overall. For 2,483 civilian positions in the first four military
governments, the average rate of military penetration was 10.6
percent, up from 6.9 percent in the Goulart government.[22] In
1968, Daland found military officers in 10 percent of 321
second- and third-level positions in the civilian bureaucracy
(1981, 285). My survey of top positions in the economic bureaucracy turned up ex-officers in 15 percent of the appointments.[23]
In comparative terms, military penetration of the Brazilian bureaucracy was low. In Peru, for example, officers took over
around half of the top positions in state enterprises (Sorj 1983,

87). In Chile military officers (mostly active army officers) occupied 52 percent of the 237 top executive positions (Huneeus 1988, 126).

Presence does not necessarily mean commensurate power, especially in Brazil. On the one hand, the percentages may understate the relative power of these officers. Sometimes they had access to top decision-making circles, and hence their policy weight was greater than the percentages convey. On the other hand, these percentages may overestimate the military content of the penetration, because officer-engineers and anfíbios may not always act like military men. Some argue that these officers militarized the bureaucracy, but it seems more likely that nonmilitary bureaucrats would civilianize the minority of military appointees (see Barros 1978, 207). Golden paratroopers might, in greater numbers, militarize the bureaucracy. They have spent their entire lives in the military and will probably not work long in civilian positions. They are more socialized by military service and not dependent on civilians for further promotions.

For anfíbios and military engineers, the action of doffing their uniforms is more than symbolic. This is especially significant when Brazil is contrasted to Chile and Argentina, where line officers were "stationed" in civilian positions, remained in uniform, and returned to active duty after serving out their time in civilian bureaucracy. In Brazil active-duty officers can take up to two years of unpaid leave to work in the civilian bureaucracy, after which they must retire or return to the military (Barros 1978, 266fn). In sectors such as steel that military técnicos ran for decades, career patterns are more technical than military. At about age thirty an officer-engineer has the option of active or technical service. Those in state enterprises usually choose the latter and apparently hang on to military promotions until they can enter the reserve (at an early age). Their técnico careers are then largely dependent on their performance in the state enterprise or government agency. For anfíbios, their departure from active duty also means that career advancement will depend on political rather than military criteria.

Anfíbios and engineer-officers have split careers. They share the same lengthy and forceful socialization in their formative years but then spend much of their careers working in civilian environments. To some extent the degree to which these hybrid officers act "in type" depends on the length and strength of early socialization (internal) versus the force of their ambitions to succeed in the civilian world (external).[24] These conflicting pulls may not, however, affect the preferences associated with the social type: nationalism, developmentalism, and national security. Military engineers especially were trained in a field deemed essential for national security and presumably continue to think of it as such. Overall, ex-officers are unlikely to militarize the bureaucracy but likely to hold on to toned-down military preferences.

The force of the military social type is not limited to its representatives in the civilian bureaucracy. The Brazilian military has been very successful in formulating and propagating its blend of nationalism, counterinsurgency, developmentalism, and *grandeza* (superpower destiny). This ideological offensive encouraged civilian policy makers to drape their proposals in these ideologies. Top appointees knew that they were dependent on the military and that they had to please them to remain in power.

The presidency was thoroughly military and had a potential voice in all major policies. The president was a general, as were most of the ministers of the inner cabinet (see Schneider 1987a, chapter 2). This inner circle clearly had the power to intervene in any policy, but actual intervention varied greatly from president to president, and across sectors and policies (see chapter 9 below). It was through the presidency that the "militarization" of policy was most visible and profound.

The appearances of military rule in Brazil can be misleading. The military did hold all the trump, but power should not be confused with direct policy impact. In fact, some officers complained about the *lack* of military influence in economic policy. In 1968, General Albuquerque Lima called for a national development council, which he claimed "would allow members of the armed forces to play a larger role in shaping development policy, as against the current system dominated by civilian técnicos" (Flynn 1978, 419). Nonetheless, through the various channels considered above, the military had a powerful but not overweening or consistent influence in industrial policy.

Técnicos

Técnicos are far more common than officers in the economic bureaucracy. They have university degrees and work in their area of expertise often for only one or two different agencies throughout their careers. The preferences they bring to policy making are economic and technical rationality, procedural universalism, and organizational loyalty. Their impact on policy does not, however, correspond to their numbers because they are concentrated in low-level or low-power positions.

O'Donnell's caricature of technocratic roles is an extreme but apt description of what I call técnicos:

> Their training stresses a "technical" problem-solving approach. Emotional issues are nonsense; the ambiguities of bargaining and politics are hindrances to "rational" solutions; and conflict is by definition "dysfunctional." . . . That which is "efficient" is good, and efficient outcomes are those that can be straightforwardly measured; the rest is noise that a "rational" decision-maker should strive to eliminate from his decision premises.[25]

In Brazil a técnico is a man with university-level, non-humanities training in an area such as engineering, economics, administration, accounting, and law. His career starts with a bachelor's degree from one of a dozen or so top universities in the center-south states of São Paulo, Rio de Janeiro, and Minas Gerais. Upon graduation, he enters the appropriate (for his degree) division of a state enterprise or ministry department. In contrast to the political técnico, he stays in this agency and rises vertically to the top of his technical specialty: for example, an engineer rises to director of production. His career usually peaks at the level of company director or department head.

Over time all of the major state enterprises have at least a handful of directors who fit this type. For example, in 1957, Antonio Ianuzzi graduated in engineering from the University of Brazil. In 1964 he passed the BNDE entrance examination and entered the steel division. He worked his way up in this small department before transferring in 1973 to the nonferrous metals section. There he rose to become head of the department, but he resigned after a year because he found himself in an ugly political vise between his subordinates and outside policy makers. After resigning in 1977, he returned to project analysis in the same department until he retired in 1984.

Carlos Walter Marinho Campos graduated in mining and metallurgy from the University of Ouro Preto. He first went to work for the National Petroleum Council as a geologist but entered Petrobrás a year later. After two years as assistant field geologist, he was sent by Petrobrás to the Colorado School of Mines for two years. Upon returning, Campos started a twenty-year climb to the top of the exploration wing of Petrobrás which he headed during the Figueiredo government. With the arrival of the new government in 1985, Campos left Petrobrás after more than three decades to work with a research institute.

Técnicos inhabit the lower levels of the economic bureaucracy. They enter through examination and advance by merit, but only a few rise to top positions, *as técnicos.* The influence they bring is technical rationality, within the immediate bounds of the project or program, and they are likely to oppose any flawed proposal regardless of whether its inspiration is military or pork barrel. In the end, Ianuzzi demoted himself rather than endorse politically tainted projects.

Several elements of this career track socialize técnicos into their "technocratic" role. First, education in engineering and economics school can encourage many to adopt a narrow technical approach to policy, though university is a weak socializing force (and does not have the same effect on political técnicos). Moreover, extracurricular education in most technical schools includes a heavy dose of nationalism and developmentalism.

Second, initial career advancement is based on merit and confined to one institution. The técnico is rewarded for pushing technical evaluations of policy and defending the procedural turf of the agency. When a técnico rises to a confidence position, it is usually accompanied by a clear communication that his promotion is based on the assumption that he will continue to act as a técnico. It is because of this socialization and these career rewards that técnicos will oppose, often baring their political necks, projects that transgress technical ethics or endanger procedure.

The empirical identification of técnicos is not as simple as that of officers and politicians. Técnicos are quite similar to political técnicos in training and early career paths. Since all the bureaucrats in my sample have technical training, this variable does not distinguish the two groups. Rates of circulation provide a better proxy. About one-half of the officials in my sample ($N=217$ and excludes military officers and politicians) spent their careers in the state in one, two, or three agencies. This constitutes a rough upper boundary for técnicos, because managers who work for four or more agencies are much more likely to work outside their area of expertise and to care less about their agencies. Of course, some bureaucrats who do not circulate much are highly political and outside their area of expertise; others have whirlwind careers but always work on the same types of technical issues and procedures. Circulation is still the best initial indicator, according to which about one-third of the elite bureaucrats in my sample were técnicos.

This lower level of circulation contributes to another aspect of the behavior of técnicos: risk aversion. The majority of bureaucrats circulate rapidly through top positions and are unlikely to worry about the long-term consequences of their decisions. The técnico minority, in contrast, has to live with mistakes for years, if not decades. Hence técnicos anchor bureaucratic politics and temper "misplaced boldness" (Heclo, cited in Aberbach, et al. 1981, 259).

Técnicos have less power than their numbers suggest. They tend not to rise as far or as fast. When they do rise, they are further hampered by a lack of personal and political allies and experience in coalition building. Their power depends on their expertise and on outside political support for technocratic policy making (e.g., the military's support for neutral expertise in Petrobrás [see also Leff 1968, 148]). Other policy actors need their expertise to build coalitions, to fend off technical attacks, and to find technical flaws in competing projects. Technically flawed projects do get approved, but it is always easier to have strong technical arguments to deflect political attacks. Técnicos are often agenda setters as well. More political appointees often take over agencies, but they consult with the agency's técnicos on projects or policies to push.

Politicians

Although politicians were not numerous in the economic bureaucracy, they were nonetheless able to influence policy, especially during the more open periods of the military's rule. Unlike its contemporaries in South America, the Brazilian military did not board up Congress the day after the coup. The military continued to hold elections and constantly sought support from politicians (many of whom called for and approved of their intervention). Although Congress was impotent, politicians participated in economic policy making through several other channels. Military rulers appointed some politicians to top positions in the government while outsider politicians informally lobbied officials at all levels. Brazilian politicians generally pressured to change policies to favor their regions and elite constituents.

Of the social types discussed here, Brazilian politicians are second only to the military in terms of highly structured socialization, career paths, and a high sense of shared identity. Politicians attend one of a handful of law schools. In one survey, 63 percent of the politicians studied law ($N=44$), compared to 29 percent of the civil servants and 49 percent of the businessmen (McDonough 1981c, 71). After graduation they may enter private practice for a few years before running for the municipal or state assemblies. After several terms in the local assemblies they run for the Federal Chamber of Deputies. From there the successful politician accepts appointed positions in the state or federal government. The crowning achievement in a politician's career is to be elected (or appointed) governor (the position of governor of a state has ranked second to that of president throughout this century).

Rondon Pacheco's political career spanned four decades after his graduation from law school in 1943. After four years of private practice, his hometown in rural Minas Gerais elected him to the state assembly, where he served until 1951. He was then elected to the Federal Chamber of Deputies, where he served out the decade. The governor of Minas Gerais appointed Pacheco to be secretary of the interior of the state for 1961–62, after which Pacheco returned to the Chamber. He supported the 1964 coup, and in 1967, Costa e Silva appointed him to head his Civilian Household. When Costa e Silva died, Pacheco returned to Congress until he won the indirect gubernatorial election in 1971. Upon leaving the governor's mansion, he parachuted into the presidency of Usiminas (one of the three big steel plants), where he served for six years. In 1982 he returned to Congress.

Pacheco's career illustrates nicely the positions and channels open to politicians: access to the president's inner circle, appointment in the economic bureaucracy, and representation of "legitimate" regional demands. Presidents varied in their disposition to include in their inner circle politicians who supported the regime, as was the case when Costa e Silva invited Pacheco to head the Civilian Household. Military presidents usually invited politicians to the inner group to serve as liaison with Congress, to smooth things over with a feeble but potentially hostile legislature. But, while inner-circle politicians were meant to mollify their colleagues, they also had the position and influence to intervene sporadically in economic policy to further narrow interests.

Politicians who supported the regime sometimes received invitations to the economic bureaucracy. Of 450 confidence appointees over the course of the military regime, 20 percent were politicians.[26] As in the case of the supposed militarization of the bureaucracy, politicization was rare and varied from agency to agency and from president to president, increasing as the military gradually retreated to the barracks. The more important a particular agency or state enterprise to the local government, the more likely a political representative was to show up in the agency's management. This was true in Pacheco's case: steel is very important, symbolically as well as economically, to Minas Gerais.

A last avenue of influence was that of an outside governor or congressman pressing regional interests. Northern and northeastern politicians in particular could count on sympathy from some factions of the military that felt that regional imbalances or northern misery threatened national integration and hence security (see Skidmore 1985, 129, 134–35). Since this was one of the few remaining representative functions politicians could fulfill, it was all the more likely that it would be the kind of pressure they would bring to bear as a social type. To the extent that clientelist and party benefit were less acceptable claims, politicians concentrated on regional lobbying.[27]

Politicians concentrated their efforts on diverting resources to their states. They flocked to projects and programs that could be committed to any state. Few of them worried about the technical merits of the policies; if the resources were to be committed, better their state than someone else's—and better soon, while they were in a position to take credit for it. Though elected positions had little power and appointed politicians were few, politicians nonetheless did influence policy beyond what one would expect from their formal and numerical weight and from the prevailing technocratic discourse.

Political Técnicos

The military claimed to have purged the bureaucracy of clientelist temptations and patrons. The first governments achieved some success by cutting Congress out of policy formulation, firing selected administrators, and recruiting top bureaucrats from outside the *classe política* (see Nunes 1978). No sooner had they proclaimed the dawn of a new technocratic age than the emasculation of Congress and parties repoliticized the cleansed policy machinery. Closing down parties and Congress did not turn politics off; it merely squeezed them entirely into the bureaucracy. Technical training became a prerequisite to entering this politicized state, but further political skills were necessary to advance. This was the climate in which the political técnico—a cross between a politician and a técnico—was to flourish.

Political técnicos begin their careers in schools alongside técnicos.[28] Both enter the state through examination or technical qualification. However, political técnicos are more mobile across industrial sectors, administrative lines, and the boundary between the state and the private sector. They start at lower technical levels and build careers by moving laterally and up through the state, often taking years out for stints in the private sector. The more political the técnico, the more likely it is that he will sit out one government in the private sector. Specific technical training is not a barrier to moving into other areas: the research for the case studies in part II turned up electrical engineers negotiating mining investments, uranium experts co-ordinating coal imports, and economists determining steel plant expansions. Qualified técnicos were available for these jobs. Since experts were not appointed, political and general technical training were the criteria for selection.

Most of the non-politician, non-military officials who circulated through four or more agencies can be classified as political técnicos. Those who work for many different agencies are more likely to wind up outside their area of expertise and more likely to receive appointments because of their general bureaucratic effectiveness. In my sample political técnicos constitute about one-third of all top bureaucrats.

Once a political técnico has demonstrated minimum technical and administrative competence, further promotion depends on political factors. However, political técnicos are distinct from politicians because they lack a broad base. They do not seek out mass or electoral support. Rather, they thrive on visibility, a reputation for effectiveness, informal networks (regional, family, school, and/or career), and projects. Participation in projects helps form interbureau ties that facilitate future coalition building and appointments.

There are two subtypes. The first follows a *panelinha*, an informal group centered on one powerful person. The *Delfim Boys* are the archetype, but others with power formed less notorious cliques. Here promotion depends on service and loyalty to the kingpin. Long-term advancement depends on the fortunes of the central figure, although subordinate members would also help one another if this person loses power. *Panelinhas* do not predominate in the bureaucracy, but they have occasionally occupied powerful positions. A second, far more numerous group of political técnicos is not tied to any one person and has more widely distributed political allies. These independents rise through general political skills—not specific loyalty—and have steadier fortunes within the state than *panelinha* participants. The following two biographies illustrate these two subtypes.

Carlos Viacava graduated from the University of São Paulo in economics in 1962, when Delfim Netto was the big man on campus (information mostly from Museu da Fazenda 1983). Viacava went on in the mid-1960s to get his master's degree while teaching in the economics department. When Delfim Netto became the secretary of finance for the state of São Paulo, he hired Viacava as an adviser, and so began a twenty-year career that never strayed very far from Delfim. When Delfim moved to the Ministry of Finance in 1967, Viacava went along, again as an adviser.

With the ministerial shake-up in 1970, Delfim expanded his bureaucratic power by (informally) appointing Viacava to head the Instituto Brasileiro do Café which was formally subordinate to the Ministry of Industry and Commerce (MIC). With the change of presidents in 1974, Delfim became Brazil's ambassador to France, and most of his group went to the private sector. The private Companhia Cacique de Café Solúvel hired Viacava, and he remained a director there until Delfim returned to power in 1979. During Delfim's second reign, Viacava held several jobs. He started as special secretary for supply and prices in Seplan, then became the secretary general (vice minister) of finance for two years before leaving to run Cacex (the International Trade Bureau) in 1983. He remained in Cacex until Figueiredo and Delfim left office in March 1985, when Viacava returned to the private sector.

Though of the same generation, Élcio Costa Couto has had a more independent and typical political técnico career. He graduated from the Federal University of Minas Gerais in economics, and after teaching there for two years, went to work for the Development Bank of Minas Gerais. By 1969 he had risen to director of the bank, and from here his career took off. He spent the Médici government at the head of the Special Agency for Industrial Finance (Finame) of the BNDE, before Velloso invited him to be his secretary general in Seplan, where he spent the

Geisel government. With Figueiredo's inauguration he moved to Geipot (the executive group for transportation) and then, two years later, to the National Superintendency of the Merchant Marine. He spent the last two years of the Figueiredo government in the private sector before returning to public service with the Sarney government at the head of the Fundação Centro de Estudos do Comércio Exterior. In mid 1987 he was last sighted running the Secretariat of Agriculture in the Partido do Movimento Democrático Brasileiro (PMDB) government of the state of Rio de Janeiro. Costa Couto's more dispersed political support and his political skills can be inferred from his staying power; he worked in positions of confidence in two regimes, under four different presidents, and more different ministers.

Political técnicos are hybrid or swing social types. They are trained in a technical field (though they often work outside their fields of expertise) and carry an engineer's socialization to the policy process. At the same time they recognize that planning is an essentially political process, and that technically perfect projects wither on the bureaucratic vine if denied political support. They are willing to sacrifice technical purity in order to build in political support, though they may alienate some potential backers to make sure the project will function, mechanically. They are motivated developmentalists, personally ambitious, bureaucratically dynamic, and always in a hurry.

They can bring either technical or political influence (or some mixture) to policy, but they usually seek a balance. Armed with a good technical proposal, political técnicos will seek out political support among politicians, the military and/or capitalists. Faced with powerful backers of technically flawed projects, they will maneuver to gain time, make new studies, find technically oriented allies, leak technical criticism to the press, and so forth. What distinguishes political técnicos from técnicos is that the former accept political "meddling" as necessary to get decisions made. Promotion in the politicized state depends on performance; political técnicos must be able to show, through projects and programs, what they have accomplished. They also know they have at most four to six years (depending on the presidential term). The vast majority of political técnicos do not remain in the same job, agency, or even sector when the president changes. They have to act as if they are going on to new jobs in a few years, and to get a major project/program up and in operation in a short period requires political support to overcome the initial resistance, red tape, and administrative inertia.

Political técnicos differ from other elite political actors in their freedom from binding political commitments. They engage in policy politics without ideological indoctrination (military men), constituents to represent (politicians), or immediate material interests (capitalists). Independent political técnicos are freer than their colleagues who depend on a *panelinha,* but both are more likely to press technical goals farther than traditional political actors are.

Perhaps more important than the influences they bring to bear is the mediating role political técnicos play. Policy making in most bureaucracies is a process of coalition building, logrolling, and negotiation. This aspect is accentuated in Brazil because of the large number of agencies involved in any one policy, the personal ties that crisscross the bureaucracy, and the permeability of the bureaucracy to outside (elite) actors. Hence political técnicos occupy pivotal positions in mediating, brokering, and building coalitions. For instance, an adept political técnico in the top management of a state enterprise such as Petrobrás, CVRD, or BNDE mediates between committed técnico subordinates and outside political pressures. He communicates in both idioms. Political técnicos are not only brokers but also entrepreneurs in the classic Schumpeterian sense. They are political and bureaucratic entrepreneurs. They combine in new ways intrastate power, informal policy coalitions, and state agencies and instruments. And they get things done.[29]

Although numerous, their policy impact comes mostly from the support they can elicit from the powerful. In some instances powerful ministers delegate authority to political técnicos because they can be trusted politically. In other instances political técnicos, like Lenin, see power lying in the streets, or in this case in the corridors of the state, and pick it up. That is, at any given moment power is dispersed within the bureaucracy and among social elites. Unarticulated, these power points may have little impact. If a political técnico can forge several into a coalition and focus it on a particular policy, then he has made manifest some portion of the dispersed power.

Diverse Social Types, One State Elite

After this lengthy microscopic classification, these social types should be put back in their macro context. The bureaucratic elite that occupies the pinnacle of the polity numbers at any given moment in the hundreds. In contrast to a diverse country of millions, this tiny group is remarkably homogeneous and cohesive. For the fine-grained analysis of policy, the distinctions in this chapter are necessary, but for some macro examinations they collapse into an undifferentiated state elite (see Daland 1981, 259–78).

This state elite shares a common education and similar career tracks, and most top officials know their colleagues quite well. For the select few the state is a village. About one-half of the administrators in my survey attended the best universities of Rio de Janeiro, São Paulo, and Minas Gerais. Most will spend all but a few years of their careers in the state apparatus circulating through jobs into contact with one another.[30] They attend many of the same conferences and read the same publications, in which they appear and write frequently. Brazilian officials also share fundamental outlooks; almost all favor capitalism, industry, and development (see chapters 9 and 10). These elements of common socialization and mentalities and constant contact also provide non-bureaucratic bases for state coherence (Rueschemeyer and Evans 1985, 59).

That it is such a small, cohesive elite that is delegated so much power makes it all the more important to identify and distinguish subtypes. A small group of bureaucrats makes many important decisions, but to understand specific policy outputs requires attention to the different groups in the elite. The mere existence of a socially cohesive, developmentalist elite does not explain effective policy. An analysis of social types and their interaction allows one to identify the preferences that go into a particular policy, and which mixes of preferences make for more effective policy than others.

Politics, Technical Rationality, and Effective Industrial Policy

Career tracks generate social types who have stable though not invariant preferences, rationalities, or mentalities. In a static sense particular policy outputs are the result of the interaction between these types and the consequent balance of rationalities that inform the policy. The success of a project in Brazil depends first on its effective, and not necessarily efficient, contribution to industrialization. However, two projects with very different costs may both contribute effectively to industrialization. Hence a secondary criterion of relative opportunity cost must be included. In Brazilian projects, technical influences helped minimize the opportunity costs, while political influences expanded the effectiveness of the project.

Chalmers Johnson offers the basis for choosing different standards of success for different states and their policies. He first distinguishes between market-rational states, which set rules, and developmental or plan-rational states, which pursue substantive goals.[31] In comparing their rationalities, Johnson notes that "the most important evaluative standard in market rationality is 'efficiency.' But in plan rationality this takes lower precedence than 'effectiveness,' . . . [which] is the proper standard of evaluation of goal-oriented strategic activities" (Johnson 1982, 21). Brazil is a prime example of such a developmental state, and the major industrial projects are very much "goal-oriented strategic activities." Unfortunately, Johnson does not provide the criteria by which to assess a policy's effectiveness or to set a cost limit.

A policy is effective if it removes major supply and demand bottlenecks, integrates the economy backward or forward, internalizes within the domestic economy a particular technological cycle, serves as a motor to regional development, opens new markets or supplies, or otherwise has significant externalities that contribute to industrialization. However, effective but very costly projects preclude equally effective and less costly projects and cannot be deemed successful. Success in this sense eludes precise measurement and remains in part a matter of judgment (and hence of controversy). Nonetheless, it is adequate to the task of evaluating or ranking major projects. The effectiveness and opportunity cost of one project can be assessed relative to other existing or proposed projects.

Through what process is successful policy likely to result? In Brazil it was one that allowed for the articulation and combination of both technical and political rationales and influences.[32] Military officers, industrialists, and politicians usually favor political rationality and attempt to influence policies to achieve political ends. In most policy areas they meet with técnicos, who push narrower technical rationalities. Political técnicos are brokers, mediators, and swing coalition members. They can favor either type of rationality but usually work toward a compromise.

The policy process in Brazil is inherently open to politics for several reasons. First, no policy can be purely technical, because it is informed by underlying (and politically relevant) assumptions, and/or because it is subject to technical uncertainties. For any one problem, even a very specific one, there are several cost-effective, technically feasible solutions.[33] The choice between them can be made only on non-technical, often political grounds. Moreover, technical cost calculations are based on uncertain future market fluctuations. When decisions rest on projections, they involve risk taking, which is inherently non-technical. Projections such as market forecasting can be technically better or worse, but they are ultimately only probabilities (Wildavsky 1966, 296). Technical procedures may be able to narrow the risk, but taking the risk can be weighed only in political terms, in terms of other goals.

Second, the peculiarities of the policy process in Brazil bring politics in in other ways. Most industrial projects are non-routine, and planning therefore requires innovation and entrepreneurship, qualities often tied to political motives. The Brazilian state is highly fragmented. Complex projects require coordination among competing officials and agencies with overlapping, competing, or contradictory policy jurisdictions. Coordination among these agencies is possible only through standard political practices such as logrolling and personal exchange. Lastly, officials seek outside political support to get their projects going quickly and sometimes keep them going once they have moved on to other jobs.

Political and technical influences, rationales, grammars, or behaviors are analytically distinct in terms of the number of variables or relationships they factor into policy formulation. Narrow technical calculation applies efficiency criteria to factors internal to the immediate execution of the policy or project. Political influence brings in more external factors: the constituencies the project should benefit or its relation to a long-range strategy or vision of development (Aberbach, et al. 1981, 109). Economists consider externalities, but usually in a more restricted sense than the external factors discussed here (Wildavsky 1966, 297). Politics revolves around who benefits over the short and long run.

The appeal to a vision or to a present or future constituency must also have some public legitimacy. Those who benefit cannot be restricted to the friends, relatives, or clienteles of policy makers. Political influences appeal to regional constituencies, the poor, national capital-goods producers, or some other group that the proponents can publicly argue deserve to benefit from a particular project. The *public* defense of benefiting some constituency is important. Not everyone, or not even a majority, may agree that a certain group deserves special help, but at least the proponent can make it public.[34]

In sum, in successful policy, technical influences hold the opportunity cost within bounds while certain political pressures (such as pork barrel, representative, and/or ideological) give a project a broader impact and hence make it more likely to contribute to industrialization. During the heyday of development by project, Geisel would reiterate in policy meetings his desire for maintaining *a justa medida,* by which he meant a balance of technical and political criteria.[35]

This chapter was intended to open a bit the black box of the state, breathe life into faceless bureaucrats, and introduce some of the characters who will figure in the case studies. The four categories of military officer, politician, técnico, and political técnico still do violence to the rich diversity of Brazilians who work for the state. The goal was to combine a step beyond blunt aggregate analysis of the state with a manageable disaggregation into a limited number of social types. Focusing on careers overly distills or abstracts individual preferences and behaviors, but it restores more individuality and complexity to this behavior than does a focus on immediate organizational or material interest. People are more subtle and patient; they can delay gratification and subordinate present to future interests.

Sometimes, of course, organizational, material, and career interests converge, but the correlation is spurious. It depends not on the fact that the individual is in the organization but on the close identification of the individual's past and future career with the organization. The convergence of organizational and career interest is common enough in most countries so that an organizational approach applies, at least in a pinch. However, it is at best incomplete and hazardous if followed too closely, for it cannot explain the many instances in which these interests diverge.

The personnel implications of this analysis are straightforward. Rather than devising optimal organizations, procedures, or immediate incentive schemes, reformers should look for ways to tie career advancement to the types of outcomes desired. For the bureaucracy as a whole, the issue is not rational structure versus fragmentation but the interaction of careers and structures. If you have a simple, rational structure, then tying officials' careers to organizations may improve performance; however, to attempt such a linkage in Brazil's "feudalized" bureaucracy would risk complete disarticulation.

4

Appointments and Bureaucratic Politics

> The essence of power lies in four
> verbs: appoint, dismiss, arrest, and
> release.
>
> —Último de Carvalho[1]

IF FORMAL ORGANIZATION and procedure do not channel power in the Brazilian bureaucracy, what does? Are we left with a recombinant broth of career-oriented officials who bond sporadically in personalized dyads that coalesce randomly around policy issues? Not quite. Appointments (and chains thereof) create the informal hierarchy within the bureaucracy. In authoritarian Brazil appointments rather than regulations or elections distributed the primary positions of power. To the extent that politicking between social types determines industrial policy, then it is appointments that distribute different social types and structure their opportunities for coalition building and policy coordination.

Sheer volume makes appointments politically significant in Brazil. Most estimates put the number of appointed positions around fifty thousand (*Visão*, 7 January 1985). Incoming Economics Minister Zélia Cardoso de Melo estimated there were sixty-five thousand positions "de confiança" (*Jornal do Brasil*, 4 March 1990). In any event, all policy-relevant positions are filled by appointment. By comparison the U.S. president appoints several thousand top bureaucrats and the Japanese prime minister only dozens (Johnson 1982, 52). Mexico appears to match Brazil in its tens of thousands of appointments (see Purcell 1981, 201). The numbers alone have made presidential appointment power highly political throughout the postwar period.

Appointments became even more important after the coup in 1964. By emasculating Congress and the judiciary, the military forced politics into the executive. Top bureaucrats became legislators as well as executives. On most issues the president and his inner circle delegated power over economic policy to a narrow range of around two hundred occupants of top positions in the state apparatus—from ministers and presidential advisers down to chiefs of ministry departments and directors of state enterprises. With other avenues blocked, bureaucratic appointments became the primary means for recruitment and elite representation. Thus the politics of appointment mobilized would-be elites (and outside forces who wanted their interests protected), thereby making appointments *the* critical issues in the limited pluralism of authoritarianism.

Lastly, appointments matter because individuals matter in Brazilian policy making. As institutions recede, personalities grow in stature. In my policy studies, decisive policy turns were associated with particular officials rather than institutions or organized political interests. However, a more complete explanation requires that one delve back in time to examine how these officials attained positions that allowed them to influence policy. This in turn requires an examination of the byzantine politics of appointment.

Generalizing on appointment politics in Brazil is a daunting task; irregularities and idiosyncrasies complicate induction, and the paucity of general theory limits deduction. In the major empirical study of the Brazilian bureaucracy to date, Daland concludes that, "in one sense, the bureaucracy is staffed in a random or eclectic manner" (1981, 265). The Brazilian press devotes reams of newsprint to speculating about appointments, reporting rumors, and participating in the process by airing names and curricula vitae. Press predictions on nominees to the new cabinet usually bat less than .500 in the months leading up to the inauguration of a new president. Nonetheless, practiced observers can name a pool of candidates two to three times the number of available positions, and nearly all top positions will be filled from this pool. This suggests enough regularity for social science, if not precise prediction.

Political appointments escape most theorizing in public administration because they fall in the divide between politics and bureaucracy. Despite the perpetual discussion of the dichotomy between politics and administration, little work has been done on a major area where the two meet—the politics of appointing top administrators. Public administration theory has been primarily concerned with relations between offices and between officeholders—not individuals—at lower levels in the bureaucracy. Others have noted the importance of personal, informal relations, but usually as secondary and non-political factors superimposed on formal structure. Lastly, public administration focuses more on what officials do once in office rather than the politics of how they arrived. Numerous studies of elites detail the social backgrounds of top officials and from this analysis infer the bases for appointment, but very few start with appointments themselves.

One of the only book-length studies of appointments concludes with only broad observations on the process in the United States and laments that systematic generalizations may not be possible. The four major characteristics of the appointment process are that: (1) it is "broad in scope" and affects virtually all important positions; (2) it lacks "any substantial consensus on the criteria that qualify individuals for presidential appointments"; (3) it is free from "visible conflict"; and (4) it is inconsistent and unpredictable.[2] These conclusions apply to Brazil, but they do not give one much of a theoretical leg up.

In the absence of a single theoretical perspective, an eclectic clustering of concepts best conveys the general forces in the politics of Brazilian appointments. The first three concepts to be discussed—limited pluralism, bureaucratic insulation, and coalition building—focus primarily on considerations of political representation. The following subsections—on uncertainty, control, personal exchange, and performance—analyze how appointments affect relations of authority and administrative performance.

Appointments and Representation

Authoritarianism restricts the range of actors who may participate politically. However, as Linz (1964) first pointed out, the politics of limited pluralism continue in authoritarian, as opposed to totalitarian, regimes. Such politics become very intense when appointments to the executive bureaucracy are at stake. Linz specifies that representation by appointment is non-responsible: the appointee depends on appointers and lacks an external base of power.[3] Appointees can represent the groups from which they were drawn, up to ill-defined but real limits, but cannot fully mobilize their groups to maintain their positions or policy preferences.

On the surface authoritarian leaders appear to appoint representatives from the major groups that support the government, just as leaders in democratic regimes do. But in contrast to the situation in parliamentary systems, once in office, the authoritarian minister is much less beholden to the interests he represents, because they may not be able to oust him if the president and military approve of his performance. In parliamentary coalitions, the parties divvy up ministerial portfolios, decide which party leaders will be ministers (subject to recall by that party), and can threaten to bring down the government if their views are not adequately represented in the cabinet. The distinction revolves around the question of whom the minister is most dependent on for the appointment to, and therefore continuation in, the cabinet.

The flip side of limited pluralism and inclusion through appointment is bureaucratic exclusion by non-appointment. Many authors argue that bureaucratic insulation explains Brazil's success in economic policy making during the democratic interlude.[4] An adage popular before 1964 captures this notion: "Brazil grows at night when the politicians sleep." Freed from clientelistic demands, officials could formulate technically rational policies and redirect state resources from distribution and consumption to investment and accumulation. By extension, the military regime further insulated economic policy makers.

An examination of appointments helps to elaborate the concept and reveal its limits under the authoritarian regime. One of the best empirical indicators of insulation is the number of "outsiders" in an organ who were appointed by, and beholden to, patronage politicians. Effective insulation requires defeating these outsider candidates. Ultimately it is up to the president (the appointer) to enforce insulation, though in some instances other groups lobby in favor of appointing insiders or técnicos.

Several state enterprises even attempted to legislate their own insulation. In 1972 the BNDE passed a resolution requiring that three of its five directors have significant prior experience in the bank. Shortly after the transition to civilian rule (which apparently provoked fears of political intervention), CVRD's new management adopted a similar bylaw requiring that two-thirds of the directors be previous CVRD employees (*Brasil Mineral*, June 1985, 9). However, these acts appear to be largely symbolic, because the majority shareholder, the state, is free to overrule them at any time.

Complete insulation was rarely attained, before or after 1964 (see chapter 10). Vargas and Kubitschek insulated selectively, but Goulart reversed this emerging trend by appointing friends and politicians to most previously insulated positions. After 1964 the military reinsulated, but not completely. Over the five military governments, one-fifth of 450 confidence appointments in the economic bureaucracy went to politicians.

Insulation is usually defined in terms of barriers to clientelistic politicians. However, a more appropriate definition would also cover military penetration or deinsulation through the appointment of officers to civilian positions. Officers occupied 15 percent of the top positions in the economic bureaucracy ($N=450$). In instances where these appointees were also expert técnicos, some degree of insulation may have survived. However, non-técnico officers were little different from politicians in infusing policy with political concerns (though usually relating to national security rather than to patronage) at the expense of technical factors.

Even técnicos recognize that complete political isolation would banish them to the policy hinterland. Proposals, irrespective of technical merit, require political backing to become policy. More specifically, coalitions of officials in different agencies and non-state supporters make policy. Hence effective bureaucrats seek political support rather than exclusively promoting greater insulation. They do this by making appointments that link them to other significant actors in the policy area, be they military officers, governors, industrialists, or other officials. In Thompson's (1967) terms, Brazilian officials want to create a team of "boundary spanners" who mediate between their agency and its politicized task environment.

When lower-level técnicos seek out political appointees, their hope is that these politicians can enhance their position in the bureaucracy and catapult their technically rational but politically anemic proposals into top policy circles. For example, by the late 1960s, once it became clear that the military was in power to stay, state enterprises and agencies recruited retiring military officers in an effort to open channels to top military circles. In other instances técnicos accept politics as inevitable and figure that it is just as well or better to have politicians on the inside.[5]

Extending the argument in the previous chapter, appointers often embed a political and technical balance in their agencies in order to make them effective policy instruments. For instance, presidents of state enterprises appoint certain managers for technical qualifications, some for personal ties, and others for political connections that open channels to relevant political forces. It is thus through appointments that the coalitional basis of policy making is expressed (and insulation moderated).

Coalition building through appointments conforms to what analysts of policy making have called political rationality or political feasibility. In this perspective policy makers assess the political situation and redesign policy proposals accordingly in order to mobilize support and diminish potential resistance (see May 1986; Meltsner 1972). The same rationality of political feasibility can be extended to Brazilian appointments. Officials appoint subordinates with an eye to facilitating the future mobilization of support, while at the same time accommodating other strong groups so as to minimize their future opposition.

In sum, in authoritarian regimes appointments structure representation. The representation can affect the governing coalition, particular policy coalitions, or both. The next section takes a more micro view and considers the relationship between appointer and appointee and the way in which it influences the latter's behavior.

Appointments, Exchange, and Performance

Crozier (1964) demonstrated that the control of uncertainty in a rigid bureaucracy redistributed real power in the organization away from formal superiors to those who could reduce uncertainty. In Brazil controlling uncertainty is one of the major motivations that make appointment politics so intense and personal. Those responsible for a given policy area will want to control other offices and agencies involved in it. Since officials cannot invoke formal controls, they have to place trusted collaborators in these "confidence" positions.[6]

The strong personal ties that permeate the Brazilian administration are not so much vestiges of traditional Brazil as they are perfectly rational responses to complexity and uncertainty. And the crosscutting personal ties further undermine formal linkages and controls, thereby reinforcing the need for confidence appointees. One could counterargue that in fact, traditional cultural norms are the prior factor that first weakened institutions. The point, however, is moot. The uncertainties of a fluid bureaucracy are stronger and more immediate conditioners of behavior than vaguely held cultural norms. That the two are congruent does, no doubt, reinforce the practice.[7]

The administrator has two means for reducing uncertainty and ensuring the loyalty of subordinates: the power of dismissal, and long-standing family, university, or professional ties. The threat of dismissal is an extreme and not necessarily sufficient means of control. Coalitions, rather than individuals, often appoint officials, and appointees can increase their degrees of freedom by playing members of the coalition off against one another. Moreover, once in office, the appointees can use their new positions to form new networks and coalitions, which can maintain them even if they alienate their original sponsors. Personal and family ties are less coercive and more reliable channels of control.

Informal exchange relations permeate the Brazilian bureaucracy. Personal favors are necessary to keep the administrative machinery functioning. They are also important in building one's network of contacts (and hence future career opportunities) and in forging new policy alliances. The appointment exchange rests on the offer of the power and prestige of a top appointment in return for loyalty, competence, and results. Salaries and fringe benefits are often high but are not the primary concerns in accepting or competing for a top position.

That exchange relations are important in the Brazilian bureaucracy is hardly a novel observation. However, the exchange relations in the economic bureaucracy should not be subsumed under the usual rubrics of clientelism, patronage, or *panelinhas*. These concepts may apply to some, but not most, top appointments (chapters 10 and 11 reconsider these themes in the broader analysis of Brazilian politics). While exchange relations are usually dyadic, face-to-face, and unequal, they are a far cry from the clientelism and patronage politics practiced by rural landowners and urban ward bosses. In top bureaucratic positions, exchange is more specific (not generalized), short-term, and transitory, and those involved are social equals, especially compared to exchange relations in more traditional settings. Moreover, because of the restrictions of authoritarian politics, superiors cannot hope to build a support coalition out of appointees. Votes, and hence numbers of supporters, did not matter until the end of the regime. Concepts in clientelism and patronage politics are best reserved for specifying the exchange relations in rural and machine politics (Powell reaches a similar conclusion [1970, 423]).

A related conceptual approach is one that Leeds elaborated over two decades ago as a general model of informal elite organization. Leeds defines a *panelinha* "as a relatively close, completely informal primary group, held together in common interest by personal ties and including a roster of all key socio-político-economic positions" (Leeds 1965, 387). He continues, "the político-economic *panelinha* characteristically consists of a customs official, an insurance man, a lawyer or two, businessmen, an accountant, a municipal, state or federal deputy, and a banker with his bank" (Leeds 1965, 393).

Such *panelinhas* may have dominated elite organization in Brazil's major cities twenty years ago, but they do not organize the top reaches of the economic bureaucracy, though they remain part of what one interviewee called the "folklore." Interviewees usually responded that, yes, *panelinhas* existed, but they were unable to define consistently the contours and membership of any given *panelinha*. For some a *panelinha mineira* controlled steel policy; for others *panelinhas* were organizationally based (each state enterprise and government agency had one or more); still others saw them grouped around university classes; and lastly, some used the term to belittle their opponents. If top decision makers cannot reach a common understanding of *panelinha*, then it cannot be indispensable for career advancement or policy making.[8]

Personal exchange informs most top appointments, but it does not justify labels such as clientelism or *panelinha*. Such systemic terms are inappropriate for characterizing exchanges that are specific, short-term, and instrumental. Personal exchange remains the means for controlling uncertainty and ensuring effective performance, and at any given moment an official is embedded in a network of informal exchange. These networks, however, break up regularly and new ones are in constant formation.

The military changed the criteria for career advancement within the bureaucracy, a method that was more effective in reorienting bureaucratic behavior than purging officials, surveillance by the Serviço Nacional de Informações (SNI), or training. Initial observers emphasized the technocratic style the first military government attempted to usher in. However, at least from the Costa e Silva government and the arrival of Delfim Netto, the criteria shifted from technical purity to general competence and policy effectiveness. The formula for legitimation also shifted. With the advent of the economic "miracle" (1968–73), the military no longer relied so much on its mission to replace inefficient, corrupt politicians with technicians (and to combat communism) but focused more on the regime's ability to industrialize. The key words in major government speeches shifted from *democracy* and *communism* in the first years of the Castelo Branco government to *growth* after 1966 (Soares 1978, 288–89). The growth theme emerged under Costa e Silva, picked up steam with Médici's outsized projects, and peaked with Geisel's quest for *grandeza*.

Criteria for promotion became more explicitly based on the ability to get things done and thereby legitimate the regime. Getting projects off the ground—using whatever political and technical means necessary—became the goal. Effective bureaucrats or political técnicos flourished. The military rulers came to expect concrete results from their economic ministers, who in turn cast about for those political técnicos who had demonstrated ability to get projects through the bureaucratic labyrinth.

In the short run, appointments can give superiors great control over subordinates (and hence over uncertainties) and a clear means for communicating incentives for desired performance. Repeated use of the same criteria for promotion helps to build a career track—the political técnico in the case of authoritarian Brazil. It is through this control over careers that central decision makers can have the deepest impact on performance.[9]

Ideal Typical Appointments

Limited pluralism, bureaucratic insulation, coalition building, uncertainty, personal exchange, and performance influence appointments and appointment relations. Different groups strive to enhance different factors in the distribution of government positions. The president and his inner circle use appointments to gain support, insulate policy makers, and/or improve administrative effectiveness. Appointers at lower levels want to control critical uncertainties, build bridges, and promote effectiveness. Outside political elites seek representation (or in some cases insulation for their favorite agencies from opposing forces). Candidates for appointment want power, prestige, visibility, and most of all, career advancement.

These six concepts also allow us to identify three ideal types of appointment: representative, confidence, and technical (see table 4). Each ideal type creates a different informal hierarchy of control: superiors have no control over representative appointees, complete power over confidence appointees, and indirect control over technical appointees. The technical nominee may ignore superior commands but does afford appointers a type of control in that they are appointing predictable behaviors.

Pure representative appointees trade the support of their constituencies in return for complete freedom in how they use their positions. The constituencies vary in breadth from parties, sectors, and interest groups to single individuals in the case of low-level spoils appointments. Leaders in all types of political system appoint people to please or appease particular factions. Sometimes, as in party coalitions, the exchange is explicit. In other cases, such as the pre-*glasnost* Soviet Union, it is opaque or only rumored. The representative appointment expands pluralism (either limited or not), provides new opportunities for coalition building, and usually punctures insulation (though sometimes seals it, depending on the constituency represented). Representative appointments do not bring a superior's sources of uncertainty under control. They make it worse because the appointees are free to use the positions to pursue whatever they perceive to be in their political interests (at least their motives

Table 4
Characteristic Effects of Representative, Confidence, and Technical Appointments

	Representative	Confidence	Technical
Usual effect of appointment on:			
Pluralism	Expands	Limits	Limits
Insulation	Perforates	Seals	Seals
Coalition building	Facilitates	Impedes	Depends
Uncertainty	Increases	Reduces	Reduces
Exchange	Depersonalizes	Personalizes	Depersonalizes
Administrative effectiveness	Undermines	Depends	Improves

are predictable). The exchange in this case is not necessarily personal, though it is usually informal, and lasts only as long as the government coalition. Lastly, the exchange, by itself, offers appointers no opportunity to elicit better performance.

Pure confidence appointees respond only to the interests of the appointers. They cannot be much help in expanding pluralism (though they can help limit it because they are completely non-responsible to the groups from which they are drawn). They can help insure insulation because they are deaf to outside interests, but for the same reasons they are not helpful in building coalitions because they are so partisan and partial. Their great appeal comes in the appointer's ability to gain control over uncertainties and elicit the desired performance, because, in its pure type, the exchange is completely personal and the appointee absolutely dependent.

Technical appointees are not loyal to superiors or responsive to outside demands. They exercise their responsibilities purely in accordance with the rationality of their area of expertise (such as economics, engineering, or law). Technical appointees are effective insulators, steeped in the technical field (and the organizations in it) and oblivious to outside interests. They cannot expand pluralism or join coalitions except when outside groups support their positions. The exchange is in this instance impersonal—the appointer need not know or talk to the appointee. Hence the appointer has little hope of changing the appointee's behavior. Nevertheless, technical appointees usually serve to reduce uncertainty or are expected to control the technological sources of uncertainty.

In real life it is difficult to find a pure appointment. Most mix the ideal types, and any one appointment can exhibit facets of each over time. As I mentioned above (and explore below), most appointers prefer a range of types: confidence appointees for their closest advisors (who are usually young) and trusted intermediaries, more technical appointees for the mysterious sides of agency operations, and representative ones if outside coordination and support are critical. In some cases appointers managed to combine confidence and technical criteria to achieve partisan competence (as opposed to the neutral competence often advocated in the literature on public administration), which promoted effective policy. The following sections apply some of these concepts and ideal types to concrete situations in state enterprise and in the Brazilian bureaucracy generally.

Appointment Politics and State Enterprise Autonomy

Issues of control and autonomy have generated libraries within the subfield of state enterprise studies. As normative concerns, these issues propel the perpetual-motion debate over the correct relations between the state and its enterprises. Other empirical research has revealed the substantial power of state enterprises that in turn often bedevils those attempting to perfect the relationship.

Why are control and autonomy such central topics? Many analyses have diagnosed the cause of lethargy in state enterprises as bureaucratic sclerosis. Centralization and hierarchy stifle the rapid, flexible responses that firms need to succeed in their markets. Red tape and routinization snuff out whatever entrepreneurial spirit may have slipped in. The antidote is greater decentralization and autonomy. Others find the root cause of deviant state enterprise behavior not in overweening bureaucratic control but in the absence of all but the flimsiest of tethers. Free to follow their own interests, rogue enterprises trample the public interest they were designed to serve. The solution lies in greater control.

Regardless of the specific prescription, nearly all agree that too much of either autonomy or control is a bad thing. The nub lies in an elusive administrative arrangement that allows both flexible control and the necessary, limited autonomy. There may well exist a composite of rules, regulations, and procedures that achieve this. Failing this, the Brazilian experience suggests that judicious manipulation of the power of appointment may provide an acceptable informal balance of control and autonomy.

The authority of the president and his inner circle to appoint presidents of state enterprises (and the power of these presidents to appoint directors and scores of other subordinates) provides several means for adjusting the leash to an optimal length. Superiors can use confidence and/or technical appointments for different degrees and kinds of control.[10] In confidence appointments, the prior personal bond between appointer and appointee establishes the subsequent working relationship between government and enterprise and gives the appointer deep and easily adjusted control over the management of the firm.

In technical appointments superiors select reputations or roles. They may not personally know the appointees, but the nomination carries a tacit or explicit understanding that the appointees will persist in the behavior that gained them their reputations. For example, Ozires Silva became known as one of Brazil's most effective state managers after more than fifteen years at the helm of Embraer, the efficient aircraft manufacturer. When Sarney appointed him to run Petrobrás, few were surprised that Ozires declared that "a state enterprise is justified only if it earns a profit" (*Veja*, 31 December 1986). The approach to control via reputation applies most directly to the pure technical appointment. However, it can be expanded to include other impersonal appointments of a broader range of roles. Appointers have a pool of candidates who are known to be development visionaries, consummate political brokers, project hounds, efficiency engineers, or financial alchemists. Depending on the goals appointers want the state enterprise to achieve, they can then appoint the appropriate reputation or reputations.

The flip, coercive side of appointments is the power of dismissal, or the threat thereof, which allows the appointers to shorten the leash very quickly. The power of dismissal is a blunter instrument usually reserved for cases of flagrant deviation from expected behavior. Dismissal cannot be employed to fine-tune what a state enterprise does, but it can put it back on course should it stray noticeably. One dismissal, or making an example of one appointee, can be effective in changing the behavior of other appointees by making clear the limits of acceptable behavior.

Another strain in the literature on state enterprises focuses less on the optimal government-firm relationship and concentrates on the structural economic factors that thwart efforts at control. The common view is that state enterprises that are big, complex, and self-financing tend to have power and autonomy.[11] This seems to be the case in Brazil: revenues, profits, and political power co-vary. But the causal argument that economic strength creates political power misses the key intervening variables: appointments. The size and vast resources of a state enterprise make it a coveted political prize. Its capture is negotiated at the political peak. In fact, this intervening variable can invert the relationship between size and autonomy: larger enterprises attract greater political attention and interference while politicians ignore small firms, which therefore retain greater autonomy.

In most cases ministers and presidents of state enterprises have different types of appointments and political bases. Ministers rarely appoint or remove their "subordinate" state enterprise presidents, who deal directly with the president. Presidents and other top political leaders in Brazil have no political incentive to allow ministers to appoint the presidents of the state enterprises they supervise. The revenues of several of the largest firms exceed those of the federal government proper. A minister of mines and energy who was left free to appoint the presidents of Petrobrás, Eletrobrás, and CVRD would control an enormous fiefdom within the state that would rival all the other government agencies combined. Clearly, such power can be centralized only in the president, not one of his subordinates.[12] Economic power is the basis for political struggle, which ends in (relative) *political* autonomy for enterprise presidents.

Attention to the intervening political variable makes for more discriminating and dynamic analysis. It allows one to account for rapid shifts in relations between state enterprises and formal supervisors when the economic position of a particular firm has not changed. In some infrequent instances ministers handpick the presidents of state enterprises and these presidents have little independent base besides the minister. Open efforts to exercise autonomy are not suitable for such situations. When the formal controller has the informal power to appoint the presidents of state enterprises then "government" control can be quite effective.

Attention to the appointment process highlights the political nature of state enterprise autonomy. For instance, huge integrated steel plants owe much of their autonomy not to economic power but to the fact that this economic clout mobilizes a powerful regional lobby that defends the plant against central government controls. In Brazil the federal government cannot appoint the presidents of steel enterprises without consulting regional elites, and the presidents nominated are often active in regional politics.[13] In cases where presidents of state enterprises resign to return to regional politics, it is unlikely that their first loyalty while president was to their federal superiors.

The major issue of control is how peak power groups jockey to put someone loyal to them in state enterprise management. For most purposes the appointee remains loyal and beholden to these interests. However, some entrepreneurial appointees attempt to parlay their positions into broader political support, making them less beholden to, and controlled by, the powers that appointed them in the first place. With such appointees the firm may begin to look more autonomous, but not for the reasons usually supposed: the interests of the firm and the struggle for *managerial* autonomy. These are political entrepreneurs using state enterprises to advance their careers.

Incorporating an analysis of appointments reduces the distinctiveness of enterprises belonging to the government and recommends against examining them separately as a peculiar breed of government agency. The key to understanding the behavior of enterprises (public or private) is the individuals who occupy top management positions and the pressures to which they respond. Managers may be constrained by the recalcitrant bureaucracies below them and swings in their markets (or in their task environments more generally), but their longer-term strategies depend mostly on their preferences and those of the people who appointed them. The most significant difference between managers of public and private firms is that state managers are appointed by, and hence accountable to, political leaders. This power of appointment (and dismissal) constrains the economic and political decisions the manager of a state enterprise can take.

If political appointment is the most important constraint, then state enterprises are not much different from other government agencies.[14] That is, the pressures of operating in markets or the ability to generate an investable surplus (some of the key factors that other authors claim make state enterprises a breed apart) are not as important as the mandate and responsibilities communicated through appointments. Political leaders may opt to appoint managers who are primarily concerned with markets and profits. This gives the impression that state enterprises are different from traditional government agencies, but it is merely coincidence. Managers with other interests or charged with meeting other political goals behave quite differently. In short, the behavior of state enterprises depends more on the managers who run them (and the people who appoint the managers) than on the logic of market or profit.

Staffing the Brazilian State

How did the military and its civilian allies fill the top 150–200 positions in the economic bureaucracy? The process of forming a cabinet (including heads of major enterprises) begins well before inauguration, and speculation about appointments becomes a national pastime for six to nine months. For example, more than a year before taking office, Geisel and his closest advisers had already matched an average of two names to each of the top 23 positions.[15] The president first makes confidence appointments to his inner circle (usually to the advisory or liaison cabinet positions that have offices in the presidential palace).[16] Next he rewards the military and civilain factions that supported his candidacy with some military, advisory, and top economic appointments.

Beyond these core appointments, presidents must also give their cabinets rough geographic representation. This "requirement" demonstrates the staying power of regionalism even under authoritarian rule and reveals one of the bases of limited pluralism in Brazil. Regional appointees (who may fulfill other criteria as well) can pursue their region's interests in nondisruptive ways. These appointments are intended less to bolster representation than to preempt regional opposition to the regime.

For example, northern politicians demanded that they be included in the Interministerial Council for the Greater Carajás Program (CIPGC) since its decisions dictated the future of their states. In response to these criticisms the executive secretary of the council, Oziel Carneiro, claimed in congressional testimony that Pará was indeed well represented: "Being from the Amazon, I was very surprised to hear . . . that Pará is without power within the Greater Carajás Program. Imagine what Maranhão and the rest of Brazil would say [considering] that I, a native of Pará, am the executive secretary of the program.[17]" That Carneiro felt he could respond to such criticism in such a forum demonstrates the legitimacy of representation through appointment. Because of a decades-long practice, important states and regions came to expect representation, and the military in many instances saw no reason to disappoint them.

Ministers, while under less pressure than presidents to reward supporters, have less leeway in appointing their subordinates in ministry departments, state enterprises, and *autarquias,* because they face pressures from all sides. First, the minister has to contend with the president and his inner circle, who will nominate officials for major firms and who have additional names that still lack positions. As a former finance minister, Simonsen, related it, the members of this inner group know they want to appoint certain people, but they have to shuffle them around until they fall into place, often preempting ministers in their own backyards (interview, 13 November 1984).

Then, depending on the position, the military, other ministers, regional elites, and/or business will pressure the minister. For instance, coffee producers and the minister of agriculture took a great interest in the head of the Instituto Brasileiro de Café which was formally subordinate to the MIC. Or the military insists on reviewing appointments in sensitive areas such as communications. The money ministers (finance and planning) know they cannot control spending without some say in appointments to financial intermediaries such as the state banks, agricultural price support agencies, and the Central Bank. One ex-secretary of the Secretariat for the Control of State Enterprises (SEST) said it would be much easier to control the spending of state enterprises if he could appoint the financial directors of all major firms (interview, 26 June 1985). In São Paulo the secretaries of planning and finance sign off on all nominations for finance directors in that state's firms. Often, because a minister's effectiveness will depend on cooperation from these interested parties or clienteles, he will want to represent them.

For the remaining positions, ministers and other top-level officials seek confidence and technical appointees to reduce their sources of uncertainty. For some positions they appoint friends and loyalists; in more technical areas they rely on experts. Lastly, for organs that must coordinate with others in the state, ministers want appointees skilled in inter-bureaucratic politics.[18]

Since subcabinet appointments respond to a range of forces and motives, possibilities for coalition and coordination exist from the start. Appointments in any one policy area can include officials with ties to the president's inner group, to other ministers, to outside private interests, to the military, and/or to regional elites. Furthermore, the range of vectors that bears on appointments—technical, confidence, representation (coordination)—endows a policy area with a mix of técnicos, political técnicos, and politicians who will push varying combinations of political and technical factors in the policy process.

Presidents of state enterprises play out a similar though more restricted drama in appointing their directors.[19] Sometimes they are obliged to accept higher orders. Beyond this they attempt to reduce uncertainty by appointing qualified directors with whom they have worked closely before, especially in critical areas of finance and technical operations. Often they promote an insider who knows the firm well to head internal operations. Lastly, presidents of enterprises often reserve one directorship, usually a marginal one such as administration, as an outside liaison post. This is especially true of a steel plant: the governor of the state where it is located directly nominates one director whom the president of the firm puts in a position where the appointee can do little damage. This arrangement is convenient for all concerned. Governors are assured that their interests will not be forgotten, and the firm managers can call on a powerful ally in conflicts with the central government.[20]

Much has been made of the SNI's (military intelligence's) responsibility for conducting security clearances and issuing a bill of political health for all top nominees. The SNI has an agent in all major state enterprises and agencies who formally reviews appointments to that agency. If appointments structure the informal hierarchy in the bureaucracy and communicate incentives for expected behavior, the power of the SNI to remake the bureaucracy would appear formidable. However, this power was rarely exercised. Although the SNI collected massive dossiers on top officials, they could only recommend against the appointee. This was in fact rare, and several civilian appointers managed to override negative recommendations. Of course, SNI surveillance no doubt had an indirect effect in narrowing the pool of candidates by dissuading some people from even considering a public career.

Further evidence for some of these unwritten rules of appointment comes from the rare cases of dismissal. These demonstrate limits for using representative and confidence appointments. For instance, Geisel fired Severo Gomes for carrying his defense of national capital too far (see Evans 1982). Gomes was also too outspoken in supporting *abertura* and criticizing previous military governments. In other words, Gomes went too far in representing his base of "democratizing," Brazilian capitalists. In terms of confidence appointments, both Costa e Silva and later César Cals (Figueiredo's minister of mines and energy) went overboard in appointing family members to senior positions for which they had neither training nor experience. This nepotism provoked public criticism and military and bureaucratic opposition. Cals at least was obliged to reassign his son. Trusted, confidence appointees with kinship ties are fine only if they are also minimally competent and trained.

Antônio Delfim Netto: *L'État c'est lui?*

Delfim Netto was the single most important economic policy maker during the authoritarian regime. He served in three governments in three ministries: as minister of finance (1967–74), minister of agriculture (1979), and minister of planning (Seplan) (1979–85). Regardless of his position, he was the economic superminister for thirteen of the twenty-one years of military rule. Few economic policy makers incite such passions as Delfim. His defenders and collaborators had difficulty expressing their awe, and his detractors rarely refrained from ad hominem abuse. In part this is because no name was so closely associated with the strategy of capitalist industrialization during the military regime. Few countries have experienced such rapid economic expansion (in the seven years Delfim served as finance minister, the Brazilian gross national product doubled), but rarely in the twentieth century have the poor been so mercilessly subjected to the ravages of capitalist development. Delfim personified both sides of the strategy.

Nearly all general policy studies discuss Delfim and his policies. Fishlow (1973) notes that in the 1960s the critical change in economic policy and Brazil's economic fortunes came with Delfim's arrival. Skidmore, in his analysis of the Costa e Silva government, concludes that Delfim had "greater personal control than any predecessor since 1945" (1985, 139). Flynn notes that "the role of Delfim Netto is . . . a key to an understanding of Brazilian politics from 1967 to 1973" (1978, 382). Vianna (1987) devotes much of her book on this period to an analysis of the mechanisms Delfim employed to amass his power. Like a bureaucratic black hole, Delfim drew agencies and policy instruments to him.

What was the basis for Delfim's power? It depended ultimately on the military (Skidmore 1985, 139), but this was true of nearly all policy makers. Why did Delfim have so much more of it? For a while his power appeared to have roots in the Ministry of Finance, which he revitalized. But he ran the economy from that ministry in the Médici government and then from Seplan in the Figueiredo government. Hence the formal powers of each ministry meant less than Delfim's informal power. In each instance, Delfim, over time, abrogated formal powers from other ministries and centralized them in his ministry of the epoch.

However, in the Brazilian bureaucracy it is not enough to centralize formal policy instruments. To achieve real control, Delfim deftly wielded his considerable powers of appointment.[21] Delfim reputedly admitted that he was a better politician than economist (and few of his critics would disagree), and his political acumen was quite evident in appointing and dismissing other officials, from ministers on down. He first appointed confidence subordinates to positions formally in the domain of his ministry (something not all ministers have the power to do). Next he appointed several officials formally outside his ministry but in important policy positions. Delfim's power of appointment over subordinates increased over the course of each government. He did not participate in many appointments at the start of each government, but as appointees left, he positioned himself to participate in replacing them.

The nature of Delfim's appointments and the subsequent hierarchical relationship differed from the norm. More than other appointers, he demanded (and got) complete personal loyalty; his authority frequently bordered on charismatic.[22] Most of his appointees were young, recent graduates of the economics departments of the major São Paulo and Rio de Janeiro universities, and often his ex-students. His personal network gained such notoriety that his appointees became known, in Portuguese, as the *Delfim Boys.*

The absolute number of appointments Delfim made is a small fraction of those in the economic bureaucracy. He concentrated on the critical ones such as the Central Bank, other public banks, agricultural credit agencies, and price councils. Where he could not appoint, the threat of dismissal was a strong functional equivalent in setting power relations within the bureaucracy. Those who opposed Delfim sometimes found themselves without an office. One of the more publicized cases in the 1980s was the dismissal of Douglas Luz, the president of Eletronorte, which Delfim engineered to increase his authority over state enterprises. He created a central watchdog agency, SEST, in Seplan to control state enterprise spending. Some presidents of state enterprises ignored SEST's budget ceilings (because formal commands are initially tentative). The most convincing way for Delfim to communicate how serious he was and how much enforcement power he had was to get Figueiredo to fire a president for exceeding budget ceilings (*Gazeta Mercantil*, 7 September 1984). Firing the spendthrift president of Eletronorte sent a strong message to other managers to respect SEST's limits.

Delfim Netto is an illustrative but extreme example of a master appointer. He is unique in recent history in that he held more power for a longer period than any postwar money minister. He is also different in that he fully recognized and exploited the powers of appointment. He exacted greater personal loyalty than is usually the case, but at the same time he maintained high technical standards. The *Delfim Boys* were qualified confidence appointees. Delfim demonstrated the possibility of resolving the apparent contradiction between neutral competence and partisan appointments by surrounding himself with competent partisans.

Presidential Succession and the Argument So Far

Chapters 2, 3, and 4 have elaborated the three essential concepts for understanding bureaucratic behavior in Brazil: circulation, careers, and appointments. To recapitulate, high circulation weakens formal organization and inhibits organizational loyalties and hence institutionalization. Although unencumbered by organizational commitments, officials do follow identifiable career paths that, through socialization and the exigencies for advancement, shape social types with distinct sets of policy preferences. Then it is appointments, rather than formal authority, that distribute these social types through the bureaucracy and structure power relations between them.

The authoritarian regime in Brazil is nearly unique in that it had regular and scheduled presidential successions. It is difficult to overemphasize the impact of this regular succession on rationalization and institutionalization of the bureaucracy, circulation, bureaucratic careers, and policy change. After Castelo Branco, successive presidents succeeded in de-institutionalizing the bureaucracy. Each pursued short-term economic and political goals, and to achieve them they undermined institutions. They changed procedures capriciously, created hundreds of new, often redundant, agencies, and dramatically altered existing ones. Institutionalization requires stability; people do not value nor commit themselves to uncertain organizations or procedures. Paradoxically, the same dictatorial powers that in 1964 were considered necessary to create rational planning structures allowed subsequent presidents to undermine the same structures.[23]

The impact of succession was most direct on circulation. Almost all top officials changed jobs when presidents changed. Had only one or two generals ruled Brazil for these two decades, circulation might have slowed to a trickle. This high circulation, coupled with the propensity to go forth and multiply agencies, further undermined formal organization by eliminating the career bond between officials and their agencies.

Presidential succession maintained career uncertainty for all top-level officials. They knew they would be leaving their jobs at the end of the presidential term. Their task was to use their position, policy responsibilities, and personal contacts to gain a better position in the next government. Such an endeavor is always uncertain because no one knows who will be the next president. In the authoritarian regime the knowledge that the next president would be a general mitigated the uncertainty. Officials could bank on the general wanting to promote industrialization and therefore needing effective officials. So they could use their positions to demonstrate their abilities to get policies implemented. They would also need personal contacts, but not personal liabilities. Some top appointees would probably come from within the bureaucracy, but officials could only guess which ones. One's best bet was maintaining ties to all possible candidates. Other officials, and those closest to them, would be banished, and it was wise to maintain one's distance. In short, the climate was ideal for political técnicos.

The policy consequences of succession were direct and often dramatic: major policy and project changes usually come with new appointees. The fact that different economic doctrines circulated through the bureaucracy meant that projects were often subjected to different evaluations and modified to fit the orientations of the new economic team. Moreover, a policy or project begun in one government would mobilize those most affected to have some representation (read "participation in appointments") in the policy area in the next government. This mobilization adds a dynamic dimension to the analysis of bureaucratic insulation and representation through appointment.

Part II tells the stories of four projects, which illustrate the weakness of institutions and the policy impact of circulation, social types, appointments, and the dynamics of presidential succession. While most elements of the arguments presented in this first part crop up in all of the stories, each chapter highlights some of them.

The creation of Siderbrás, a holding company in steel, is an administrative reform and most likely to arouse organizational interests. But when the behavior of officials does not further their organizational interest, their career paths explain the divergence. While all the stories involve state enterprises, chapter 5 considers most explicitly alternative hypotheses from the literature on them. Finally, Siderbrás's chronic difficulties illustrate the impracticality of devising new administrative structures that do not take into account informal powers.

Chapter 6 recounts the building of Açominas, a gigantic integrated steel mill. This story demonstrates how easy it is to circumvent formal procedure and organization, how powerful politicians could be under military rule, and how disastrous an overly political policy can be. The subbattle over who was to supply equipment for the plant brings into high relief the coalitions that span the boundaries of the state and the political técnicos who broker them. This chapter in particular explores the balancing of technical and political rationalities and its effect on policy outcomes.

Carajás, the huge mining complex in the Amazon, is the subject of chapter 7. The initial decisions illustrate the influence of some of the nationalist concerns of military officers and other officials. Appointments in subsequent governments stand out in structuring power and coalition possibilities. Informal politics in this case strengthen CVRD and contribute to its more institutionalized participation in policy. Lastly, Carajás was slow to fulfill its potential as an engine of regional development, which reflects and overemphasis on technical rationality and the exclusion of other political concerns.

The last case study chapter follows three projects in bauxite and aluminum. Again the major agency is CVRD, but its behavior is less institutionalized, mostly because political técnicos dominate policy making. This chapter uses the analysis of political técnicos to reassess competing state capitalist and organizational interpretations of the behavior of CVRD (and state enterprise). Aluminum policy also provides a window on the informal bases of effective planning and the accelerator effect of circulation.

Part II

Case Studies

5

Siderbrás: The Politics of
Administrative Reform in State Steel

Two chapters analyze policy making in state steel. This one examines administrative reform and the creation of Siderbrás, a holding company for state enterprises; chapter 6 analyzes the decision to build Açominas, a huge integrated steel mill (see appendix B for a partial list of interviewees). Both policies were largely ineffective over the medium run, but for quite different reasons. Siderbrás was a good administrative and technical idea, but it was politically weak, a factor that diminished its effectiveness compared to other projects of the time and other holding companies. Açominas erred in the opposite direction: it was politically inspired and backed but technically flawed.

The politics of Siderbrás illustrates particularly well a subset of the issues raised in part I: the general lack of institutionalization in steel policy, the impact of appointments on the power of officials and the agencies they head, and the effect of presidential succession on policy. This chapter closely examines how career patterns rather than bureaucratic position determine how officials engage in bureaucratic politics. The case of Siderbrás reveals many weaknesses in prevailing notions of the behavior of state enterprises such as the arguments that firms tend to capture the agencies that are meant to control them and that managers seek primarily to maximize their autonomy from hierarchical controls.

Brazilian Steel in the 1980s

Steelmakers in Brazil do not tire of pointing out that Brazil has a "vocation" for steel. Brazil has some of the largest reserves of high-grade iron ore in the world, and since 1983 it has been the world's second largest producer (*Gazeta Mercantil,* 22 November 1984). The other metals used in steelmaking are available in modest to abundant quantities. The weakest link in natural resources is the lack of coking coal, but with low modern transport costs, this deficit is not crippling. Labor is cheap and skilled. Brazil has been producing steel for over forty years, so it can now draw on an experienced pool of engineers and workers. Moreover, capacity in state-owned steel tripled over the last ten years of the military regime, and the largest firms installed the most modern equipment available.

Brazil has capitalized on this vocation (see table 5). By 1983, it was the largest steel producer in Latin America and the second largest in the Third World (after China); and in 1985 it outproduced France to take seventh place in world rankings.[1] In 1978, Brazil became a net exporter and subsequently increased exports steadily (though initially less by design than in response to the severe contraction in domestic demand in the early 1980s). In addition, manufactured exports grew dramatically in the 1970s and 1980s, which increased Brazil's *indirect* steel exports to over 1 million tons by 1984 (IBS 1985, 18).

By the late 1980s, before the incoming Collor administration unceremoniously abolished the firm in 1990, Siderbrás had become one of the giants of the Brazilian economy and the third largest steel conglomerate in the world. By 1984 it owned ten steel firms, including the three largest producers, which accounted for nearly all flat-rolled steel. In the 1980s, Siderbrás firms stabilized their share of total production at around two-thirds. In 1988 they employed seventy-six thousand workers who produced 17 million tons of steel. They exported 7 million tons, which generated over $2 billion or 11 percent of Brazil's trade surplus (Siderbrás, *Relatório* 1988, 1).

Siderbrás dominated the formal organizational universe of the operating enterprises. In principle, it held much of their debt and shares, allocated federal budgetary resources, decided on expansion plans and market shares, and determined export strategies. However, as state holding companies and conglomerates go, Siderbrás was weak and fragmented. It usually ran at a loss, had in fact few of the resources the firms needed, and could not plan effectively. Eletrobrás had more power in pricing decisions and controlled a special electricity tax, while Siderbrás always had to seek new budgetary funds and was never able to get the prices it and the enterprises demanded. In 1988, an oth-

Table 5
Brazilian Steel: Total Production, State Enterprise Production, Exports, and Imports, 1965–1988
(millions of tons)

Year	A. Total Production	B. State Output	B / A (percent)	Exports	Imports
1965	3.0			.5	.3
1966	3.8			.1	.3
1967	3.7			.6	.3
1968	4.5	2.5	57	.4	.3
1969	4.9			.4	.5
1970	5.4	3.0	54	.8	.6
1971	6.0			.4	1.2
1972	6.5			.6	1.0
1973	7.1			N.A.	1.8
1974	7.5	4.0	53	.5	4.2
1975	8.3	4.8	58	.7	2.9
1976	9.2	5.3	58	1.1	1.1
1977	11.1	7.1	63	1.3	1.0
1978	12.1	7.8	64	2.1	.8
1979	13.9	9.0	65	1.5	.6
1980	15.3	9.9	65	1.5	.7
1981	15.2	8.2	62	1.9	.9
1982	13.0	8.2	63	2.4	.4
1983	14.7	9.7	66	5.1	.1
1984	18.4	12.1	65	6.5	.1
1985	20.5	14.0	68	7.1	.1
1986	21.2	14.5	68	6.1	.6
1987	22.2	15.8	71	6.5	.5
1988	24.7	17.9	72	10.9	.1

Sources: For 1965–74, IBS 1974. For 1975–88, CONSIDER 1985 and SDI 1989. State production in 1968 and 1970 from Villela 1984, 50.

erwise excellent year for production and exports, Siderbrás had to find $4.3 billion (half in transfers from the Treasury and half in bonds) to cover its costs and investment. The firm calculated that it had to come up with $750 million just to cover losses due to delays in price readjustments, which are critical in an economy running nearly 1,000 percent inflation (Siderbrás, *Relatório* 1988, 3).

Planning and Administrative Reform, 1965–1970

As major new firms came on line in the mid 1960s, the administrative disorder in state-owned steel became apparent (see figure 1). The government had no sectoral plan, and its control of its firms was sporadic and intermittent. Although they followed no central plan and did not report to any one central agency, managers were still responsible to those who appointed them, but the power to appoint was as dispersed as ownership.[2] To most involved in the sector, there was a clear need to rationalize planning and the administration of these firms.[3]

Between 1965 and 1968, three different entities wrote three separate plans for state steel. The first was the Booz Allen study, completed in August 1966.[4] Simultaneously the Escritório de Pesquisa Econômica Aplicada (Office of Applied Economic Research) in the Ministry of Planning prepared its own global economic plan, which included a section on steel. The incoming Costa e Silva government created the Grupo Consultativo da Indústria Siderúrgica (GCIS) and charged it with molding these proposals into a third and official national plan.[5] In December 1967 the GCIS released the first National Steel Plan (PSN).

The Booz Allen Report devoted little attention to administrative engineering but concluded that the BNDE should coordinate steel planning. The report cites the bank's well-trained and experienced steel técnicos, its major financial commitment in steel, and the fact that the "BNDE is best qualified to make financial evaluations" (BAHINT 1966, 96). The plan of the Office of Applied Economic Research made only closing remarks on administrative reform. It endorsed the BAHINT suggestions but further recommended that steel policy be decided at a ministerial level and that the government create a holding company to resolve dispersed state ownership in steel.[6]

The GCIS plan, PSN, went to much greater lengths. It proposed extensive and detailed reforms (and even appended

Figure 1
The Dispersion of State
Ownership in Steel, ca. 1967

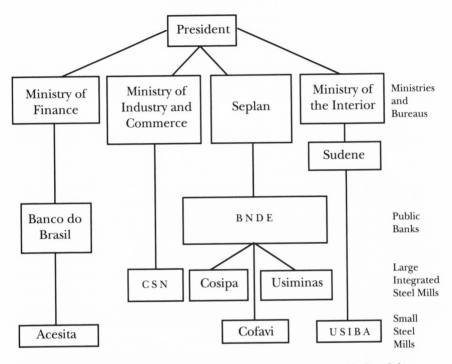

KEY: Acesita = Companhia Aços Especiais Itabira; BNDE = Banco Nacional de
Desenvolvimento Econômico; Cofavi = Companhia Ferro e Aço de Vitória;
Cosipa = Companhia Siderúrgica Paulista; CSN = Companhia Siderúrgica
Nacional; Sudene = Superintendência do Desenvolvimento do Nordeste;
Usiba = Usina Siderúrgica da Bahia; Usiminas = Usinas Siderúrgicas de Minas
Gerais

drafts of appropriate legislation), including: a Commission for
Steel Development, a permanent interministry body (à la GCIS)
to set global steel policy; Brassider (as Siderbrás was first
known), a holding company for all state-owned steel plants; a
Commission for the Development of Private Steel Firms, to coordinate the expansion of private firms; and a National Fund
for Steel, an entity to finance steel expansion. As a piece of
administrative engineering, this proposal was remarkable. It

isolated the significant types of policy decisions—global planning, operational rationalization, and financial evaluation. It then created a separate agency for each type of decision and incorporated myriad formal channels of consultation and coordination. However, the plan's beauty on paper was not going to make it any more palatable to the powers it would constrain, especially the BNDE.

The reforms would deprive the BNDE, known informally by the mid 1960s as the "National Steel Bank," of its central role in steel. It came to hold a majority share in Cosipa and Usiminas, two of the three largest producers, and between 1960 and 1965 it devoted 63 percent of its funds to steel (Abranches 1978, 332). The PSN was cautious and ultimately evasive on how to ease the BNDE out of steel.[7]

The keystone of the reform was the holding company Brassider, which, as proposed, would have become one of the ten largest firms in Latin America (GCIS 1967, 5/26). The PSN reviewed the British, French, and Italian experiences (and praised especially the last, which it found apt for transferring to Brazilian conditions [GCIS 1967, 5/8–5/13]). The PSN claimed that Brassider would centralize ownership, standardize management practices, rationalize expansion programs, and allow firms to reduce costs by dividing markets to lower transport costs and achieve greater economies of scale. The Brassider idea was not a radical departure. The government had already created two other holding companies for state enterprises in railroads (1958) and electricity (1962). Furthermore, the BNDE had been a moving force behind the creation of both of them.

Compelling technical arguments against such a holding company are not easy to find. The inauguration of Cosipa and Usiminas created a clearer need for coordinated market and expansion strategies. In steel, economies of scale are probably the best means for reducing costs, and a holding company could force the operating firms to specialize to achieve these economies. A holding company was not necessarily the only or best administrative option; however, in other countries (since at least the formation of US Steel at the beginning of the century) holding companies have been popular in both public and private steel. The record of these companies is mixed, but at least a few, especially Finsider in Italy, have achieved just the results sought by Brazilian developmentalists: an expanding, efficient steel industry that contributes to both national and regional development (Wormald 1972).

In March 1968, three months after the release of the PSN, the government created the National Council for the Steel Industry (CONSIDER), an interministry council. The members of the council included the minister of industry and commerce (president); the presidents of CSN, BNDE, Banco do Brasil, and CVRD; and representatives from the ministries of planning and of mines and energy. However, the holding company became a paper company only in 1973 and was not consolidated until 1975. As created, CONSIDER could not resolve the administrative problems in steel. The continued dispersed ownership thwarted coordinated policy. Moreover, the new steel plan called for massive financing. Distributing investment among the firms required active administration and technical expertise—both of which CONSIDER lacked.[8] CONSIDER could not remedy the situation, and a strong holding company would have been better able to do so. However, through the two and a half years of the Costa e Silva presidency, Brassider languished in plans debated among lower-level técnicos.

CONSIDER:
The Path of Least Political Resistance, 1970–1972

In 1970 the economic and political situation in steel began changing rapidly. The early 1970s were the high point of the economic miracle, and excess capacity in steel quickly evaporated (see table 6). This was to be the heyday of steel, which became one of the top sectoral priorities of the government. To handle steel policy, Médici appointed a new young minister of industry and commerce, Marcus Vinicius Pratini de Morães, in February 1970. Médici was not an activist, hands-on president: he left economics largely to Finance Minister Delfim Netto, the economic "prime minister," and left sectoral policy to the relevant ministry (Skidmore 1988, 105–06).

In July 1970, Pratini trimmed CONSIDER into a better policy-making body. He removed the representatives of the private

Table 6
State Enterprise in Steel: Production, Installed Capacity, and Investment, 1966–1985

Year	Production[a]	Installed Capacity[b]	Investment[c]
1966		3.8	
1968		3.8	
1970		3.8	
1971		3.8	
1972		4.0	.2
1973		4.0	.3
1974		4.0	.7
1975	4.1	4.6	1.0
1976	4.5	5.6	.7
1977	6.2	6.8	.9
1978	6.9	7.8	1.7
1979	8.0	9.0	2.2
1980	8.6	9.3	2.0
1981	7.1	9.3	2.3
1982	7.0	9.5	1.6
1983	8.5	9.5	.5
1984	10.7	12.2	.4
1985		13.0	

Sources: Production from CONSIDER 1985, 14–15. Capacity and investment from Siderbrás communication, 30 March 1985.

Note: State enterprise refers to only the largest integrated producers: CSN, Usiminas, Cosipa, CST, and Açominas.

a. In millions of tons.

b. In millions of tons per year. CST capacity became available in 1982. Açominas was projected to add another 2 million tons of capacity in 1986.

c. In billions of dollars. Açominas investment began in 1976; CST in 1978. A flood destroyed investment data for Cosipa for 1965–71, so before 1971 (and before centralized record keeping) total investment cannot be calculated. Investment here includes modernization, expansion and new plants, excluding miscellaneous investments.

sector and brought in Delfim as a voting member. Pratini also hired a new technical staff, which gave CONSIDER the ability to evaluate policy options. The council in 1970 had a staff of about thirty to forty, twenty of whom were university-trained técnicos.

Formally, CONSIDER assumed the following responsibilities: co-ordinating national steel policy; setting priorities for government financing of new plants and expansion; authorizing accelerated depreciation; programming sectoral development; and coordinating policies with the agencies in control of prices and tariffs (Abranches 1977, 47; see also Abranches 1978).

The formal attributes look impressive, and at first glance it appears that Pratini was able to centralize policy instruments from other parts of the state. However, it was by and large a re-organization within the MIC.[9] Moreover, CONSIDER still did not control all the major levers. For example, it determined priorities for government funding, but the BNDE, the major financial agent, still evaluated steel projects according to its own procedures and was not obligated to accept CONSIDER's recommendations. Nonetheless, the council became a greater force in steel planning than its predecessor, GCIS.[10]

Why did Pratini strengthen CONSIDER but ignore Siderbrás? The setting was more propitious for Siderbrás, and the need to coordinate steel expansion was increasing. Steel consumption (production and imports minus exports) had doubled in only four years (from 3.4 million tons in 1967 to 6.8 million tons in 1971), and it became clear that Brazil would have to invest massively and rapidly in order to continue to supply its own steel. CONSIDER was obliged to assume commercial tasks, which confused its planning role. For instance, in 1971, it began coordinating steel imports, a function better suited to a commercial enterprise. Furthermore, the inauguration of several new state firms, including USIBA (steelworks of Bahia) and Piratini, would soon further complicate the administrative scene.

However, this suboptimal setup was Pratini's deliberate design (interviews with Pratini de Morães, 5 February 1985, and Sarcinelli Garcia, 12 March 1985). Upon taking office in February 1970, he and his adviser on steel, Luiz Fernando Sarcinelli Garcia, set about studying the best organizational framework for steel expansion and policy making. After four months of study they settled on the path of least bureaucratic resistance, which resulted in CONSIDER, described above. Shifting instruments within MIC and centralizing steel policy in

CONSIDER did not require interbureaucratic negotiation (or formal congressional approval). As was clear from the initial reaction of affected parties to Brassider (and as would be clear later during the creation of Siderbrás), to create an effective holding company would require mobilizing political resources and engaging in protracted struggle that would not necessarily speed steel expansion. Pratini and Sarcinelli opted to create an imperfect instrument immediately rather than waste energy struggling for the optimal organizational solution as the steel crisis snowballed.

Most importantly, CONSIDER was not a state enterprise, but rather an initially insignificant council directly subordinate to the minister of industry and commerce. Pratini could therefore appoint alone a close and loyal collaborator. A full-blown Siderbrás would have controlled massive resources—more, probably, than any other state firm. Pratini would not have been able to appoint the company's president on his own and would consequently have had much less control over the firm and over steel policy. Pratini preferred complete control over an imperfect instrument to shared influence over a more appropriate agency.[11]

Pratini's stewardship was a substantive success and an institutional failure. He and CONSIDER planned, for the first time in Brazil, a major expansion in steel production (though it did not come on line in time to avert the import crisis of 1973–74), but they left state ownership in the same organizational mess as they had found it. By keeping policy and planning within MIC in CONSIDER, Pratini hived off a policy area. It was politically astute because it fitted the ministerial distribution of power under Delfim Netto and Pratini's position in the cabinet as a privileged but nonetheless junior minister.[12] But this accommodation meant that CONSIDER failed in technical terms, because it was an unwieldy business unit and incapable over the longer run of rationalizing decision making and administration.

Like regulatory agencies elsewhere, CONSIDER had to recruit qualified staff from the very firms it was meant to regulate. In many interpretations the "controlees" thus capture the controlling agencies. In Brazil the added, unusual practice of requisitioning personnel—where the state enterprise pays the administrative técnico's salary—would seem to seal this argument.

Career patterns provide the most compelling evidence for rejecting the "capturing" argument. Siderbrás and CONSIDER técnicos rarely return to their firms. They know when they leave their firm that their future career is no longer dependent on their ex-superiors. Aluísio Marins, formerly executive secretary of CONSIDER, summed up the career choice as follows (interview, 29 January 1985). Officials invest in their human capital when they go to CONSIDER (or later, Siderbrás). They learn how the central government operates, have much broader planning tasks, deal with more issues and sectors, and establish contacts with the private sector. These new skills make them more eligible for the jobs they normally take next in private firms and other government agencies.[13] CONSIDER provides a stepping stone from which to launch a political técnico career. The "capturing" state enterprise no longer controls the técnico's career and must rely on sentimental or other persuasions, which are unlikely to have much effect in agencies wary of regional favoritism.[14]

Managers versus Siderbrás: The Missing Battle

CONSIDER served Pratini's purposes initially, but by 1972 his attention returned to Siderbrás. Even then he did not set out to rationalize the basic confusion of state ownership, but rather needed to resolve immediate, logistical problems. Pratini was negotiating at least three new joint ventures.[15] Dividing the government share between the existing state enterprises was unnecessarily complex and would delay negotiations by incorporating new actors with potentially divergent interests. Moreover, foreign minority partners could exploit divisions and thwart overall state and national control. A state holding company was a better option, and Pratini set about to create it.

However, other officials (considered in the next section) stopped Pratini from getting the Siderbrás he wanted. This section considers the preferences of managers in state firms who in principle had the most to lose were Siderbrás created. The theoretical argument that state managers are most interested in furthering their autonomy would lead us to expect them to oppose the creation of an entity that would be formally responsible for appointing managers, doling out their finances, and instructing them what to produce for whom (see, for example, Aharoni 1982). An early empirical analysis corroborated this theory and claimed that the long delay between the first Brassider proposal "and the creation of Siderbrás can be attributed in large measure to the resistance of the firms to losing their autonomy" (Dutra and Salles 1975, 121).

In fact, in 1972 state managers had no clear and united position on Siderbrás in large part because they belonged to different social types. Some clearly and publicly opposed it. Others pressured Pratini to create it in hopes that it would give steel a more prominent organizational and political profile within the government (see also Abranches 1978, 336). An analysis of careers, social types, and appointments illuminates why they did not mobilize to oppose the holding company, and why the preferences of many managers diverged from those to be expected from their positions and those of their firms.

Most interviewees agreed that CSN directors opposed Siderbrás and that the president of CSN, Alfredo Américo da Silva, supported it. As early as 1968, Américo came out in favor of the Brassider proposal. He claimed that a holding company endowed "with the necessary authority and mobility will in principle bring only benefits to this basic sector of the national economy" (*Revista do Clube de Engenharia*, no. 378, December 1968). This split derives from the difference between técnicos and military officers. The directors were técnicos who had risen from the ranks of CSN and were therefore more likely to defend its interests in opposing Siderbrás.

Américo was an outsider. He was a military engineer who parachuted late in his career into the CSN presidency in 1966 (see chapter 3). He knew that his career depended not on CSN but on his general skills as a manager and his ties to the military. He also knew that, if Siderbrás were created, he was the leading candidate to run it. The press cited him early on as the likeliest candidate for the presidency of Siderbrás (*Estado de São*

Paulo, 4 August 1972). As president of CSN and classmate of Médici, Américo would be a prime candidate for the Siderbrás presidency, and his nomination was no great surprise. His view of Siderbrás confirms my rephrasing of Allison: his position on Siderbrás depended less on where he sat (CSN) than on where he thought he was going (Siderbrás).

Of the big three, Cosipa was most dependent on the BNDE and most subject to its interference. Cosipa already lacked autonomy, and Siderbrás offered at least the potential of more palatable intervention. Moreover, the president, Mário Lopes Leão, was not in a position to campaign against Siderbrás. Lopes was an outsider, a political técnico and not a "steel man," and he lacked the credentials to enter a public steel dispute.[16] Prior to his appointment to Cosipa, he had worked for thirty years in municipal transport and electricity generation. It made little sense for Cosipa's managers to oppose Pratini's Siderbrás proposal, which probably would not affect their careers much anyway.

Managers of Usiminas had more motives and means for opposing Siderbrás. Most observers considered Usiminas the most efficient of the big three steel firms. Hence it felt fewer price and funding constraints. More importantly, as a joint venture with Nippon Steel, it was less subject to BNDE intervention.[17] Amaro Lanari, president of Usiminas (1957–75), was also in a better position to lobby against Siderbrás. He was a steel man par excellence (a técnico, in terms of social type) and was in his fifteenth year as the president of Usiminas, having survived six presidents and even more ministers of industry and commerce. He was not personally dependent on the Médici government and had the support of the attentive and active political elite in Minas Gerais (where steel is much more important to the regional economy than in Rio de Janeiro or São Paulo). Furthermore, Lanari had the most to lose in that Siderbrás posed a greater threat to his job. In March 1972 he stated publicly that state steel needed a financial and regulatory body but by no means an administrative holding.[18]

In sum, the presidents had different careers, different views on Siderbrás, and different political bases from which to defend them. Lopes (Cosipa) may have opposed Siderbrás but was not in a position to lobby. Américo (CSN) favored Siderbrás and had the informal military connections to push for it. Lanari (Usiminas) opposed Siderbrás and could afford to fight it.

Beyond these specific career interests, high circulation in state steel firms undermined potential resistance by managers to Siderbrás. Managers could oppose it in principle but still offer no resistance because it would not affect their careers. Managers knew that the odds were better than even that they would have different jobs after the 1974 presidential succession. Twelve of twenty directors in the big three firms had moved on to different jobs after the 1967 and 1970 successions, and six of eleven would do so in 1974. Hence Siderbrás would probably not affect their careers, and they were not going to make a big stink, because they were leaving soon anyway.

In the end, managers' opposition or support had little impact on the final decision. Nonetheless, this section provides a clear illustration of the effect of careers on preferences and the effect of appointment relations and informal ties on the ability of managers to pursue their preferences.

Siderbrás Is Stillborn, 1973–1974

Besides the state enterprises, the other interested officials were in CONSIDER/MIC, BNDE, and the ministries of Finance and Planning. Officials in the last three agencies did not share common interests, nor did they appear to be allied. However, the combined effect of their differing oppositions diluted the powers of the Siderbrás created in 1973.

Within MIC (and especially among the technical staff of CONSIDER) the tendency was pro-Siderbrás. Many of the council's técnicos wanted to rationalize state steel (including increasing CONSIDER's power). Also, they felt that the BNDE used ill-adapted short-term banking criteria.[19] As one ex-técnico of CONSIDER put it, BNDE's intervention in its steel firms "was not the most brilliant." The staff at CONSIDER had no real power, and their preferences were marginal in the major decisions on Siderbrás. However, having a permanent staff allows an agency and its técnicos to keep proposals on the agenda, even if they remain at the bottom of it.

The career and pro-Siderbrás crusade of Benedito Andrade, a técnico and former executive secretary of GCIS, illustrates CONSIDER's impact (interview, 13 March 1985). His career as a técnico began in the 1940s in CSN. In 1961 he transferred from an operations position there to one as special adviser to the president of the firm, where he worked on special projects. The minister of industry and commerce, Macedo Soares, knew and apparently admired Andrade's work from their years together at CSN in the 1950s. He invited Andrade to fill the small organizational crack he had opened for steel with GCIS.

Andrade was one of the two or three full-time técnicos at GCIS. From 1967 on, he struggled for eight years in various ways to create Siderbrás. He was the executive secretary of the GCIS that drafted the PSN, which strongly advocated Brassider. Pratini tabled Brassider until the end of his ministry and demoted Andrade to adjunct secretary. With the shift of government in 1974, Andrade started lobbying again. He circulated an article (cleared with Américo in Siderbrás) that either directly or through Américo reached Geisel and, according to Andrade, influenced Geisel's reform of Siderbrás.

This brief biography demonstrates the overlapping interplay of political técnicos and técnicos and of organizational and personal powers. GCIS and CONSIDER gave técnicos the organizational platform for drafting and redrafting proposals that met with varying responses and were pursued by different higher political actors with varying *personal* powers. This organizational basis is key in that it allows proposals to continue to percolate up, increasing the likelihood that—over changing governments and ministers—strong technical proposals will one day encounter the requisite political backing.[20]

In terms of its organizational interests, one would expect strong BNDE opposition to Siderbrás. Throughout the 1960s the bank pumped half or more of its resources into steel: two-thirds of its loans in 1966–67 (Naves 1977, 17). By the early 1970s its shares in steel firms represented about one-third of its total capital (interview with a BNDE manager, 11 September 1984). Taking the bank out of steel would require restructuring it and redirecting its lending. Without compensation for its shares, the BNDE would lose a large part of its resources. Finally, steel was still one of the most important sectoral programs, and the bank stood to lose prestige and its vanguard role in development.

Surprisingly, the BNDE had seemed initially willing to surrender its prominent position in steel in the interests of administrative rationality. Técnicos at the bank were active in drawing up the PSN, and BNDE president Jayme Magrassi Sá was an active GCIS member. They had all approved the Brassider concept. However, to the surprise of some GCIS técnicos, Magrassi strongly opposed the final proposal.

In October 1970, Médici and his planning minister Velloso appointed Marcos Vianna to replace Magrassi. The change in presidents did not signal a major shift in bank policies, and Vianna seemed to want the BNDE to stay in steel. The press continued to highlight the bank's supposed veto. The *Estado de São Paulo* (28 April 1973) wrote that "the BNDE has been . . . the big opponent of the creation of Siderbrás, because it does not want to hand over its [majority] shares in Cosipa and Usiminas."

However, it was not a simple question of whether or not the BNDE opposed Siderbrás. Interviews with presidents and técnicos of the bank revealed that they were not opposed to a holding company per se but wanted a "better" one than Pratini's Siderbrás. Their concerns were: to keep the BNDE at the forefront of state-led industrialization; to group together the state enterprises in such a way that the lowest common denominator would not predominate; and to secure adequate compensation for the bank's shares.

The BNDE was well respected, and its técnicos considered it the best development agency in Brazil. Steel was to be a major issue in industrial policy in the 1970s, and many in the bank did not want to entrust it to a second-rate agency. That it was to be the major conduit for steel financing was never really challenged. Even after Siderbrás was fully constituted in 1975, the BNDE continued to be the largest domestic source of financing. However, the creation of a holding company would mean that the bank would not control all the massive resources the state would channel into steel expansion.

Many in the BNDE worried less about the organization than about personnel, the quality of Siderbrás management. The bank's managers did not have a strong hand, as they did in setting up Eletrobrás and the railroad holding, in designing Siderbrás (though they did in Brassider) and would not have much say in who would run it. Their fear, which came true, was that CSN managers would dominate Siderbrás, and that the BNDE's firms (Usiminas and Cosipa) would be underrepresented. One bank técnico rated the management of the enterprises on a scale of one to ten: Usiminas 9, Cosipa 6, and CSN 3.[21] Hence they feared that CSN's dominance of Siderbrás would homogenize the firms, but at the level of CSN.

BNDE's deepest concern, noted by observers in and outside the bank, was capital. Vianna was emphatic about not relinquishing the bank's shares without compensation for their *real* value. The bank had a development role to fulfill and was not about to hand over its capital to some unknown agency. It was also unwilling to give Siderbrás its shares as a loan, mostly because the bank's managers doubted that Siderbrás would ever be able to repay (and their fears were borne out).

On the issue of compensation, BNDE managers acted to defend organizational interests. It never came to a pitched battle because no one was proposing a transfer of shares without compensation. However, the posture is worth noting because it is one of the rare instances in which an agency appeared to act like an organization and stand its institutional ground. As I argued in chapter 2, agencies will be more likely to behave this way if they are among the handful of older agencies (such as the BNDE) and if the stakes are very high (as they were in the case of the bank's steel shares).

Once it became clear that the BNDE would struggle for full compensation, the Siderbrás decision rose to a higher level of decision making because it required creating enormous new government capital, on the order of $850 million (*Estado de São Paulo*, 28 April 1972). Such large sums of money brought in other constraints and actors, especially superminister Delfim Netto, who was not enthusiastic about Siderbrás.[22]

The Médici government finally created Siderbrás six months before leaving office. It had little capital, few employees, no shares, and no earmarked tax. The decree endowed the holding company with an initial capital of only $16 million and gave it full ownership of two *future* state firms. All new equity investment by the government would become Siderbrás shares, so that someday (though no one could tell when) all government firms would belong to Siderbrás. Commenting on the final form Siderbrás took, the *Estado de São Paulo* (1 August 1973) wrote, in faint praise, "The formula discovered . . . overcame the resistance that existed." The solution hurt no one's interests but could hardly have pleased anyone, though it was hailed as a victory for Pratini. However, in light of its meager capital, its lack of real controls, and its dependence on future capital subscriptions, the outcome would have to be considered a victory for its opponents.

Epilogue: The Rise of Siderbrás, 1974–1984

Though legally constituted in 1973, the real structure for Siderbrás, CONSIDER, and the more lasting framework for steel policy were products of the Geisel government. President Geisel, and incoming ministers Simonsen (finance) and Gomes (industry and commerce) radically changed the administration of steel policy in the first year and a half of the new government. They started by retooling CONSIDER. They made it an exclusive decision-making body by restricting voting membership to only four ministers (industry and commerce [president], planning, finance, and mines and energy) and also widened the scope of its policy responsibilities to include nonferrous metals as well as steel.

Then in May 1974, two months after the new government took office, Américo, the president of Siderbrás, submitted to Gomes, the minister of industry and commerce, a proposal for changing the legislation governing Siderbrás. Six months later new legislation, based on this proposal, was handed down (Siderbrás 1983). It gave the agency more money and made it clear that it would get all state-owned steel firms, including those the BNDE owned. The following year these plans started taking effect. In April, Siderbrás received a healthy boost in capital to $615 million, and from then through the end of 1975 all state firms (save Acesita) were transferred to it.

For most purposes the decade-long story of the establishment of Siderbrás ends here. Subsequent legislation changed its role and composition little. However, though Siderbrás in 1975 was in a position to become a real holding company, the process of consolidating its formal mandate was protracted and only partially successful. Many argue that it never had the financial and policy muscle it deserved, and chapter 6, on Açominas, illustrates just how irrelevant Siderbrás could be to steel planning.

When Siderbrás entered the Brazilian administrative structure, the steel firms were midway through the execution of Stage II (1972–75) expansion plans. According to an ex-director, Siderbrás had to "swallow" these plans. Thus its participation in longer-range planning had to await Stage III (1974–78). Though Siderbrás's capital may have been fairly respectable, it controlled precious few new funds to dole out to its subsidiaries.[23] State enterprises were still responsible for arranging most of their own financing and negotiated loans directly from the BNDE and international banks. Critics maintained that Siderbrás could not expect to control the firms because it was not the holder of the purse. All of the investment in 1970–71 was self-financed. From then on the proportion of internal financing dropped to one-half in 1972–73, then to one-quarter in 1974–75, and finally to 17 percent in 1978–79 (Trebat 1983, 207). By 1985 Siderbrás liabilities were 91 percent debt and only 9 percent equity (*Gazeta Mercantil* 12 August 1985).

However, Siderbrás's financial role grew. First, it became a conduit for some foreign financing. Even in this activity, which seemed to be one where a holding company could facilitate and coordinate external borrowing, outside officials determined its role. In the words of João Camilo Penna, minister of industry and commerce (1979–84), "Siderbrás was asked to seek external financing to meet the needs of the Central Bank" (*Jornal do Brasil*, 9 February 1984). Second, with the onset of recession and government attempts to reduce its deficits, the Figueiredo government created a new agency, SEST, to cut state enterprise spending. SEST held Siderbrás responsible for the performance of its operating enterprises. Siderbrás became more powerful financially not by allocating resources but by meting out budget cuts. In sum, Siderbrás, "was unable to achieve on its own a position of financial strength or political influence" (Trebat 1983, 229).

Interpreting the Siderbrás Saga

Siderbrás was a good administrative (technical) idea, but its political shortcomings reduced its effectiveness. It failed to achieve what its proponents hoped for and what other holding companies in Brazil and elsewhere have accomplished. The sector needed administrative rationalization, and the Siderbrás created in 1975 was on paper a technically sound means to achieve it.[24] Where the reform failed was in not accommodating the real powers in steel. When outsiders wanted something from steel, they were usually able to overcome resistance from Siderbrás and undermine its managers' efforts to plan and rationalize. Regional elites sought and got investment funds not authorized by it; steel consumers lobbied successfully to keep prices low (often below cost); and macro-economic policy makers kept prices low to rein in inflation while forcing Siderbrás to contract international loans to help balance Brazil's external accounts.

Siderbrás's shortcomings arise partly from design flaws— some of these outside powers could have been incorporated into the administrative structure. The result would have been unwieldy, but Siderbrás would have been more powerful. To be fair to the designers and subsequent managers who attempted to make it work, the major flaw is systemic. In Brazil's goal-oriented system, outcomes take precedence over procedure. Few rules or "institutions" can resist strongly backed outcomes. This is particularly true of an agency born into a universe already crowded with contrary interests and powers.

For example, Siderbrás had little impact on the powers of appointment. In the 1960s and early 1970s, the major forces were the president, the minister of industry and commerce, the regional elites, and the BNDE. The arrival of CONSIDER and Siderbrás cut BNDE out but did not detract much from the power of the others. One would have expected presidents of Siderbrás to replace outside confidence and representation appointees in the operating firms with their own technical and confidence appointees. Siderbrás president Brandão Cavalcanti appeared to accumulate appointment power over the course of his eight-year term, though regional politicians maintained influence. In 1984 he even engineered the dismissals of the presidents of Açominas and Cosipa. The process was not, however, one of consolidating Siderbrás's power. Brandão Cavalcanti's successor in the Sarney government, Amaro Lanari, encountered enormous political pressures and resigned in 1987 in part because he had lost influence in appointing subordinates (*Jornal da Tarde*, 18 April 1988).

Why regional elites are so interested in steel requires some explanation. Broadly speaking, hard tax revenues, vaguer notions of prestige, and less-than-fully-baked ideas on development spark this interest. The revenue side explains much of the interest, though it depends on the weight of steel in the regional economy. Beyond direct revenues, state governments are also interested in direct employment and indirect growth multipliers. However, these impacts are not great, especially considering the enormous investment ($120,000–$280,000) per job created.[25] Of course, the investment is federal, and the job is in the individual state.

Other, less tangible factors such as tradition, prestige, and patronage also motivate regional elites. Tradition is especially strong in the state of Minas Gerais, which has relied on metallurgy for centuries (see the chapter 6). Prestige comes to those state governments that build steel plants. By their very size, steel plants dominate the industrial landscape and at least symbolize industrialization. Lastly, participation in appointing managers to huge public enterprises can be a valuable resource in local politics. Besides some limited opportunities for direct patronage, state governments also have input into the policies of some of the largest buyers and employers in the area. As long as public firms in steel satisfied these regional political appetites, appointments and hence control remained politicized and dispersed, and Siderbrás's administrative effectiveness thereby diminished.

On the surface, administrative change in steel over the past twenty years can appear gradual and incremental. Proposals percolated up to top policy makers, who then debated and revised them before implementing incremental versions. From afar it seems an impersonal, bureaucratic process. When the new minister Macedo Soares arrived at the MIC in 1967, he inherited several proposals for administrative reform and implemented the top priority by setting up CONSIDER. It was easy to create an interministry council with a vague mandate (in its first decade, the military regime created seventy councils [Barros 1978, 255]).

When Pratini arrived in 1970, he inherited a formally functioning, though feeble, CONSIDER. Rather than confront a drawn-out bureaucratic fight to create Siderbrás he chose the incrementalist path of reorganizing within the MIC and giving CONSIDER a staff. In 1974, Pratini left a Siderbrás on paper without resources—like the CONSIDER that Macedo Soares had bequeathed him—which Geisel took and made reality. By 1975 the administrative structure had reached an incrementalist plateau, though tinkering continued at lower levels. This incrementalist view highlights the impact of regular presidential succession. The main changes came soon after incoming presidents, ministers, and in some cases second- and third-level appointees took office.

However, once we acknowledge the significance of changing the individual actors, we come closer to a stronger personalistic interpretation where people prevail over formal organizations. Individual actors and their varying *informal* powers determined administrative change and general steel policy. The incrementalist argument is based largely on organizations—people are constrained by existing organizations to incremental change. The personalistic explanation focuses on the powers, goals, and styles of individuals.

Formally, change looks incremental, and the formal result seems pretty rational. However, the informal powers of the officials in the agencies have varied dramatically over time according to who is heading the agencies. The story of CONSIDER is illustrative. Under Macedo Soares, the council was a center for debate and planning, but not execution. Under Pratini it shared in the minister's power, planned, and even implemented policies (which was beyond its formal authority). Under ministers Gomes, Calmon de Sá, and Camilo Penna, it again languished and did not participate in major decisions. CONSIDER reached its political apogee under Pratini, but, because its power depended on the minister, it fell when he left.[26]

Briefly, the fortunes of state steel and in particular its position in intrastate politics depended mostly on personalities. Reflecting on the failure of Siderbrás and CONSIDER to consolidate the position steel had enjoyed during his ministry, Pratini concluded that "what's important is not structures but strong individuals" (interview, 2 February 1985).

6

Açominas: Regional Politics and the Institutional Bypass

> Steel plants are not created by decree
> or to respond to requests by aldermen
> and deputies, or by whoever it might
> be. A steel plant is not a marginal
> project . . . and cannot be the result of
> a mere political decision.
>
> —Amaro Lanari, Jr.[1]

AÇOMINAS BEGAN PARTIAL operation in 1985 and soon became Brazil's fifth, most modern and most controversial, integrated steel plant. It made Minas Gerais the only state with two of these mammoth steelworks. By the early 1980s critics were classifying it together with the other dubious "Pharaonic" projects such as Itaipú, the Ferrovia de Aço, and the nuclear program. Açominas was scheduled to come on line six years earlier, in 1980, to supply a market niche for which demand did not yet exist. With the severe contraction in domestic demand in the early 1980s, the need to add another 2 million tons to capacity evaporated, and the government slowed Açominas. Since the investment relied on short- and medium-term loans, by 1985 the delays rolled up accumulated interest of $2 billion, equal to one-half the amount actually invested (Souza 1985, 116). Had the federal government not assumed much of Açominas's debt, the financial burden would have left this industrial cathedral operating forever in the red.

With hindsight, the project is easy prey for criticism, but many critics hold that it made no sense from the beginning and from then on the errors just accumulated. Supporters are just as tenacious in their defense. For many, especially *mineiros*, Açominas is not a business undertaking or a mere steel plant, but an article of faith.[2] Such controversies are not new to steel politics in Brazil. Since the 1940s skeptics have criticized each new integreted steel mill as too big, too costly, and too soon. Over time each has proved itself a capable and necessary contributor to Brazilian industrialization. This is likely to be the case with Açominas.

Focusing on its long-term potential glosses over the short-term mistakes. Four major errors figure in most critiques: building a plant without a market niche;[3] exaggerating projections of future steel demand; raising costs through ad hoc financing; and slowing investment in existing plants with lower expansion costs (i.e., Açominas had very high opportunity costs). Without a clear market niche and predicated on exaggerated projections for future demand, the new plant lost its justification for existence when demand fell sharply in the 1980s. Defenders chalk this up to bad market luck. However, it was clear to many even in the mid 1970s that steel demand would not continue growing at the very high rates that would have justified the construction of Açominas (see, for example, World Bank 1972, app. 2, p. 4). The financing was not long-term, and much of it came due before the plant was completed, let alone producing at capacity and able to generate a surplus. Most importantly, though, is the fact that other steel plants and expansions that made more economic sense lost potential investment resources to Açominas.

In the Açominas project the purely political element stands out, from creation, to implementation, to paralyzation, to final completion. As one ex-director of Siderbrás pointed out, the fact that the original decisions were so politicized encouraged and justified subsequent attacks and counterattacks on political grounds. Furthermore, coming in the wake of major efforts to institutionalize policy making in steel, the decision in 1975 and subsequent elaboration of a plan in 1976–77 demonstrate how easy it was to circumvent formal organizations and procedures.

Açominas, like all major projects, entailed many decisions. The following sections focus especially on the battles over whether to build a plant, what it should produce, who should supply the equipment and capital, and when the project should reach completion.

Mineiros and Steel: The Dream through 1974

Ever since the gold rush in the eighteenth century, *mineiros* have been quick to condemn simple extraction of ore, whether it be destined for export abroad or for other states of Brazil. *Mineiro* politicians bring an awareness of past exploitation, ranging from paranoia to alert sensitivity, to policy politics. It is a long-standing *mineiro* creed that the resources of the state of Minas Gerais should be processed *in* Minas Gerais for the benefit of *mineiros*. The story of Açominas clearly illustrates the force of this creed in the politics of steel.[4]

Indignant over Vargas's decision in 1942 to locate CSN in what is now the state of Rio de Janeiro, the *mineiro* political elite stepped up pressure to get their own plants. Their efforts finally resulted in the creation of Usiminas in 1957. However, this did not sate the steel appetite of Minas Gerais politicians. In 1963 the governor of Minas Gerais officially authorized the creation of Açominas. The measure was largely symbolic, for the firm would not be constituted until three years later, and then still without capital. Since the state government lacked the resources, the project would have to await federal capital, which was in short supply in the 1960s. Furthermore, two national steel plans of the 1960s both recommended that future expansion take place through incremental investment in the three existing firms rather than building whole new plants.[5]

By the early 1970s the impending supply shortage in steel improved the prospects for federal approval of Açominas. In November 1972, CONSIDER announced that it was accepting proposals for integrated plants in semifinished and nonflat steel. In March of the following year, Açominas duly submitted a feasibility study for a grandiose plant to produce 3.5 million tons of nonflat steel per year.

Although market conditions were more favorable for fulfilling the *mineiro* dream, the political conjuncture was not. The Rondon Pacheco government in Minas Gerais was nearing its term and was already overextended in a series of other ambitious industrial projects (including a new Fiat plant) (see Diniz 1981). Besides, Pacheco was one of the few *mineiros* who at least privately opposed Açominas (*Veja*, 28 April 1976). Moreover, for Pratini, the minister of industry and commerce, a huge state project in nonflat steel was an enormous political risk. Pratini's 1972 proposal for a state firm in this sector had met virulent opposition from the private sector, forcing him to beat a hasty and awkward retreat. It was highly unlikely that he would risk similar political embarrassment for the sake of Açominas, especially since a private concern had also submitted a proposal to produce nonflat steel. Not surprisingly, Pratini's CONSIDER rejected the Açominas proposal and approved the smaller, privately owned plant (Mendes Jr.) in Minas Gerais and a plant on the coast (CST) to produce semifinished steel. Açominas would have to await the "illustrious . . . statesman" and "steel man of the heart" *(siderurgista de coração)*, Aureliano Chaves (Souza 1985, 93).

Steel in Minas Gerais is serious politics, and has been for decades, if not centuries. Little does it matter that Minas Gerais was, by the mid 1970s, already making more steel than any other state. In 1975 it produced 45 percent of Brazil's steel (compared with São Paulo's 24 percent). By 1984, on the eve of Açominas's inauguration, the share of Minas Gerais had dropped to 34 percent, but it was still the largest producer among the states (CONSIDER 1985, 12–13). More relevant in political discourse was that Minas Gerais was also the largest exporter of iron ore. The trainloads of ore were so much unmade steel that constantly reminded *mineiro* elites of the continuing status of their state as a mining enclave.

Açominas Prevails

In his inaugural speech of March 1975, Governor Aureliano Chaves graphically summarized the *mineiro* dream and what his government would do to realize it: "Among the natural vocations of our State, there is one that penetrates deeply, to its entrails [*entranhas*]—the steel vocation. Because it is in the nature of things in Minas, my government will struggle, stubbornly, to consolidate a powerful steel pole in our state."[6] Within a year and a half, Usiminas elaborated a feasibility study for Açominas, the appropriate government organs approved it, President Geisel laid the cornerstone and signed financing agreements in

London, and bulldozing began. Project elaboration delayed the project longest—from approval to initial construction only some nine months passed (see the chronology in appendix B).

Given the organizational confusion in steel, the billions of dollars involved, and the many conflicting interests, how was such a policy blitz possible? The short answer is that an alliance between Geisel and Aureliano Chaves overwhelmed the weak institutional arrangement for steel policy before opposing interests could mobilize. When asked how Açominas happened, nearly all of the dozen or so people I interviewed responded simply, "Geisel and Aureliano" (see appendix B for a partial list of people interviewed). This pact was the cause of Açominas's dash through the policy bureaucracy *as well as* the subsequent crippling delays in implementation.

Aureliano Chaves enjoyed a special link to Geisel for two reasons. First, there was a strong personal and political bond that continued unabated through at least 1985. As federal deputy (1970–74), Chaves chaired the Mines and Energy Commission of the Chamber of Deputies and participated in numerous others, including those on nuclear energy, pollution, Itaipú, science and technology, and a special joint commission on the creation of a Petrobrás subsidiary, Braspetro. These commissions kept Chaves in constant contact with the then president of Petrobrás, Geisel. Their developing friendship contributed to Chaves's selection as the keynote speaker at the convention of the National Renewal Alliance (Arena) in September 1973 that launched Geisel's presidential candidacy. Despite intra-Arena opposition, Geisel later "appointed" Chaves the governor of Minas Gerais (see CPDOC 1985, 786). Throughout the Geisel government, Chaves had easy access to Geisel and conversed with him regularly.

Second, Geisel's political project was to begin a gradual liberalization (*distensão,* and later *abertura*) of the military regime and to mold the government party into the civilian bearer of the military's revolutionary project (see Skidmore 1989, 9–11). Chaves seemed to be just the sort of popular young pro-regime leader who could shoulder this burden. Açominas fulfilled a long-standing *mineiro* demand and would strengthen the governor who realized it. Also, it would have a political impact in that it would project Chaves nationally as a dynamic developmentalist. Nearly all interviewees said that the Chaves-Geisel pact infused Açominas with what one ex-director of Siderbrás called "political charm" that made it unstoppable.

Beyond this political rationale, Açominas also gained support by meshing fairly well with Geisel's economic plan and policy style. Like other outsized projects, it conformed to Geisel's vision of *Brasil Grande*. Açominas was also an easy conduit for the international financing that Geisel relied on to maintain investment without absorbing the recessionary impact of the oil shock. Geisel's National Development Plan II (PND II) also planned sustained substitution of imported industrial inputs such as steel.

The Açominas juggernaut did not pause even to pick up natural allies, let alone stop to weave together a lasting base of support. For instance, Brazil's huge construction firms are usually active members in coalitions favoring huge projects. Their influence may not be decisive, but it can help to articulate a favorable convergence of interests while speeding the bureaucratic processes. The rapidity of the decision caught construction firms off guard; by the time they could mobilize to support Açominas, Geisel had already approved it.[7] These contractors are strategic in their use of scarce influence, and they therefore push projects that already have some technical rationale within government priorities and have a minimum political base. Apparently construction firms felt that Açominas, prior to 1975, lacked these characteristics, and they were unprepared to support it when its political star rose. Lastly, pressure from construction firms would have been superfluous; Açominas already had sufficient political support, and the firms would all get a piece of it anyway.

Açominas also lost some apparent early allies in the first few years of the project. Overall, Usiminas and CVRD were not prominent protagonists in policies relating to the new plant. They had, however, agreed initially to enter an Açominas joint venture with around 40 percent of the capital. Had backers of Açominas been able to secure this investment, they could have woven these firms into a far stronger coalition within the bureaucracy. However, the firms dropped out as direct investors in late 1976 because of unresolved disputes over product lines and management (*Veja*, 8 September 1976). Regardless of the specific disputes, this falling out demonstrates that backers of Açominas were not particularly disposed to compromise or worried about isolating themselves politically.

Geisel, Chaves, and the *mineiro* political elite propelled Açominas in the early years.[8] However, this coalition was very narrow and would prove precarious over the longer run. It did not seek out partners to sustain the project, nor was it overly concerned with fitting the project more than obliquely into national planning and political objectives. The coalition quickly got the Geisel government to approve the project, but the approval was, because of the haste, necessarily vague. Subsidiary decisions on fitting Açominas into the steel plan, arranging financing, buying equipment, and determining product lines remained pending. That CONSIDER's approval left even the product line for a future decision highlights Açominas's political force and roots and demonstrates how little the council was able to influence the project. It can hardly be considered effective planning to approve a 2 million ton plant that needed to be adjusted to meet the "necessities of the market" and to call for joint study between Açominas and CONSIDER of necessary alterations of the project originally presented (CONSIDER Resolution no. 37/76, in Souza 1985, 181–82).

The Institutional Doormat

Within the state, Açominas met little resistance. In formal terms, many agencies had a chance to stop it: the minister of industry and commerce could have shelved it as a political liability, Seplan as a budget excess, CONSIDER as a low sectoral priority, or Siderbrás as a technical lemon. Officials at all levels opposed the project, but they lacked the power or will to put up a fight.[9] Gomes, the minister of industry and commerce, was not close to Geisel and did not emerge as one of the more powerful ministers (Geisel accepted his resignation in February 1977). Regardless of his own evaluation, Gomes took the decision as final and accepted the task of implementing it (interview, 14 June 1989). As minister of industry and commerce, he was the president of CONSIDER, which rapidly approved Açominas.

Aluísio Marins had been appointed from within CONSIDER to be its executive secretary. Other officials thought he had slim outside political support and little taste for political infighting. Since the council's power varied primarily with that of the minister of industry and commerce (and his interest in steel), it had little to do but approve the project. CONSIDER thus accepted Açominas as a political given and began working on the margins to render it more technically palatable.

The newly established Siderbrás also offered little opposition. Its managers were setting up the holding company and trying to gain ownership of existing steel plants when Açominas became a policy issue. Siderbrás's president, Américo, strongly opposed the new plant (interview, 13 June 1985). He feared that it would drain funds from Stage III expansion of the existing three integrated plants and from Siderbrás's top priority, the new CST plant. However, the holding company lacked formal responsibility in steel planning, and Américo and his directors lacked informal influence. They were Médici appointees and not well linked to the top levels of the Geisel government. Hence Américo also accepted Açominas as a fait acompli and worked to incorporate it into Siderbrás. First, he fought successfully to keep Açominas from stopping other Siderbrás projects. Açominas would encounter less opposition if presented as a positive-sum option, and Geisel made it so by deciding to fund all steel projects. Second, if Açominas was to be the fifth integrated steel plant, then it should belong to Siderbrás. Américo gained this "control" in October 1976.[10]

Lastly, the BNDE, often a pivotal actor in huge government projects, was not directly involved. Vianna, the president of the bank, thought Açominas was a disastrous idea (interview, 8 April 1985). He opposed it from the beginning and argued against the international financial package for $1.1 billion that Geisel signed in London in May 1976. However, this package, plus capital promised from the Minas Gerais government, Siderbrás, and CVRD, meant that Açominas did not need BNDE funding, in the short run. The bank was poorly positioned to modify or block the project.

As a political project, Açominas suffered the pressure of time. Under the best of circumstances it takes about a decade to present a project, obtain approval, draw up engineering plans, take bids for equipment, arrange financing, and construct the plant. Chaves and Geisel had four years.[11] The solution was a disarticulated forced march that advanced on all fronts at once; Açominas managers worked apace on engineering, equipment, and financing, and at the same time began bulldozing.[12]

The Opposition Mobilizes

Geisel's ramrod technique caught other interested parties off guard, but they quickly regrouped to oppose Açominas. At various times and on differing issues, this opposition included private steelmakers, cement makers, producers of capital goods, and officials in agencies such as BNDE, MIC, and Siderbrás.

In 1972, Pratini had proposed a government plant in nonflat steel, but the private sector counterattacked, effectively stunning and stopping the young minister. Shortly after the official announcement of the Açominas project in nonflat steel, the private sector mobilized again. In its opposition it had the prevailing political winds at its back. In 1974 industrialists launched an *anti-estatização* campaign, which soom became a major point of contention between the government and the bourgeoisie.[13] The rallying point was opposition to excesses of state enterprises and their encroachment on private turf. Açominas was a perfect case of unjustified state entry into a market that private firms were supplying adequately. The Geisel government was publicly sensitive to the general criticisms and went so far as to include strengthening private industry as a central goal of the PND II (see Evans 1982).

Although unable to kill the project, the private sector did manage to modify it out of the most sensitive markets. To CONSIDER fell the task of expressing technically this political outcome. To have a major, visible impact, Açominas had to be an integrated plant, which meant a minimum scale of over 1 million tons of annual capacity.[14] The first projects planned to divide this output between light and medium shapes. The private sector forced the project out of light shapes into heavy shapes. However, the market for heavy shapes could not absorb total output, so CONSIDER had to come up with other final products to absorb the output of the blast furnace—semifinished steel (slabs) and some medium shapes.

Domestic producers of capital goods mobilized not to stop Açominas but rather to raise the proportion of equipment orders placed with them. National producers could produce most of the equipment and felt they had lost out with the Stage II steel expansion in the early 1970s, when the nationalization index was only 22 percent (Klein 1980, 5). And steel was to be one of the three sectors that ordered the most equipment in the Geisel period. From 1974 to 1982 over one-half of all capital goods made on order went to the steel or energy sectors. Steel went from 11 percent of total orders in 1974 to a high of 28 percent in 1979, before dropping to 18 percent in 1982 (Villela 1984, 116).

Two factors account for the success of national producers of capital goods in raising their share of state investment (particularly steel). First, the PND II targeted this sector for priority government action, which raised expectations of producers and gave their demands greater legitimacy.[15] Second, the sector was well organized and politically effective within the state. The industry associations such as ABDIB and SIMESP were classically simple to organize, and their interests aggregated naturally into focused pressure. A small number of large firms produce for a small number of clients in an environment of extreme political capitalism. State enterprises bought most of their output (capital goods on order), the BNDE, through Finame, financed most of their sales, and Cacex protected them from import competition. That they were few in number, large, and not engaged in market competition made it easy to organize; that they were so dependent on the state made it imperative.

Klein (1980) argues that these associations and their prominent leaders established a close informal alliance with the BNDE and especially its president, Marcos Vianna. In some instances, this was enough to achieve their goals, because the bank had discretionary control of funds it could devote to expanding the production of capital goods. In other cases this alliance gave these producers access to higher officials.

In steel expansion generally, this access allowed producers to forge an alliance with Vianna (BNDE), Gomes (MIC), Marins (CONSIDER), and Velloso (Ministry of Planning) in favor of setting a minimum percentage of nationalization (Klein 1980, 12). They ran into opposition from Américo (Siderbrás) and Simonsen (Ministry of Finance), who wanted to avoid making a commitment to a set percentage and favored freer bidding. CONSIDER originally set the minimum national participation in Stage III at 40 percent. However, the political force of the producer alliance managed to exact a government commitment of 65 percent (Klein 1980, 8, 13).

In the case of Açominas the outcome was similar, but the alliance and process were less bound by organizations and more personalized. Over the course of two years, national producers and their in-house allies got successively higher shares of the equipment contracts for Açominas. The initial viability study stated that the project would buy only 30 percent of its equipment from national industry (Souza 1985, 175). The project was submitted in November 1975, but in the same month the president of Açominas was already announcing that the firm would in fact order 40 percent of its equipment from Brazilian industry (Klein 1980, 15). Three months later, CONSIDER decreed that the nationalization index would be 50 percent.[16] Finally, after another ten months of politicking, Brazilian producers got a higher order from the CDE to raise national participation to 60 percent (*Veja*, 8 December 1976).

Since Açominas had not requested financing from the BNDE, the keystone in the producers' alliance, the bank was not formally drawn into policy formulation. Usually formal procedures were no obstacle for a political técnico such as Vianna, the bank's president, but in the case of Açominas, the previous champion of national producers abruptly turned his back on his erstwhile allies. Not only did he desert them, but he also criticized them publicly for causing unnecessary delays in government projects and for their "unjustified hostility" in negotiations with the state.[17] Also, because Siderbrás did not obtain formal control of Açominas until late 1976 and because its managers were weak within the state, Siderbrás did not figure prominently in these negotiations. Brazilian producers and their associations had to rely more on the channels of communications established previously with other ministries— Planning, Industry and Commerce, and Finance. They also waged a public press campaign.[18]

The national capital goods producers were fortunate in finding another pivotal ally in Paulo Vieri Belotti, the general secretary (vice minister) of MIC, who could plead their case within the bureaucracy. Belotti, a classic political técnico, was an ideal ally.[19] He was socialized in the BNDE's nationalist developmentalism and very well connected to Geisel, who would make the final decision. From 1956 to 1970, Belotti had risen through the ranks of the BNDE and likely shared in its early esprit de corps. In 1970, Geisel, then president of Petrobrás, appointed Belotti director of Petroquisa, a Petrobrás subsidiary in petrochemicals, where the two worked closely together. In fact, from the late 1960s on, Belotti owed much of his career to Geisel. Geisel appointed him directly to his position in MIC and relied on him as one of his main informal advisers in economic policy matters (interview with Severo Gomes, 14 June 1989). This link helped bring the dispute between the managers of Açominas (who favored a nationalization index of 50 percent) and the national producers (who favored 80 percent) to the CDE and President Geisel for the sort of compromise solution political técnicos are famous for (60 percent).

In sum, Geisel's pact with Chaves and the pro-regime *mineiro* elite made some sort of major steel plant nearly inevitable. On specifics the pro-Açominas coalition was willing to accommodate the interests of other affected parties, inside and outside the government, as long as these modifications did not compromise the plant itself. The Geisel government had little reason for rejecting these accommodations, especially if it wanted to maintain a coherent economic program and cordial relations with private producers. Furthermore, officials were dealing with organized and mobilized groups of industrialists with a "legitimate" foothold within the state apparatus.

In each conflict officials attempted to make it a positive-sum negotiation. The pro-Açominas coalition muted opposition from Siderbrás and state enterprises by assuring them that Açominas would not divert funds from Siderbrás's expansion plans. CONSIDER soothed private sector emotions by shunting Açominas into unoccupied market niches. And Açominas was amenable to increasing equipment purchases in Brazil, as long as it did not seriously constrict the flow of suppliers' credits, without which the project would have languished in loan negotiations. These compromises were easy to make in the Geisel government; however, they weakened the project technically, making it an easy prey to a successor government with different priorities and political bases.

By accommodating various opponents and capitalizing on its "political grace," Açominas made it, to most intents and purposes, to the point of no return by the close of the Geisel government in 1979. By the end of 1978 most of the plant and infrastructure still remained to be built, but equipment and loan contracts had been signed, contractors were making their respective pieces, and parts of the blast furnance were already arriving. By the end of 1979, four-fifths of the contracts were out and the project as a whole was about half done (Mendes 1981). The question of whether or not the plant would be built had been resolved. However, supporters were to be shocked to learn that the date of completion was far from a settled matter.

The first four years of decisions on Açominas reveal several aspects of policy politics, both in the Geisel government and in the authoritarian regime more generally. First, the authoritarian regime (especially during *abertura*) sought support through economic policy by pleasing or appeasing both regional and industrial elites. Second, formal policy organs are little match for presidential pacts and other powerful political alliances. Third, policy coalitions are fluid and not necessarily based on organizational position. Lastly, these coalitions can be quite accommodating in a positive-sum environment in which the president (the appointer) sends unequivocal signals that the project should go through.

The Tables Turned

In a lecture delivered in the first week of the Figueiredo government, Moacélio Mendes, president of Açominas, succinctly analyzed the opportunities and constraints for the plant in the overall economic and financial conjuncture. Among the constraints *(ameaças)* he noted with remarkable clairvoyance: possible inversion of government priorities in economic policy; priority expansion of flat-rolled steel and indecision in the area of nonflat steel; restricted ability to import capital goods; crisis in international steel markets; insufficient financial resources in national markets; and lack of support from associations representing the capital goods industry (Mendes 1979). Some of these constraints (such as the restrictions on imported capital goods) were already realities; the others constitute pretty much just what would happen in the next few years.

For Açominas the composition of Figueiredo's cabinet in March 1979 looked propitious. Chaves was Figueiredo's vice president, and MIC went to another *mineiro,* João Camilo Penna, who had been Chaves's secretary of finance in the Minas Gerais government. At the second level, the pliable president of Siderbrás and the accommodating executive secretary of CONSIDER survived. Simonsen was to have general control of the economy, and he had at least acquiesced to Açominas as Geisel's minister of finance. Lastly, politician outsiders were appointed to BNDE. They were more likely to accept political arguments for financing the project (and ultimately did). The Açominas coalition was formally close to the president, had one of their own in MIC, and seemed less likely to encounter intransigence in other parts of the economic bureaucracy.

However, within months this bureaucratic advantage collapsed when Delfim once again took over and centralized control of government spending in Seplan.[20] Over the period 1978–80, growing budget and external accounts crises moved Açominas from the positive-sum situation (which had made it possible) to zero-sum politics. In addition, Delfim had not thought much of the project to begin with. He decided to channel government investment into projects that were close to completion (and likely to generate the most revenue in the shortest run) and/or designed for export (interview, 3 September 1985). Açominas lost on both counts: in comparison with other projects it was not near completion, and it was to produce for the domestic market.

Most of the steel projects begun during the Geisel government reached the peak of actual investment in the first years of the Figueiredo government (see table 7). State investment in steel grew nearly threefold from the mid 1970s to the peak

Table 7
Açominas and State Enterprise Investment in Steel,
1972–1984

	Total State Enterprise Investment	Açominas	Açominas as a Percentage of Total	Apparent Steel Consumption[a]
1972	176			6.9
1973	316			N.A.
1974	701			11.2
1975	995			10.5
1976	708	4	—	9.2
1977	906	159	18	10.8
1978	1,688	536	32	10.8
1979	2,175	869	40	11.8
1980	2,017	791	39	13.4
1981	2,316	412	18	11.2
1982	1,648	308	19	10.1
1983	512	144	28	7.5
1984	419	97	23	
Total		3320		

Sources: For total investment and Açominas, Siderbrás communication. Apparent consumption calculated from IBS 1974 and CONSIDER 1985.

Note: In millions of current U.S. dollars. State enterprise refers to only the largest integrated producers: CSN, Usiminas, Cosipa, Açominas, and CST (begun in 1978). Investment includes modernization, expansion, and new plants but excludes miscellaneous investments.

a. In millions of tons. Production minus (exports minus imports).

years of 1979–81. Steel was a major drain on the state and a prime target for budget cuts.

The three major projects underway were CST, Stage III expansion of the big three, and Açominas. The first two fitted within Delfim's stated priorities. CST was an export venture, and Stage III would generate more resources with less investment than would Açominas. Moreover, when it became clear that investment was to be cut, the other potential victims mobilized. Siderbrás, CST, and the other big three and their regional backers rallied to protect their projects and to cut Açominas, which never generated much enthusiasm among these producers even in the positive-sum days of steel expansion.

In April 1979, the first month of the Figueiredo government, Planning Minister Simonsen delayed the completion of Açominas from 1980 until late 1981 or early 1982. Even after Delfim took over in August 1979, investment continued at a normal rhythm through early 1980 (*Folha de São Paulo*, 28 February 1985). Economic crisis hit in late 1980, and demand for steel fell sharply in 1981 (see table 7). To redress the growing disequilibria in public and external accounts, Delfim resolved to decrease further government investment, contain imports, and promote exports. For steel these goals spelled financial disaster; Delfim cut Treasury resources for steel by 70 percent and dropped steel prices 30 percent below their "real" level.[21] This financial vise forced all steel firms to borrow heavily.

Delfim's strategy hit Açominas particularly hard, and by 1981 the project was almost completely paralyzed and rescheduled for completion only in 1983–84. From 1981 through the end of the Figueiredo government, construction continued sporadically, picking up in 1982 but coming again to the brink of paralysis in late 1983. Investment in Açominas dropped steadily in absolute terms, though after 1982 it rose somewhat as a percentage of total state enterprise investment in steel (as other projects neared completion and reduced their investment requirements). *Mineiro* officials in the top ranks of the Figueiredo government managed to sustain a trickle of resources. Souza, the president of Açominas, argued that it survived "only as a result of the vigilant and tireless activity of the minister [of industry and commerce] João Camilo Penna, a *mineiro* par excellence [*belo exemplo de mineiridade*], as well as the support of the productive classes of Minas Gerais" (1985, 123).

Delfim's policy style was ad hoc, centralized, and politicized. He kept Açominas in a state of permanent uncertainty. Each year SEST would approve a very low investment ceiling for the project. The money would quickly run out. The construction firms would threaten to lay off thousands of workers, and these firms and the Minas Gerais government would mobilize the press and pressure Delfim. Delfim would send off an order to pay the construction firms, and work would straggle along until the next crisis.

In 1984 this recurring subplot was played out in the press. Delfim and SEST had approved about $50 million (at the January 1984 exchange rate) for investment in Açominas in 1984. However, the project already owed more than this in late payments to contractors for work already completed. The president of Açominas declared, "We found ourselves in a paradoxical situation of having already surpassed the investment ceiling at the moment it was set" (*Gazeta Mercantil*, 30 March 1984). By February 1984, Açominas had not paid the construction firms for six months. In early March the firms gave a month's notice to 2,500 employees.

The threat of wholesale layoffs mobilized *mineiro* politicians. A *mineiro* deputy went to see Delfim on 1 March (*Gazeta Mercantil*, 1 March 1984). The following week, Camilo Penna promised a healthy infusion ("*uma quantia bem boa*") of funds soon (*Jornal do Brasil*, 10 March 1984). On 9 March the BNDE gave Açominas $3 million, $2 million of which went straight to the contractors. The firms considered the sum "ridiculous" and stuck by their decision to fire the workers (*Gazeta Mercantil*, 20 March 1984). The governor of Minas Gerais, Tancredo Neves, then entered negotiations. On 22 March the firms fired 1,100 workers, and Tancredo announced that the federal government would disburse another $3.2 million (*Gazeta Mercantil*, 23 March 1984). Even after receiving part of this money, the contractors fired another 350 workers, which got them another $4.5 million from the BNDE in the first week of April (*Gazeta Mercantil*, 4 April 1984).

This tug-of-war was only resolved by the new management of

Açominas appointed in late April 1984. From then through the end of the year, resources flowed more abundantly. The story of these two months nonetheless illustrates Delfim's style of waiting for a political crisis to flare up before stepping in to direct the BNDE to release funds incrementally.

Personnel changes over the course of 1984 improved Açominas's chances of getting the final 5–10 percent of the total $5 billion investment required to complete the plant. At the end of April, Brandão Cavalcanti, president of Siderbrás, fired Mendes, who had been president since construction began nine years earlier. Shocked and hurt, Mendes speculated on the motives for his dismissal: "I have the qualities of a técnico. The authorities may have decided that more political action will facilitate the negotiations and articulations necessary to complete the project."[22]

The past career of Mendes's replacement, Miguel Augusto Gonçalves de Souza, confirms his analysis. Two previous governors of Minas Gerais had appointed Souza to the sensitive positions of secretary of finance, secretary of political coordination, and president of Fiat (in which the state government held a minority share).[23] Shortly after his appointment, Souza made clear what his political conditions were for accepting the job, which had been offered to him the previous October;[24] "My purpose and my agreement in accepting the job are to inaugurate the plant during the Figueiredo government" (*Jornal do Brasil*, 6 May 1984; see also Souza 1985, 124). Whether because of his political skills, of the conditions of his appointment, of Figueiredo's desire to inaugurate government projects, or simply because so little remained to do, the funds began flowing. In Souza's first month the BNDE released another $18 million.

The next propitious personnel change came in August 1984, when Figueiredo replaced Camilo Penna, the minister of industry and commerce. Delfim had effectively hemmed him in throughout his five years as minister. Camilo Penna had been the central *mineiro* in the cabinet (along with Vice President Chaves) but was generally considered one of the weaker members of the pantheon of ministers, and no match for Delfim.[25] His replacement, Murilo Badaró, was a loyal Democratic Social

Party (PDS) senator from Minas Gerais but no political power-house. But he too had discussed funding for Açominas with Delfim prior to accepting the job (*Gazeta Mercantil*, 28 August 1984). He wanted to be sure that he would be the minister to inaugurate it.[26]

And he was. The resources continued to flow from Siderbrás and the BNDE, and two weeks before leaving office, Figueiredo went to Açominas for one of the most symbolic inaugurations of his government. In fact, the only thing ready to inaugurate was the cokery. The politics of the inauguration were pretty petty. Conspicuously absent and uninvited were Chaves, Camilo Penna, and Tancredo. A skeptical report by the *Folha de São Paulo* (28 February 1985) noted that in his speech, "the minister of industry and commerce, Murilo Badaró, took credit [*chamou para si as glórias*] for having been the principal person respon-sible for Açominas's entry into operation, even though he had been in the ministry for only six months." Even in the last gasp of the military regime, Açominas was still valuable politi-cal capital.

Well before the inauguration it was clear that Açominas would never be commercially viable. Loans started coming due long before it commenced production, and financial costs pushed total costs well out of the realm of competitive produc-tion. Through 1984, Açominas had invested a total of $3.3 bil-lion. However, interest continued to accumulate (see table 8) over the years of paralyzation and semiparalyzation so that the total cost of the project was over $6 billion and its outstanding debt in 1985 stood at about $3.5 billion (*Folha de São Paulo*, 28 February 1985).

As of 1985, Açominas was a financial fiasco and would con-tinue to require substantial infusions of government "invest-ment," even once it was producing at capacity. A study by the Organization for Economic Cooperation and Development cal-culated the base cost for a plant of the same size (2 million tons per year) in a developing country to be on the order of $2.8–$3.1 billion depending on labor costs and location.[27] Açominas cost more than double this average. Speaking at the "inaugura-tion," Siderbrás president, Brandão Cavalcanti, stated that until

Table 8
Financial Evolution of Açominas

	1978	1979	1980	1981	1982	1983	1984
Finance Costs as percentage of total budget[a]		10	23	40	59	87	86
Debt/equity ratio	2.7	4.9	5.3	3.8	3.8	2.1	2.1

Sources: Finance costs from Souza 1985, 116. Debt/equity ratio for 1978–80, Mendes 1981; for 1979–84, Souza 1985, 116.
a. Includes interest and amortization payment.

it was operating at capacity in final markets "this firm cannot live with the voluminous financial burden it has accumulated." He suggested converting outstanding government loans from the BNDE and the Banco do Brasil into equity. Without such a substantial subsidy, Açominas would continue losing money.

The Politics of Industrial Failure

"Political charm" facilitated the approval and start-up of Açominas in years of political favor and (artificial) abundance of resources under Geisel. However, by 1981 changes in the political and economic environments left the project politically cursed. Nobody wanted the mess it turned out to be, but the dispute continues over whom to blame. Critics charge that it was misconceived from the start and merely ran its naturally disastrous course. Defenders see Açominas as a victim of both the unforeseeable economic crisis and contrary political interests that gained power with the change of presidents. Both arguments have merit; Açominas was both technically and politically flawed, and these flaws operated in perverse synergy.

Açominas was born with a heavy political burden, which laid it open to *political* attacks by private steel, national capital goods firms, other state governments, and other officials. A less political and technically sounder project could have won over technical supporters. This support would not have precluded political attacks, but it could have deflected them and diminished their legitimacy.

Moreover, this political baggage forced a number of technical compromises that weakened Açominas's defenses and made it vulnerable in times of budget crisis. For example, the effort to find an undisputed market niche put the firm in a market with no supply shortage. This sin proved mortal when it came time to assign increasingly scarce resources to competing projects. The rush to get Açominas constructed meant that its managers left full financing pending. Had funding been at least contracted, cutting investment would have been somewhat more difficult.[28]

Building steel plants in developing countries, and especially in less developed regions of those countries, is inherently politicized. All of Brazil's steel plants had powerful (and victorious) political encouragement, and after initial difficulties most became effective and efficient. In other words, successful policy is perfectly feasible in a highly politicized environment. In fact, if left to some technical criteria, Brazil would still be importing much of its steel and what it produced would be concentrated in São Paulo.[29]

Successful policy results from a balance of political and technical rationales, a balance Açominas lacked. Its great political force enabled it to ignore technical objections. Technical considerations entered the project as afterthoughts, not as compromises that would have helped to even the balance.

Chapter 3 argued that the mix of rationales that inform any one policy depends on the mix of social types in and around the policy area who bring different rationales to policy politics. In the case of Açominas, *mineiro* politicians provided the impetus and showed a characteristic indifference to technical issues. They did not even care what the plant produced as long as Minas Gerais got it. Técnicos in Siderbrás, CONSIDER, and BNDE opposed the project but were overwhelmed by their political opponents. In such a skewed confrontation, political técnicos cannot do much; brokers are useful only when opposing sides are more evenly matched or amenable to compromise. On the issue of capital goods (where in fact Açominas can be considered a greater success in that it promoted the substitution of imported capital goods), Vianna and Belotti fulfilled their roles as political técnicos. They brokered a compromise between state enterprises and *mineiros,* who wanted to import equipment, and domestic producers and BNDE técnicos, who wanted to promote domestic production.

However, the normal interaction of these officials was distorted by Geisel's heavy backing of Aureliano and other *mineiro* politicians. Geisel involved himself directly in all major decisions about Açominas. He and Aureliano decided the project should be undertaken in the first place. In 1976 he broke ground for construction and then flew to London to sign the first major financial package (while of course attending to other matters of state). Also, the conflict over capital goods ultimately came directly to him for resolution.

All presidents have pet projects. However, the noninstitutionalized Brazilian bureaucracy is particularly susceptible to overcentralization, especially under military rule. Hence the quality of policy in Brazil is a much more direct result of the president's values and actions. In the case of Açominas, this vulnerability to centralization had disastrous consequences because it permitted Açominas to skirt técnico opposition and thereby obviated the need for a compromise, which could have improved the project and built a broader coalition.

The fact that Geisel's support was so intense highlights the enduring force of regional politics. On many issues the military was willing to accede to regional demands and found the accommodation paid high dividends in elite support for the regime. This support was marginal in the heyday of the "miracle," but in the context of slower growth, the electoral defeat of 1974, and hostility from within the military to *abertura,* Geisel must have found the prospect of regional support very attractive (see chapter 10). Regional sensitivity was acute in the pivotal state of Minas Gerais. Many *mineiros* have felt wrongly overshadowed and exploited by Rio de Janeiro and São Paulo, and they have historically depended heavily on the federal government to prevent being completely eclipsed (see Schwartzman 1982, 104). Hence the combination of Geisel's immediate political fears and traditional *mineiro* preoccupations welded a very solid alliance.

I emphasize the extraordinary nature of this alliance because more moderate regional politics had a salutary effect on other policies. Centrifugal regional pulls help mitigate the extreme centralization of power in the federal government and over-concentration of industry in São Paulo. In fact, prior to Açominas, regional rivalry promoted competition in steel between Minas Gerais, Rio de Janeiro, and São Paulo, often with beneficial results. Tendler noted a similar beneficial impact in hydroelectric development, where regional elites backed different companies that competed for federal resources. She notes that "disaggregated development of power supply . . . harnesses the growth of [electric] power to the virulence of local drives and personal ambitions."[30]

Regular presidential succession and consequent circulation had a strong impact on the evolution of Açominas. Knowing that the grace of the Geisel-Aureliano pact would last only four years, the project's managers and supporters worked feverishly to get it to the point of no return. They initiated planning, engineering, financing, and construction almost simultaneously and began each phase well before its normal sequential order. In this haste, high circulation and short tenure contributed indirectly to the technical flaws in the package. For instance, Brazilian steel plants have traditionally relied in part on World Bank financing, but Açominas managers did not have time to go to that source because they knew it would take years of planning to convince the bank. Açominas preferred to take easily obtained suppliers' credits, which, however, diminished the project's overall contribution to industrialization by forcing it to buy foreign equipment.

Presidential succession and circulation did have a beneficial effect after 1979 when a new set of policy makers reevaluated Açominas and found it lacking. Despite the haste under Geisel, there was still at least the opportunity for damage control. Because of its delayed completion, the project of course accumulated enormous additional debt; however, it was less than it would have accumulated had it contracted additional debt and been unable to sell its output upon completion. Moreover, in this period of scarcity of resources, further Açominas investment would have had a higher opportunity cost in terms of the forgone investment in other projects that were nearing completion.

The changing coalition possibilities illustrate how appointments structure power relations within the bureaucracy. For example, under Figueiredo the initially favorable distribution of ministers and other top appointees turned sour when Figueiredo appointed Delfim and gave him free rein to reorganize economic policy. The earlier example of Belotti and his defense of domestic producers of capital goods demonstrates how appointments can open channels without which a particular policy output is impossible. Geisel wanted someone loyal and competent in the MIC (in part to take care of petrochemicals in which Geisel had been very involved as president of Petrobrás). Belotti thus had never previously worked much in steel. However, one of the unintended consequences of appointing a petrochemical expert to this position was to give an ex-BNDE developmentalist a pivotal intermediary position between national producers of capital goods and Geisel.

7

Carajás: CVRD and the Politics of Ore in the Amazon

Aos técnicos cabe a tarefa válida de estudar e propor soluções viáveis. Aos políticos, optar por aquelas melhor afinadas com os legítimos anseios do povo. Não se pretende que a construção das nações seja obra exclusiva dos políticos, mas, sem eles, isto não seria possível.

—Aureliano Chaves[1]

THIS CHAPTER and the next move out of steel into iron ore and aluminum, the two greatest export successes in mining during military rule.[2] The projects shift from the center-south to the north of Brazil, though the decisions stay in the Rio-São Paulo-Brasília triangle. The organizational universe also changes. CVRD is the major state enterprise, and it is more efficient, insulated, and institutionalized, though not irrevocably, than its sister steel firms. However, these characteristics of CVRD are not the major factors in the success of these projects.

Carajás, the world's largest mining complex, is also a different kind of project. The organizational framework was simpler within the state, but the addition of an MNC partner complicated the picture. Politically, the other interested parties were weaker and fewer than in steel. Lastly, technological "determinants" conditioned decisions more (for example, location was non-negotiable).

However, the pace and specifics of the project, and hence its medium-run developmental impact, depended on policy politics and the policy preferences of several "generations" of state mining managers. And, though CVRD manifested a higher degree of institutional force, the winning coalitions were largely made by and with outsiders. The subdecisions an-

146

alyzed in this chapter include the initial decision to force US Steel into a joint venture, the option for a railroad rather than a waterway to transport the ore, and CVRD's initial reluctance to broaden the project beyond a mining enclave into a more integrated program.

From Runt of the Litter to Institutionalized Giant

By the 1980s, CVRD had established itself, nationally and internationally, as an efficient, effective iron ore exporter and a respected, diversified conglomerate. It became the largest mining firm in the world and the largest ocean-borne exporter of iron ore (CVRD 1982: 76). Within Brazil also, the company is a giant. After Petrobrás it is the second largest state enterprise and the fifth largest Brazilian firm in terms of net revenues.[3] CVRD is Brazil's largest mining firm, responsible for 14 percent of the country's nonpetroleum mining output (*Brasil Mineral,* April 1988). It produces just over half of Brazil's iron ore (and Brazil is the world's largest exporter and second largest producer after the Soviet Union) and owns 46 percent of MRN, which accounts for two thirds of Brazil's bauxite production (*Brasil Mineral,* April 1988). In 1985 the CVRD conglomerate had total revenues on the order of $2 billion and employed directly 37,000 workers (including subsidiaries and joint ventures, *Journal da Vale,* July 1985).

With the creation of Docenave, a shipping subsidiary, in 1962, CVRD began integrating vertically into transport, marketing, and iron ore processing. By 1985 it had a fully integrated transport system including railroads, ports, and ships. During the 1970s it diversified into activities farther afield, and by 1985 its thirty-four subsidiaries and joint ventures were involved in engineering, geological research, reforestation, cellulose, aluminum, and steel, as well as bauxite, manganese, and iron ore.

CVRD's recent strength, exuberance, and reputation mask the difficult beginnings and the arduous struggle in its first thirty years after creation in 1942. The company was born through peculiar negotiations with the Allied powers, who were preoccupied with securing the raw materials necessary to wage a protracted war and with keeping Brazil on the right side.[4] In one of the simpler nationalizations in the history of Third World mining, the British government expropriated British holdings in Brazil and turned them over to the Brazilian government in return for guaranteed supplies of iron ore (at one-third of the international market price [Fernandes 1982, 16n]). That CVRD was created was something of a fluke: state enterprise was an expedient vehicle at a time when few if any private Brazilian firms could undertake the enterprise.

Compared to other agencies of its generation, CVRD was born politically weak. That it was state owned because of the extraordinary circumstances of World War II meant that it lacked from the beginning both a strong justification for being a state enterprise and an articulated coalition that could defend it.[5] Over the years its managers built up the company's legitimacy and support coalition by 1) generating foreign exchange; 2) adopting a "public/social" development role; and 3) promoting a company esprit de corps and loyalty among its employees. In addition, it gained legitimacy by stemming the penetration of multinational capital. These factors promoted institutionalization, or infused CVRD with value for its officials and outside supporters.

Few CVRD publications fail to note its export earnings and their contribution to Brazil's trade balance ($2.1 billion in 1988, or 6 percent of Brazilian exports (CVRD, *Relatório* 1988, 7). Brazil's import-substituting industrialization generated recurring crises in the balance of payments, and the government increasingly responded to these crises by intervening to promote exports. Thus, by emphasizing its role in generating foreign exchange, CVRD moved itself into a legitimate area of government intervention.

As it became profitable in the 1970s CVRD took on the role of a development agent (another public function) in its mining districts while diversifying in Minas Gerais, where investment was falling off. *Mineiros* often criticize the company for exploiting their state. One saying claimed that CVRD took the ore and all it left for the state was "a hole and the whistle of a passing train." Despite its self-proclaimed development role, the firm's diversification in Minas Gerais has been profitable and integrated into its "southern system." Outside its principle lines of business and "natural" diversification, it has been less successful as a development agency. Its original statutes created a special development fund, the Reserve for the Development of the Rio Doce Zone. Profits above a rate of return of 15 percent would go into this fund. However, real improvements in the region have been "very modest" (Fernandes 1982, 10, 18n). In the 1970s contributions to the development fund averaged $2.3 million per year or 2.7 percent of total after tax profits (calculated from Raw 1985, 307, 332).

Lastly, CVRD systematically fostered strong esprit de corps and loyalty on the part of its employees. Part of its profits have gone into two funds for employees' housing and pensions. The drive for efficiency also contributed to the esprit de corps; the company's positive reputation means that being a CVRD employee commands some respect. In the end it was difficult to find employees critical of the company, and in its first forty-three years there had never been a strike. This employee support was an added political and institutional resource.[6]

In sum, arduous and consistent efforts created a firm that, entering the 1970s, was huge, efficient, and profitable. Its nationalist, developmentalist, and export orientations gained broad-based political support, though its regional backers were often ambivalent. In addition, the firm achieved higher levels of institutionalization and commitment of the part of employees than is usually the case in the economic bureaucracy.

Carajás: From Discovery to Joint Venture, 1967-1971

Manganese is essential for steel production, and the uneven world distribution of deposits makes it a great strategic concern in industrial countries. In the 1960s steelmakers in the United States were dependent mostly on African production. As African colonies became independent, MNCs began to worry about the political future of these sources and began prospecting in other, more politically stable parts of the world. The Amazon was one of the great unknowns. It had the general geological characteristics of a province rich in mineral resources, but the difficult logistics of exploration and extraction had discouraged research. But by 1966, Bethlehem Steel, Union Carbide, and US Steel were set on exploring the eastern Amazon, where a vast network of navigable waterways made exploration possible.

US Steel established its Brazilian Exploration Program in 1966. In August of the following year, through a combination of chance and curiosity, its field team discovered Carajás.[7] The geologists wanted to find out why some of the hills in the area lacked the normal vegetation. After landing on top of several hills in the range called the Serra dos Carajás, they confirmed what several had speculated but none could believe: they were hills of iron ore so rich that nothing but scrub brush could survive in the topsoil. On 20 September 1967 the head of the US Steel program sent the following breathless telegram to headquarters: "Discovered 2-35 [billion] tons iron. Strongly recommend you or person equivalent authority come Belem next few days. Paperwork underway here. Will require a large number of signatures. Estimate lid will depart pot within 7 to 10 days."[8] Though still more interested in the nearby manganese, US Steel sent a vice president to Brazil, and the company filed for research claims on the area.

From the beginning, some officials balked at the idea of leaving Carajás to US Steel, and a coalition formed to block the MNC. The central players were the president of CVRD, Antônio Dias Leite, the general director of the National Department of Mineral Production (DNPM), Moacyr Vasconcellos, and the minister of mines and energy, José Costa Cavalcanti. In general, Dias Leite had a profound impact on mining in Brazil and especially in the Amazon, both as president of CVRD (1967-69) and subsequently as minister of mines and energy (1969-74). Dias Leite was an economist with no specific training in mining. By most accounts, Costa e Silva appointed him to CVRD because his well-publicized views on economics fitted the more nationalist, developmentalist orientation of the new government, and because he had written a great deal on state enterprises (see Dias Leite 1966).

As CVRD's president he set up joint pelletization ventures with international consumers, establishing a precedent in vertical in tegration that the company was to follow in future ventures. After two years as president of CVRD Dias Leite was appointed minister of mines and energy by Costa e Silva.[9] As minister he promoted research and diversification through the creation of Companhia de Pesquisa de Recursos Minerais (CPRM), a state enterprise in research and exploration, and approved the creation of CVRD subsidiaries in engineering (Rio Doce Engenharia a Planejamento [RDEP]) and research (Rio Doce Geologia e Mineração [DOCEGEO]). In short, Dias Leite was an active political técnico and bureaucratic entrepreneur.

Vasconcellos had a more técnico career. He graduated from Brazil's best mining school in Ouro Preto in 1942 and went directly to work for DNPM. He worked his way up (taking three years out to work in a private firm) before reaching the top position there after two decades in the department. In 1970 he became a technical director in CPRM. In 1974, with the change in government, Vasconcellos ended his thirty-year career in the state and went to work in the private sector. Like most técnicos, he stayed in his sector of expertise and rose to a top technical position.

Two factors probably contributed to his more political behavior in joining a coalition to stop US Steel. First, early socialization in engineering schools usually includes a strong dose of nationalism especially when it comes to exploiting natural resources (see J. Carvalho on nationalism at Ouro Preto (1978, 112-14)). Second, openness to MNC capital was the source of tension within the military in the 1960s. The Castelo Branco government provoked great opposition within the military because of its generally favorable policies toward MNCs, and mining was one of the sorest points.[10] The Costa e Silva government was more ambivalent about them, an attitude that encouraged mining officials to act on their nationalist preferences.

Costa Cavalcanti was an anfíbio (an officer who runs for elected office, see chapter 3). He was an important conspirator in the coup and subsequent broker between the military and the *classe política*. He apparently had no experience in mining but shared with the nationalist faction of the military a deep distrust of MNCs (Flynn 1978, 380).

In March 1968 the DNPM, the department of the Ministry of Mines and Energy (MME) in charge of conceding and monitoring mineral claims, sent a DNPM and a CVRD geologist to visit

Carajás. After they confirmed reports of vast reserves, Vasconcellos, the general director of DNPM, took the "courageous and
nationalist" initiative of informing other government authorities of his preoccupation "over the risk of leaving the control of
such fabulous potential in the hands of a multinational firm"
(B. Santos 1984, 32).

In 1968 Dias Leite, president of CVRD, and Vasconcellos went
to the minister of mines and energy, Costa Cavalcanti, who approved of their idea that CVRD approach US Steel with a proposal for a joint venture. A US Steel representative came to Rio
de Janeiro in 1968 and, over fondue, discussed possible joint
ventures with Dias Leite, Costa Cavalcanti, and other CVRD
directors.[11] The most powerful incentive to reach an agreement
came from Vasconcellos and the DNPM, who sat on US Steel's
requests for prospecting rights while waiting for a revised proposal from a joint venture. CVRD and Meridional (US Steel's
Brazilian subsidiary) formed the partnership, and in October
1969, DNPM granted them joint research rights. In April 1970
the two companies created Amazônia Mineração (Amza) (51
percent CVRD, 49 percent US Steel). Though US Steel was apparently reluctant to enter as a minority partner, it knew that it
was politically risky to attempt to go it alone.

Transportation Politics, Delays,
and Buying out US Steel, 1971-1977

From 1970 to 1972, Amza completed the geological mapping
of the area. It confirmed that Carajás held reserves of 18 billion
tons of high-grade ore and discovered along the way significant
deposits of manganese, nickel, chrome, copper, and other minerals. As more information trickled in, interest spread. The politics of the first phase was confined to the nationlist técnicos
and political técnicos of MME and CVRD. However, as the scope
and scale grew, other interests began to converge on Carajás.

Intense regional interests focused in on CVRD's studies of
transportation options. Carajás lies hundreds of miles from
the coast. Since there were no existing transportation systems
in the area, Amza would have to build a railroad or waterway
from scratch. Spending some $9 million on viability studies,

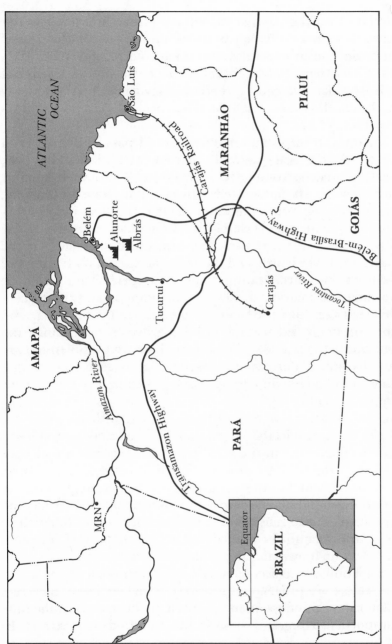

Map 2. CVRD's Northern Projects

CVRD combed the northern coastline in search of a deepwater port and settled on three possible locations—two in the state of Pará and one in São Luis, Maranhão (Fernandes 1982, 107). Carajás was close to the Tocantins river, which, with a series of locks and dams, could be rendered navigable for the roughly 600 km to the Pará coast. The other option was a 900-km railroad to São Luis.

Since the transportation system could pass through one of two states, the issue naturally became politicized. Moreover, the first studies, completed in May 1974, projected roughly equal cost for the integrated project (mine, transport system, and port) using either the waterway ($1.97 billion in 1974 dollars) or the railroad ($1.84 billion [Fernandes 1982, 108]). The battle lines were cast. Pará and Maranhão rank among the poorest states in Brazil, and the political elites of both knew full well that whichever state got the transport system would be transformed. This was the development opportunity of the century. Dias Leite and the head of CVRD studies, Costa Braga, (and others in CVRD and MME) were bombarded by politicians from both states. Dias Leite said he received monthly visits from Pará and Maranhão delegations, and legislators from one or the other state called him in to testify in Congress every three months or so.[12]

CVRD managers were mostly concerned with international markets and predictability and therefore rejected the waterway option. The rivers in the area were not well known and were subject to rapid, unpredictable changes in depth and course. Most important for the company's market strategy was that Pará ports could handle ships up to only 60,000 tons, while the Itaqui port in São Luis could dock 280,000 ton vessels. Furthermore, the amount of dredging required to keep Pará ports open was unknown and unpredictable.

A port unable to accommodate ships over 60,000 tons would tie Carajás ore to U.S. and European markets. CVRD managers did not want this dependence, especially since Japan at the time was the firm's largest, fastest growing, and securest market. In 1983, Japan was the world's largest importer of iron ore (Franz, et al. 1986, xiii), and by 1985 almost one-half of CVRD's ore exports were going to Asia (CVRD, *Relatório* 1987: 8). Huge ships were the only means for the company to compete with Australia in Asia. Euclides Triches, then a vice president of CVRD, expressed its position succinctly in his congressional testimony: "What determined the [transport] solution . . . was the São Luis port. We looked for a port; after we found it the rest came naturally."[13]

The battle over the transport system was not only between political interests and those of a state enterprise or between the interests of two states, but also over the conception of the Carajás project as a whole. If conceived as an undertaking just to get the ore onto international markets cheaply, then the railroad was clearly more reliable and more flexible in terms of markets it could serve. If Carajás mining were conceived as a lever for opening a whole region to integrated development, then the waterway would make more sense in social cost/benefit terms.[14] Because of numerous and navigable affluent rivers, making the Tocantins navigable would automatically integrate vast areas in a single transport system that could immediately be used by all. In 1975 the president of the Engineering Club of Rio de Janeiro appointed a blue-ribbon panel to assess the transportation controversy (without endorsing either option). The panel reported back that CVRD's decision criteria were too narrow and should be broadened to include among, other things, foreign debt, regional development, flood control, agricultural expansion, use of national inputs, and overall multiplier effects (*Portos e Navios*, March 1976, 8-9; and see *Revista do Clube de Engenharia*, March 1980, 10-16).

The narrow export vision, CVRD, and Maranhão prevailed. It was not, however, a major political victory for the company. Its técnicos had a string of fairly convincing technical and market arguments against the waterway, and their political opponents were from impoverished states that could not develop technically sound alternative proposals; nor could they propose to finance, say, part of the waterway. It was also a regional battle between two states that were insignificant at a national level. One of them had to win, and which did not make much difference in national political calculations.[15]

The oil shock of 1973 and the change of president in 1974 put Carajás on hold and changed the contending interests. The post-shock recession reduced world demand for steel and cooled the interests of MNC partners. On CVRD's side, Fernando Roquette Reis assumed the presidency and also thought it better to slow Carajás. He had served in the government of Minas Gerais and saw part of his political mission in CVRD as maintaining investment in Minas Gerais (interview with Eduardo Carvalho, 5 September 1985). For the first years of the Geisel government, a shared lack of interest put Carajás into slow motion. Market shifts forced further studies and negotiations. US Steel took advantage of the hiatus to probe the willingness of the new government to revise regulations on taxes and profit remittance. CVRD's top managers turned their attention to aluminum and diversification in Minas Gerais (see chapter 8).

By 1976, Reis returned to Carajás and increased pressure on US Steel to get on with the project. In 1976, CVRD finally obtained federal approval for the railroad, "after a dispute in which good sense finally prevailed" (according to CVRD's official history [CVRD 1982, 91]). Relations between the partners deteriorated as US Steel stalled. Soon it became clear that world markets and US Steel's profits were both going to have to improve significantly before US Steel would invest. So in 1977 CVRD bought out US Steel for $50 million, the sum the latter had invested in Amza through 1977. In 1978, CVRD began work preparing the railroad roadbed. However, Carajás had been relegated to the "second plane" since US Steel pulled out and since the appointment of an interim president to CVRD in November 1977 (CPDOC 1984, 348). The final decision to go ahead would have to await the new government.

The Figueiredo Government Embraces Carajás, 1979-1985

The new faces that arrived with President Figueiredo in March 1979 to occupy CVRD's organizational universe all favored Carajás. It became a positive-sum game overall (despite differences on particulars) in which the relevant actors could each benefit from Carajás. For Carajás it was appointment serendipity. None of the major appointees got their positions be cause of their stances on Carajás; however, the resulting mix of their political and technical motivations created a new pro-Carajás coalition.

Eliezer Batista returned to the presidency of CVRD after seventeen years and was intent on constructing Carajás. He had worked his way up in the company until, in the early 1960s, Goulart appointed him first president of CVRD and then briefly minister of mines and energy. The coup temporarily banished Batista from the economic bureaucracy, but after several years in the private sector he took over CVRD's operations in Europe. He used his position in Europe to help the Minas Gerais government (especially when Figueiredo's vice president Chaves was governor), which sped his political rehabilitation (see CPDOC 1984: 348). From Europe he also actively participated in CVRD's long-range policy. Many in and outside the company consider him its visionary: "Greater Carajás was born of the strategic conception of Eliezer Batista."[16]

Batista was a CVRD "lifer" and hence also likely to view Carajás favorably as it began to make better economic sense for the firm. Its reserves were diminishing in Minas Gerais, and prospects were improving in international markets. By 1979 seaborne exports of iron ore and world steel production were both back to pre-1973 levels, and CVRD projected healthy growth in the 1980s (CVRD 1981). Prices in 1979 were still 25 percent below the level of 1974, but they were up from their nadir of 1978 and higher than the projected production cost of Carajás ore (World Bank 1982a, 19; Franz, et al. 1986, 34).

César Cals, the new minister of mines and energy, was a major representative of the northeast in the Figueiredo cabinet and favored moving government investment north. Finally, Carajás sparked the interest of Delfim Netto, the economic superminister, who recognized that a massive export project could improve Brazil's international credit-worthiness. Also, since Figueiredo and others were pushing Carajás, Delfim wanted to make sure he had some say in how it evolved.

In January 1980, Delfim created a special working group on Carajás within Seplan, and in November 1980 he set up the Interministerial Council on the Greater Carajás Program (CIPGC) with himself as president. By January 1981 the council began publishing glossy pamphlets—in English and Portuguese—extolling the vast potential of Greater Carajás. The reports listed the extensive mineral deposits, mapped out the agricultural and industrial potential, and detailed the wide variety of fiscal and import incentives available to investors. The propaganda spoke of a huge integrated development pole, requiring some $60 billion investment over ten years, that would generate tens of billions of dollars in export revenues.[17]

It was a major marketing effort but, as became clear later, not a serious development plan. Neither the mining nor the agricultural projects could be begun before the railroad neared completion, which in 1981 was at least four years away. The agricultural part was even more surreal—it envisioned concessions of ten thousand hectares to export agroindustry and neglected to mention that most of the land was already privately owned. The agricultural plan was apparently thrown together in the Ministry of Agriculture without prior research, and Nestor Jost, when appointed executive secretary of CIPGC, filed it away (interviews with former CIPGC técnicos, 1985).

The November 1980 decree gave the CIPGC and its executive secretariat enormous formal powers. It charged the council with: defining general Carajás policy, approving necessary infrastructure, approving incentives for various projects, and defining conditions under which "the Executive Secretariat will exercise functions (*atribuições*) of other organs and entities of the Federal Administration" (Decree 85.387, as reprinted in IBASE 1983, 134).

The CIPGC could grant nearly the full range of incentives already existing in other legislation and projects: concession of federal lands or appropriation of private land; discounted electrical energy; mineral and forest concessions; export financing; authorization for equipment imports; treasury guarantees for foreign loans; public shares in joint ventures; reduction of or exemption from various taxes including sales tax, industrial product tax, income tax, import tax, and sales taxes on equipment bought in Brazil; supplemental federal funding; and numerous other authorizations, exemptions, concessions, and incentives (IBASE 1983, 134-35). The CIPGC had the sole right to approve all projects within an enormous area that included large parts of the states of Goiás, Pará, and Maranhão. For personnel and budget the Secretariat of CIPGC was to live off Seplan, but it could also requisition personnel as necessary from other parts of the government. Furthermore, and having learned the lesson of other ineffectual interministerial *conselhos*, Oziel Carneiro, the first executive secretary, insisted that only ministers be members and that they not send representatives.[18]

Despite criticism of its excessive centralization, CIPGC planned precious little in its first five years.[19] The major projects it approved were already well underway before 1980: CVRD's Carajás Iron Project, Albrás/Alunorte, Tucuruí, and Alumar. Little was accomplished in agriculture, and only in 1985 did work begin on pig iron production to process Carajás ore using charcoal made from the rain forest. Furthermore, CIPGC did not resolve the problem of who should mine Carajás copper while imports increased year after year.

Part of CIPGC's failure as an effective planning agency was organizational; it lacked staff. Carneiro decided from the beginning not to use its requisitioning powers to build a permanent staff (interview, 14 May 1985). Seplan offered him a whole floor of a building, but he took only two rooms. When he needed technical analysis, he sent the problem to a competent técnico in the appropriate government agency instead of bringing the técnico to work for CIPGC. Therefore policy initiatives depended solely on the executive secretary. During the Figueiredo government the council, unlike many agencies before it, took seriously its mandate of merely approving incentives for projects presented to it instead of developing those projects itself.

Delfim's dominance and the lack of political técnicos kept CIPGC from assuming a dynamic role. A permanent staff appears necessary to keep projects developing and evolving. In other words, there were no political técnicos in the agency who wanted to advance through projects in Carajás. Outside técnicos gain little from resolving particular issues for another agency and are unlikely to care about the project as a whole. The career of full-time employees of CIPGC would have depended on getting these projects, and probably others, up and performing.

However, despite CIPGC's failure to generate an integrated development plan for Greater Carajás, it did provide CVRD with a power umbrella for completing its iron mine. While not very dependent on central government resources or policy approval, CVRD could have suffered from the spending and borrowing restrictions that SEST placed on other state enterprises. But since SEST and CIPGC were both in Seplan and under Delfim, and since Delfim, Figueiredo, and others approved, Carajás had smooth sailing through the Figueiredo government. For example, in late 1983, SEST cut CVRD investment for 1984 from $429 million to $341 million. Batista went to see Delfim in mid February, and shortly thereafter SEST reinstated the full $88 million (*Gazeta Mercantil*, 28 February 1984).

CVRD put together a financial package that relied mostly on internal funds and mostly on national resources (loans and equity). It then demonstrated its usual efficiency by completing the project on schedule and nearly $800 million below projected cost.[20] In 1985, CVRD began shipping test batches of Carajás ore for clients to test in their blast furnaces. Full production at an annual rate of 13 million tons commenced in 1986 and rose to 31 million in 1989 (*Jornal do Brasil*, 29 April 1990).

In summary, the constellation of Figueiredo's appointments to economic bureaucracy graced Carajás politically. Top appointees had different goals, but each supported Carajás. This support coalition spared Carajás the fate of Açominas. Although state resources were quite scarce in the liquidity crisis of 1981-84, political support coupled with CVRD's greater financial independence allowed the project to move forward. That Carajás did not expand into an integrated project resulted partly from the absence of political técnicos (or other outside political actors), who could have harnessed this very favorable political coalition to other projects.

Narrow Success in the Carajás Enclave

Visitors to Carajás are awestruck; something historic is happening. When I flew into the newly constructed airport in mid 1985, a pioneer spirit still infused the project. Hundreds of miles from anywhere, deep in the Amazon, CVRD had built a boomtown in the wilderness. Cranes with 18-cubic-yard shovels scoop up some of the world's richest ore and dump it into 154-ton, house-size trucks, which take it to a processing plant that crushes, sorts, and cleans thousands of tons of ore per hour. The plant is a vast array of conveyers and structures that run for miles down the mountainside. Mining is a twenty-four-hour operation, and at night Carajás is all the more fantastic. The rain forest is black straight off to the horizon. But one mountain is lit up by the powerful headlights of trucks and cranes and a light-show processing structure, which cuts a line down the whole side of the ridge.

Carajás is astounding in the context of the Amazon frontier. It is also a major event in world markets (Paine Webber 1986, 52). Although capacity output of 50 million tons will be a fraction of the world market, the low cost of production and the very high quality of output will set new standards for the whole market. At the risk of hyperbole, Carajás could shift the supply curve of the industry and close not a few mines.

The basic premises of the project are very sound. Brazil does not have to worry about saving this natural resource for future Brazilian consumption. The proven reserves would allow Carajás to continue exporting at peak production well into the twenty-third century. The initiation of export is also none too soon. The increasing substitution of other materials for steel means that demand for iron ore will likely stagnate if not fall in the not so long run. The long-term profitability of Carajás was also never really in doubt (the World Bank projected a return of 11 percent [1982b, 24]). The cost of production when Carajás started up was well under world prices, which were low in historic terms. Once the railroad and port (two-thirds of investment) are paid off, Carajás will become a profit machine. Lastly, as a simple mine, the construction has been a stunning success, under cost and ahead of schedule, and the future seems equally rosy.

The success of the mine should not, however, overshadow Carajás's limited contribution to overall industrialization and development. Through 1986 it was still a classic mining enclave, and the lack of contributions by enclaves to overall development has been one of the constants throughout Latin American history. The long-term prospects for integrated development are good: if not for a Brazilian Ruhr, as some have claimed, at least for a powerful development pole. CVRD has demonstrated in its diversification in the south that ore is not its only concern, and there is little reason to suspect that it will not encourage other investment to take advantage of (and pay off) the infrastructure it constructed.[21]

Future prospects notwithstanding, Carajás began as an enclave largely because of the dominance of technical rationality to the exclusion of political considerations. The project was fraught with risk and uncertainty, and CVRD managers consistently sought to reduce the uncertainties by simplifying it and excluding unnecessary additions. They succeeded in isolating and insulating the technical core of the project. At various times they beat or excluded regional elites, US Steel, and other political técnicos. Some of these actors could have brought more political criteria to the project and rendered it more of a regional development pole earlier on.

By spending a lot on the initial feasibility studies, CVRD mustered a solid technical argument to deflate political challenges. The approval of the railroad, however, probably owed as much to the weakness of Pará politicians as it did to the power of CVRD's managers and the force of their technical analyses. During the Geisel government, Carajás was also partly insulated from the political técnico's in the new management. Reis appointed insiders to direct the company's iron ore side while the outsiders concentrated on diversification. During the Figueiredo government a different confluence of factors neutralized outside political participation. Batista had direct access to Figueiredo and Delfim, and Delfim wanted Batista to run Carajás, at the lowest cost to the government. Here resource constraints promoted Batista's narrow approach to Carajás. Moreover, the mutual agreement to keep CIPGC weak precluded its active participation in Carajás. Hence, overall, CVRD's managers insulated the Carajás Iron Project. This contributed to the mine's initial success but detracted from its contribution to overall development. A little politics could have made for a better project.

Though the railroad may have been the best transportation option for the mine in the medium run, the planning for it demonstrates the shortcomings of the purely technical approach. The major bridge on the railroad spans 2.3 km across the Tocantins. It is the only bridge for hundreds of miles and crosses the river near Marabá, which grew into a large city in the 1980s. However, some early plans projected only a railroad bridge (see Seplan 1981, 16), and it was only in response to political pressure that CVRD added a roadbed for automobiles at a marginal increase in total cost.[22] The company also planned to add rail service for passengers and cargo after the mine was in operation. Again, political pressure from local politicians encouraged it to provide such services eight months before the mine started up, to the great benefit of the communities along the railroad (Gistelink 1988, 62, 75, 91).

The other factor that limited Carajás's overall effectiveness was the delay of about five years, which had both political and technical roots. Twenty-one years passed from the initial discovery in 1967 to full production in 1988. The world average for developing a mine is twelve to fifteen years from discovery to exploitation.[23] Why the delay? The simple answers are the oil shocks, consequent steel recessions, and the Amazon. These are all real constraints, but none on its own was insuperable.

The world steel recession made Carajás less attractive, but its ore would be competitive in any market because it is of such a high grade, is so easy to mine, and requires minimum processing. Of twenty mine projects planned or under construction in the early 1980s, Carajás had the ore with the highest iron content (Franz et al. 1986, 52). Admittedly, it would be hard for CVRD to increase its market presence by 30 percent (35 million tons as a percentage of its 1979-80 output), but it could shift contracts from southern mines to Carajás, as it ultimately did in the late 1980s.[24] In any case, market projections for the five to ten years after beginning investment cannot be more than educated guesswork. The "Amazon factor" certainly delayed Carajás, but mostly in the beginning. Disease, torrential rains, and the lack of transport and other infrastructure slowed prospecting and engineering. However, once the project got strong government approval in 1979, the construction of the 900-km railroad, the port, and the mine took only six years.[25]

Another source of delay is political. From the establishment of Amza in 1970 to the completion of the first viability studies several years later, Carajás moved at a normal pace, though the 1973 oil shock dampened spirits. During the Geisel government, Carajás languished, and then it took off in 1979 under the Figueiredo administration. Had the Geisel government invested heavily in 1975, Carajás could have begun full production in 1982 or 1983. During the Geisel government there was a convergence of disinterest. The three necessary and sufficient partners for completing the project—top government, CVRD management, and US Steel—all lost interest. US Steel entered its own recession and did not have resources to invest to get ore it did not need. Geisel and his PND II were geared more to import substitution and backward linkages than to promotion of raw exports. Also, some *mineiro* managers in CVRD were not keen on massive investments in the north, especially were they to detract from diversification and investment in Minas Gerais.

Institutions, Circulation, Appointments, and Carajás Policy

In this policy story, CVRD manifested a higher degree of institutionalization than that found in steel. Fewer non-CVRD actors participated in policy (hence there were fewer transagency coalitions), and CVRD managers pressed policy outputs congruent with the firm's organizational and material interests. This is partly because CVRD was the only agency in this sector and this project, and partly because it is older and more established. Still, institutionalization is only part of the story. An analysis of circulation and appointments completes the picture and specifies when and how CVRD managers act more institutionally.

Overall, CVRD's managers circulate almost as fast as officials in the bureaucracy as a whole. However, at a more disaggregate level, managers in the technical core circulate less. Those in charge of iron ore production and transport have typically been CVRD careerists. Outsider presidents such as Dias Leite and Reis appointed insider técnicos to take care of this technical core. Also, political técnicos tend to avoid more routine jobs in established activities because they have less freedom for action. The job description is predetermined, and political técnicos can hence advance their reputations only as capable administrators, not as bureaucratic entrepreneurs. Of course, Carajás was not a routine activity, and getting it off the ground required political técnicos and entrepreneurship. Once it was in motion, though CVRD's técnicos participated more in implementation because the project hinged on an existing core activity.

The ability of the company's técnicos to formulate Carajás policy and pursue CVRD's interests depended, over time, on appointments and the favorable coalitions they permitted. The initial decision to bring the company in depended on outsiders. It was the newly appointed Dias Leite and the director of DNPM Vasconcellos, who forced US Steel and CVRD into a joint venture. When Dias Leite moved to MME, he appointed a CVRD insider as president, and he in turn maintained Dias Leite's *diretoria*, which was a combination of insiders and outsiders.

CVRD's management under Geisel was composed predominantly of outsiders (though the technical core was left to insiders), and to some extent they shifted resources from Carajás to diversification into other sectors. The timing of this deinstitutionalization was propitious for the company's técnicos who could take advantage of the lull to work through on their own the technical details required to flesh out the project. Of course, outside managers often do revise projects at this stage, but the political técnicos in CVRD at this period were not so inclined.

By 1979 the technical work was complete and US Steel was gone. The project was ready to go and CVRD had achieved almost sole control of it. In 1979, Figueiredo appointed an insider to the presidency. Batista had formally been outside CVRD management for years, but informally he had been very active. In fact, few people have been more closely identified with the past twenty-year rise of the modern CVRD than Eliezer Batista. The other top appointments in the firm's bureaucratic universe were all favorable to giving Batista the liberty to run it, and he was likely to do so in an institutional fashion.

In sum, policy making for Carajás was more institutionalized than in the other case studies. CVRD is more of an institution, but, more importantly, circulation did not intrude into its technical core and appointments reinforced the organization. However, this institutionalization is not based in the company itself. The next case study, of CVRD's aluminum projects, presents a very different picture of policy making, where circulation, interagency coalitions, and appointments deinstitutionalized CVRD.

8

Bauxite and Aluminum: The Long, Winding Road to the Amazon, Import Substitution, and Export Markets

> Nothing that has altered the face of
> the world has ever passed a prelimi-
> nary test on its rate of return.
>
> —Antônio Delfim Netto[1]

IN THE EARLY 1970s, Brazilian officials already recognized the key factors that would guide the growth of the aluminum, alumina, and bauxite industries.[2] Brazil had abundant sources of the two most important inputs for aluminum production: bauxite and electricity (hydroelectric power). The country had enough bauxite, the third largest reserves in the world, to be able to export without affecting domestic supplies for the foreseeable future, and the location of major reserves in the Amazon gave Brazil privileged access to European and U.S. markets. It was also clear that a major move into international aluminum markets would not be easy. World markets conformed to a classic enclave pattern where MNCs mined bauxite in the Third World for their aluminum plants in the First World. On the eve of Brazil's entry into world aluminum markets in 1978, industrialized countries produced 82 percent of the world's aluminum but only 16 percent of its bauxite. Furthermore, six MNCs—the Six Sisters of aluminum—accounted for 77 percent of world production outside the socialist countries (calculated from Machado 1983, 19, 24) and controlled 55 percent of the world's bauxite mining (Dantas 1980, 7).

At the same time as policy makers were considering the potential for Brazilian exports, they were also concerned about the more immediate problems of growing aluminum imports and the need over the shorter run to substitute domestic production for these (see table 9). Finally, it was clear that the total investment requirements were enormous and beyond the capacity of government and private firms. The bauxite-rich Amazon had potential but next to no infrastructure. Mining bauxite, refining it into alumina, and processing the alumina into aluminum would require not only heavy investment in mines and plants but also in shipping, ports, roads, communications, urban settlements, and, most important, a major dam.

Table 9
Brazilian Aluminum Production, Imports, and Exports, 1960–1989
(thousands of tons)

| | Aluminum | | | |
	Production	Imports	Exports	Bauxite Exports
1960	15	15		
1965	30	22		
1970	56	27		
1974	113	105		24
1975	121	79		18
1976	139	78		3
1977	167	83		4
1978	186	60		4
1979	238	52		516
1980	260	47	0	2,679
1981	256	28	2	4,126
1982	299	11	7	2,991
1983	401	3	116	3,989
1984	455	5	148	4,247
1985	549	3	179	3,317
1986	757	1	324	3,061
1987	843	2	431	2,814
1988	873	0	515	4,661
1989	888	3	472	

Souces: Aluminum (primary production) from ABAL (1989, 8, 10); bauxite from CONSIDER, *Anuário*, various years, and SDI, *Anuário* 1989.

By the early 1980s, Brazil began realizing its potential in aluminum. In 1980 it entered international markets as a major bauxite exporter, and by 1983, MRN was the world's single largest bauxite exporting company.[3] In the mid 1980s two huge aluminum plants, Alumar and Albrás came on line. Even before these two export-oriented projects began production, Brazil had reached self-sufficiency in 1982 and begun exporting in 1983. In 1988 aluminum exports reached $1.3 billion or 4 percent of the nation's exports. From an insignificant producer in the 1970s, Brazil became by 1990 the fourth largest exporter and the fifth largest producer in the world (*Gazeta Mercantil* 26 September 1990).

By 1980 the state was heavily involved in all aspects of aluminum production and contributed to increasing Brazilian control. In the mid 1970s, three private firms—Alcoa (Aluminum Company of America), Alcan (Aluminum of Canada) and the Companhia Brasileira de Alumínio (CBA)—divided the Brazilian aluminum market more or less equally. By 1982 the state, through CVRD, was heavily involved in all stages of production, and Brazilian capital (state and private) controlled much more of the sector. Brazilian capital (CVRD and CBA) controlled MRN, the largest bauxite producer. CVRD held 60 percent of Alunorte, slated to become one of the largest alumina producers. CVRD held a controling interest in the aluminum producers Valesul and Albrás. In 1988, Brazilian capital accounted for about half of Brazil's aluminum output.[4]

In the decade between potential and production hangs a tale of negotiations and renegotiations with MNCs, state enterprise diversification, state entrepreneurship, radical shifts in international markets, and delays. The story revolves around officials in numerous agencies—Seplan, MME, the presidency, BNDE, and CVRD, as well as managers in private Brazilian firms and MNCs—all jockeying to pursue their (often divergent) interests and to secure the necessary investment within a context of changing international markets. The aluminum story illustrates clearly several major themes, including the entrepreneurial function of political técnicos; the accelerator effect of presidential succession; the chimera of the autonomy of state enterprises; and

Map 3. CVRD's Bauxite and Aluminum Ventures.

coalition building across organizational boundaries based on contacts from previous jobs.

The protagonists were archetypical political técnicos. Antônio Dias Leite, Fernando Roquette Reis, and Eduardo Carvalho had the biggest impact on aluminum policy and the state's role in the sector. They were all economists who lacked training in mining and metallurgy. None of them worked in CVRD, MME, or the aluminum sector before (or after) they held top policy positions in the sector. All of them were committed to getting aluminum out of the Amazon and keeping a healthy measure of Brazilian control. Lastly, all of them (particularly Reis and Carvalho) had well-developed notions of political feasibility and coalition building with the state. That they managed to overcome formidable political and economic odds attests both to their political skills and to their concern with at least minimum technical efficiency. More than the three previous projects, this one shows best how political and technical rationality can combine to produce a better project than either on its own.

In most respects the aluminum projects were successful. As of 1985 they had a greater potential for a more effective contribution to industrialization than Siderbrás, Açominas, or Carajás. Because there were large, integrated projects, they brought greater multiplier and spin-off effects for the eastern Amazon region: electricity, roads, ports, communications, and other infrastructure. These projects transformed untapped resources into products that first substituted for imports and then grew to major exports. CVRD projects and MNC investments in aluminum in the Amazon resulted in over $500 million in foreign exchange gains (imports substituted plus exports) over the early debt crisis years of 1982-84 (Castro and Souza 1985, 90). Though the projects have yet to achieve full integration, the concept pursued from the beginning was that of avoiding raw mineral exports and attempting to add the greatest value possible.[5]

These projects are not perfect. Critics find them lacking in several respects. They contribute little directly to the regional economies because they employ few people and pay little in taxes. Further, through tax exemptions and low electricity prices, MNCs reap indirect subsidies from Brazilian taxpayers. Critics also charge that these highly polluting industries will destroy the delicate ecology of the Amazon. There is some truth in these charges. However, in the end the benefits outweighed the costs, and officials attempted to lower these costs as much as possible within the constraints imposed by world markets. In a recent and exhaustive analysis of aluminum in Brazil and the world, Machado comes to a similar "favorable" evaluation of state intervention in aluminum in the 1970s and 1980s (1988, 288).

CVRD is widely considered one of the most autonomous state enterprises in Brazil. Observers cite its ventures in aluminum as classic examples of an uncontrolled, profit-seeking firm pursuing its own interests. However, in the aluminum story, the major actors were outsiders with little concern for CVRD's interests. In fact, many within the company opposed these ventures, though later, once it was decided that it would produce aluminum, lower-level técnicos molded the margins of the projects to give them a recognizable CVRD shape.

The major market shifts were all in Brazil's favor and made costly projects in the Amazon economically viable. The political instability in other bauxite-producing countries brought MNC prospectors to Brazil in the 1960s. The increase in oil prices of 1973 knocked out many First World (especially Japanese) producers, which encouraged MNCs to consider joint ventures in Brazil and opened up huge new export markets. The bauxite cartel formed in 1974 had the classic cartel effect: overnight it made uneconomical projects in remote regions viable.

CVRD has one venture in bauxite (MRN), one in alumina (Alunorte), and two in aluminum (Valesul and Albrás). Each has a different history that could be told separately, but from the beginning, CVRD and other government officials conceived of them as an integrated complex. Thus the following analysis considers the projects together.

The 1960s: Bauxite and Dias Leite

Shortly after World War II a small Brazilian firm began producing aluminum using the limited bauxite reserves in the southeast. In the 1950s, Alcan bought this plant, and another private, Brazilian firm, CBA (part of the Grupo Votorantim, currently the largest private Brazilian conglomerate), also began production. Alcan and CBA, operating small-scale plants, managed to fulfill much of Brazil's limited demand through the 1960s, but they were slow to respond when the economic "miracle" (1968-73) radically increased demand.

Limited bauxite deposits in the south, growing domestic demand for aluminum, and the shifting pattern of world bauxite production combined to focus MNC and government attention on the Amazon. The interest of MNCs began with political changes in the 1960s in countries that supplied the bulk of the world's bauxite. In general, these years were trying for U.S. raw materials firms. From 1900 to 1965 governments in Africa and Latin America had taken over only nine MNCs; in the subsequent decade they took over thirty-four (Krasner 1978, 218). The situation in aluminum was particularly uncertain for MNCs. Through geological happenstance most bauxite deposits were located in countries such as Jamaica, Guiana, and Suriname that were working toward or had recently achieved independence. The nationalist rhetoric that accompanied decolonization frightened MNCs, which began looking to diversify their sources of bauxite.

The geological formation of parts of the Amazon was known to be promising for bauxite, and it did not take Alcan long to find significant quantities of exportable bauxite in Trombetas. The difficulties of constructing a mine were not insurmountable, since the deposits were only some thirty kilometers from a navigable river, but the complete lack of infrastructure made the project less promising in the short run. Alcan's interest revived when Guiana, source of over half of its bauxite, gained its independence in 1966. In June 1967, Alcan created MRN as one of several exploration subsidiaries, then, in 1969, reorganized it into a company to exploit the Trombetas deposits and applied successfully for government approval. Through 1971, Alcan forged ahead with the construction of a mine with a capacity for 1 million tons of annual output.

Suddenly, to everyone's surprise, Alcan dropped MRN flat. It did not delay the project; it informed the minister of mines and energy, Dias Leite, that it was going to pull out altogether.[6] This cancellation caught MME officials off guard, but they moved quickly to salvage the operation. Alcan's withdrawal opened the door for Dias Leite and state intervention, which paved the way for subsequent expansion of the state into this previously private sector. Dias Leite took a special interest in the Amazon. He had first become involved in it through his negotiations, while president of CVRD, over Carajás. In addition, President Médici himself took a great interest in the north and northeast.[7]

In general, Dias Leite wanted to get projects going quickly; involve Brazilian capital (private if possible, state if necessary);

scale projects to the requirements of the Amazon; and add as much value as possible to minerals slated for export (interview, 11 June 1985). He pressured all firms that showed any interest to undertake research and complete construction. He called in potential national firms to get them involved, alone or in joint ventures. Dias Leite especially wanted Votorantim/CBA (the sole Brazilian aluminum producer) to enter bauxite mining in the Amazon, and even before Alcan's cancellation of MRN, he had gotten the president of Votorantim, Antônio Ermírio de Morães (who usually avoids joint ventures), and Alcan to agree in principle to a minority CBA share in MRN. Dias Leite could not remember who first came up with the idea of having CVRD join MRN (which may in part be because he and CVRD managers worked so closely together on various projects that they in effect fused the ministry and the enterprise).[8] In any case, Dias Leite was convinced that, without CBA/Votorantim, the only firm capable of standing up to the MNCs was CVRD.

In mid 1971 a CVRD subsidiary approached Alcan and offered to participate with 20 percent if Alcan expanded MRN's capacity. Dias Leite used a sophisticated bargaining strategy. He told Alcan (and other MNCs prospecting in the Amazon) that legally they had the right to exploit mines alone, but that it was politically wiser over the longer run to bring in Brazilian partners, especially since they were operating in the politically sensitive Amazon. The military considered the few inhabitants, little infrastructure, various Indian groups, and lack of integration with the rest of the country potential threats to national security or in Golbery's words "paths of penetration" (Alves 1985, 125).

In December 1972, Alcan and CVRD signed an accord to study a larger bauxite project and the potential for adding an alumina plant. While Dias Leite encouraged national partners to join MRN in a *tripé* (three-way, or tripod) arrangement (which he called the government's general "thesis" at the time), he also tried to bring in other MNC partners. It was not until almost a year and a half later—after Dias Leite and CVRD's managers had traveled around the world looking for partners, customers, and loans—that Alcan, six other MNCs, CVRD, and CBA met to approve a joint venture.

Aluminum and Adding Value in the Amazon

Dias Leite favored adding value to mineral exports. As its president, he continued CVRD's forward integration into processing iron ore; as minister, he promoted forward integration into aluminum. In this promotion Dias Leite went beyond his formal authority. He was the minister of *mines* and energy; other ministries (MIC) and agencies (CDI and CONSIDER) had general responsibility for projects such as industrializing ores. However, in the early 1970s state intervention in the aluminum sector was slight, and within the state no agency had specific responsibility for aluminum, which left policy in an organizational vacuum.

An activist minister of mines and energy could step into the vacuum, especially if he had a subordinate state enterprise that he knew well and controlled. As in the case of Pratini's reformulation of CONSIDER, Dias Leite combined, in new ways, the instruments he already had at his disposal. These instruments gave him a full arsenal of carrots and sticks with which to cajole MNCs into integrating forward or entering joint ventures. He could use the stick of withholding mining concessions to persuade them that they should follow his plan. He could bring in CVRD as an executive instrument to make the project go. Lastly, in the case of aluminum, he also controlled the major carrot, the price and supply of electricity. Producing 1 ton of aluminum consumes about 15,000 kwh, which gives the metal the name "packaged energy." As minister of mines and *energy*, Dias Leite could juggle the price and supply of this major input to serve his policy goals.[9]

By 1973, Dias Leite was already discussing possible aluminum ventures with Japanese producers, but the negotiations were very tentative because of the lack of electricity.[10] In December 1973 he proposed the Law of Participation as a means of getting around this obstacle. The proposal allowed big electricity consumers to invest in hydroelectric plants and receive energy at cost in return. In January 1974, in the last months of the Médici government, CVRD and a Japanese consortium Light Metal Smelters Association (LMSA) agreed to finance a viability study of Albrás.

Through his activism, Dias Leite was able to lay the foundation for CVRD's entry into bauxite, alumina, and aluminum in the north. However, this voluntarism could not overcome the "Amazon factor," which raised investment projections above the point that would justify projects, especially in the eyes of foreign investors. Since the Amazon required projects of massive scale to justify the huge investment in basic infrastructure, and since the Brazilian market could not absorb the output of these massive projects, the ventures had to be planned for export. This led Dias Leite to look for MNC partners and made the viability of ventures subject to international markets and hence beyond direct state control. In fact, before these projects got off the ground, the state was going to have to invest more in infrastructure to reduce the total cost to investors. International markets were also going to have to change.

Some observers think market shifts were critical: "The IBA [bauxite cartel] made MRN viable, and OPEC made Albrás viable" (Machado 1985, 244). Before the increases in oil prices of October 1973 the Japanese had little immediate interest in producing aluminum in Brazil. The Japanese aluminum industry had expanded at 20 percent per year in the 1960s and could think of producing off-shore only over the longer term. However, Japanese smelters ran an oil-generated electricity, and OPEC turned Japan into an aluminum importer almost overnight (by 1976 the industry was operating at only two-thirds capacity).[11] OPEC indirectly spurred MRN on as well. Inspired by the oil cartel, the major bauxite producers formed IBA in 1974 and increased the price of bauxite, which made MRN investments viable. Despite these propitious market shifts, the government was still going to have to assume more of the investment burden in order to bring MNCs in.

The Geisel Government and Aluminum, 1974-1977

Centralization under Geisel meant that no project went anywhere unless he approved.[12] It also confused the hierarchical chain of command and the division of labor (i.e., specialized sectoral ministers) within the bureaucracy. One curious consequence was that, while centralization limited ministers' discretion, it also weakened their control over subordinate presidents and directors of state enterprises who often had direct access to Geisel and could bypass their ministers. These channels of communication strengthened the second and third levels within the state at the expense of their immediate superiors.

Geisel's appointment of his close collaborator at Petrobrás, Shigeaki Ueki, to the MME, changed the position of CVRD and aluminum in government planning. To the extent that ministerial power is dependent on the personal relationship between the president and the individual minister, Ueki and the sectors under his supervision could have a privileged position in the government. Ueki came from Petrobrás and did not share Dias Leite's concern for mining and aluminum, nor did he have experience or expertise in these sectors. In combination these changes meant that CVRD was free to develop its projects (unhindered by ministerial meddling) while, if Ueki agreed with them (which he usually did), the company could count on a powerful ally within the ministry.

CVRD's management also changed dramatically. During the Médici government, its president and many of his directors were CVRD careerists. Geisel appointed an outsider president, Fernando Roquette Reis, who retained two of the previous directors while appointing five from outside. Reis had made his career in the Minas Gerais government, as had three of his seven directors. Neither he nor these three colleagues had training or direct experience in mining or metallurgy.

Reis and Eduardo Carvalho (another outsider appointed in 1975 as director for new projects, including aluminum) were archetypical political entrepreneurs, and they were the major forces in this period behind CVRD's diversification, especially in aluminum. Both were political appointees and knew that the new government in 1979 was unlikely to invite them to stay on. Over the longer run, they both had political bases outside CVRD that would determine more of their future careers than would the firm. Reis was linked to the *mineiro* elite, and Carvalho had headed Delfim Netto's technical staff (1970-73) and was viewed as an *homem do Delfim*. Carvalho knew that when Delfim's political star rose again, Delfim would probably call him to a position of confidence.[13] In short, Reis and Carvalho were not from the ranks of CVRD, their future careers did not depend on it, and they were free to use their power over it to further personal, career, and political goals.

Table 10 chronicles their disregard for CVRD *as a firm*. Even as revenue from ore sales stagnated, they embarked on major investments through debt financing, leaving the company in sorry financial shape by 1979. After 1979, Batista claimed that he spent the first two years of his presidency cleaning up the financial mess (interview, 23 August 1985). That Reis and Carvalho knew they had only four years encouraged this disregard for annual balances: they had to get their projects to the point of no return before the next president appointed their replacements.

Table 10
CVRD Revenues, Profits, Investment, and Financing, 1969-1980

	Revenues[a]	Profits[a]	Investment[a]	Percentage Self-Financing	Percentage Loans
1969	294	105	105	85	14
1970	397	149	182	73	20
1971	433	155	254	55	30
1972	442	142	366	51	27
1973	625	220	424	75	13
1974	790	261	411	57	30
1975	985	347	341	67	32
1976	1075	320	542	36	57
1977	939	95	448	32	40
1978	938	76	370	49	49
1979	1172	−36	237	60	34
1980	1276	204	340	69	24

Source: Raw 1985, 327-29, 332, 350.
a. Millions of constant 1965-67 cruzeiros.

Beyond the changes in personnel and policy styles, the Geisel government also brought substantive policy changes that favored investment and diversification by CVRD. Geisel's PND II was a major invitation to state intervention in aluminum. It was a medium-run plan to reduce imports and a long-run program to complete the vertical integration of Brazilian industry by promoting the domestic production of capital and intermediate goods, among them aluminum. The Geisel government was not at all adverse to increasing government investment and foreign indebtedness to achieve the goals of the PND II. Thus CVRD had the broad approval for diversification and the government's commitment to maintain its investment. From 1974 to 1979 the government's share of total fixed capital formation went from 40 to 43 percent (the state enterprise share rose from 23 to 26 percent), the foreign debt tripled from $17 billion to $50 billion, and the public sector's share of incoming loans jumped from 35 to 77 percent.[14]

However, these policy opportunities and the organizational niche that Dias Leite had carved out for CVRD in aluminum were not in themselves enough. The necessary counterpart was a new management team interested in, and capable of, taking advantage of them. The company, under other managers, could still have pulled out of the bauxite and aluminum projects. A great deal of insistence by the Reis team was necessary to bring the projects to fruition.

In the first year of the Geisel government, Reis finished some of the work begun under Dias Leite. In April 1974, MRN partners signed a final agreement on shares, and in August, RDEP presented a viability study for Albrás. A month later, Japanese Prime Minister Tanaka came to Brazil and signed protocols to go ahead with Albrás and Cenibra (another of CVRD's joint ventures with Japanese MNCs in cellulose). However, this exuberant beginning was soon bogged down as MNCs in all projects decided they wanted to renegotiate in light of new market developments and lingering doubts over the original projects.

If in 1974 it looked as though the new MME and CVRD managers were merely executing Dias Leite's policies, by 1975 the slate was mostly clean again, and CVRD managers had to redesign the northern aluminum projects. Because of changing interests of the foreign partners, MRN suffered restructuring in 1974 and 1975. Problems of scale, worsening terms of trade between raw materials (the bauxite) and manufactured goods (the investment), and the Amazon factor caused various MNCs to reconsider their commitment.[15] In April 1975, CVRD and LMSA met and admitted that a 640,000 ton Albrás was not viable, and that the aluminum project could not finance the construction of a major hydroelectric dam. Moreover, the Japanese lost interest in an alumina plant for export to the aluminum plants they were busy closing. Hence Reis and Carvalho found themselves in 1975 with the opportunity to go into aluminum (the way having been paved by Dias Leite) and wide latitude in deciding how CVRD should do it.

The following sections consider separately the evolution of MRN, Albrás, and a new project, Valesul, over the first three years of the Geisel government.

Mineração Rio do Norte

The final package and the resumption of mine construction came in 1976, four years after Alcan had abandoned the project. Once resumed, construction proceeded at the projected pace, and MRN started exporting Trombetas ore in 1979. Though this project was still fairly undefined when the Reis team took office, they followed the basics Dias Leite had established. The partners and scale changed, but the basic concept of having a joint venture between CVRD and consumers remained the same. The MNCs assured a market for the output, while CVRD maintained national control and government leverage.

Why did government officials tolerate the initial delay? CVRD could have done the project alone. Several top officials in the Médici government said that the technology and capital were not major constraints, but neither they nor their successors in the Geisel government wanted to go it alone. Government officials, particularly CVRD's técnicos, were wary of entering international markets unaccompanied (the company had been badly burned before), and they were favorably impressed with the joint ventures CVRD had worked out in iron ore.

Bauxite and aluminum markets are especially dicey. International aluminum production ranks among the most vertically integrated in the world, and there was, at least until the political changes of the 1960s and 1970s, no free international bauxite or alumina market. The entry of new producers has since "freed" markets up somewhat, but still it is no small risk to enter this kind of market with 3-4 million tons of bauxite, or about 10 percent of world exports in the mid 1970s (Machado 1985, 183). In other circumstances, CVRD might have been able to enter the bauxite market alone with smaller amounts and gradually expand as the market permitted. Here, the Amazon forced it into collaboration with MNCs: to lower unit investment costs to viable levels, initial capacity had to be enormous.

Albrás

The same factors, in differing degrees, influenced the evolution of Albrás. Negotiations were not so advanced when Reis arrived, but market conditions again encouraged the joint venture option. CVRD's managers were favorably disposed to working with MNCs, and the Amazon factor inflated the scale, making an all-Brazilian alternative very risky.[16] Aluminum production is more complicated and requires greater investment than bauxite mining, so in Albrás other actors participated in resolving or creating obstacles. The Japanese partners dragged their feet, but Albrás also encountered obstacles within the Brazilian state. Overcoming these obstacles would depend on intragovernment coalition building.

When CVRD and a reorganized consortium, the Nippon Amazon Aluminum Company (Nalco), met in May 1975 and rejected the first viability study, Albrás passed from the realm of project to that of a continued willingness of the Japanese and Brazilian governments, CVRD's new managers, and the Japanese MNCs to undertake some kind of venture at some future date. Albrás's market was less problematic than that of MRN. The oil shock made it clear that Japan would soon be the world's largest importer of aluminum. The remaining elements that had to be pieced together were: infrastructure, electricity, capital, and the details of the joint venture (such as market division, pricing, investment shares, and pace). Albrás, as joint venture and technical project, floundered through the rest of 1975 into 1976. CVRD cast about for other Brazilian and MNC partners, and RDEP proceeded to scale down the project.

Over the course of 1976 the pieces began to fall into place. Ueki, the minister of mines and energy, moved quickly to resolve two key variables: availability and price of electricity. He was keen on getting the Tucuruí hydroelectric project going. It would be the major public work of his administration. Previous negotiations had stumbled on a simple "you first" impasse. The Japanese did not want to invest in Albrás until the dam was there; the Brazilian government did not want to build the dam until they could be sure someone would buy the electricity (*Veja*, 25 September 1974). In 1975, Ueki and Geisel had decided to go ahead with Tucuruí, even though Albrás negotiations were in limbo. The decision to halve Albrás's capacity to 320,000 tons complicated projected demand (and hence the justification) for Tucuruí, but Ueki pressed on.

Ueki's relations with cvrd managers on Albrás were harmonious, and he accepted most of their recommendations. In January 1976 he agreed to Carvalho's sliding electricity price. Known as the "Ueki price," it was a floor price that would rise with the international price of aluminum. This and subsequent pricing policies have drawn fire on charges that they constitute a government subsidy to foreign consumers. In the end, though, electricity prices to aluminum producers around the world are much lower than to other consumers. The Brazilian price ranked eighth among sixteen exporters and is above the average price charged by seven exporting developing countries (gti Alumínio 1986, Anexo I-3).

The government also withdrew demands that Albrás build some of the remaining infrastructure: ports, roads, water, and electricity transmission. In essence, the government was trying to reduce Albrás's investment to those elements found in any more developed area and felt pressured to do so because the Japanese were getting similar government commitments in other developing countries. At a political level, the project sailed ahead. Geisel traveled to Japan in August 1976 and signed a protocol proclaiming that Albrás was of "national interest" to both Japan and Brazil.

In July 1976, rdep presented the revised viability study for a 320,000 ton plant. With reduced investment requirements, emphatic political support at the highest level, and a concrete project, it remained only to reach an agreement between the partners. In October 1976, cvrd and Nalco signed the first of a series of accords. However, nearly two years were to pass before they agreed on a definitive shareholders' agreement. In the interim two factors held the process up: the global strategies of the Japanese and the BNDE (discussed below).

On the Japanese side negotiations were bound to drag on. The Japanese "partner," Nalco, was itself a hodgepodge of thirty-three aluminum producing and consuming companies and several government agencies. Each item and change in the agreements had to undergo a whole series of approvals.[17] To complicate matters, some of the Nalco partners were hesitant participants. The Japanese government had cajoled many of them into the deal, and some (such as the aluminum producers, who were busy closing down plants and losing money on remaining production) were not in a position to undertake overseas investments.

Another source of delay was the global Japanese strategy to obtain aluminum from diversified sources over the long run. By 1982, Japanese companies (and sometimes their government) were negotiating or participating in a dozen major aluminum ventures in Indonesia, Australia, Venezuela, China, Brazil, and elsewhere slated to produce 2.5 *million* tons of aluminum (Samuels 1983, 506-07). Simultaneous investment (or promise thereof) in different countries allowed the Japanese to force each host government to the highest common level of incentives and subsidies. This strategy helped persuade Brazilian officials to assume more of the investment (Dantas 1980, 30). It was clear that one day the Amazon was going to be one of the four or five major world centers of production, and the Japanese wanted to be in on it, but they had no reason to hurry Albrás.[18] From the Brazilian side it appeared that it had offered sufficient incentives, and that it was time to start pressuring.

Valesul

CVRD managers conceived of the southern 80,000 ton aluminum project, Valesul, as just such an instrument to pressure the Japanese on Albrás, as well as a means of getting into aluminum and substituting for some imports while the Albrás negotiations dragged on. The Valesul idea emerged early on in the protracted Albrás negotiations. As I recounted in chapter 1, the idea in fact came up during a meeting with the Japanese. Reis, while waiting impatiently for a translation at the bargaining table, passed a note to Carvalho with the Valesul idea. Carvalho wrote back "Yes," and the note went around to the other directors present, who also approved it.

Valesul is the best case in this research of political entrepreneurs overcoming formidable obstacles to implement a project for which there was no precedent. Valesul was the only aluminum project that Reis and Carvalho started from scratch, and they designed it to overcome opposition at all levels: other government agencies, private aluminum firms, and regional politics.[19] At the level of government planning, they presented the project as part of PND II's goal of substituting for imported basic inputs. Further, they argued, Valesul would be a small project in the south, which could start producing well before Albrás. Aluminum imports were high and increasing, and the private producers were not racing to meet demand.

This case illustrates how bureaucratic entrepreneurs are useful in fulfilling the goals of indicative planning. The skillful entrepreneur will try to build legitimacy and a potential support coalition into the proposal before taking on the opposition. One central element, then, is adjusting the dimensions of the project to fit official planning objectives. Carvalho stated that, when Valesul ran into opposition within the government, he would call up and say, "Look, it's in the Plan," or, "Listen, this is what Geisel wants." If plans work, it is not because officials read them and proceed to implement them, but because they change the resources in bureaucratic politics. To the extent that top decision makers back the plan, subordinates know that they can win allies by redesigning proposals to fit it.

The CVRD team wanted a regional ally to help push Valesul through the federal government. Reis used his close ties to top officials in the state government of Rio de Janeiro (they were ex-colleagues from Minas Gerais) to form an alliance to locate the plant in that state. Rio de Janeiro was in the midst of a difficult process of uniting the old state of Guanabara with the former federal district of the city of Rio de Janeiro. The new state government of the merged entities welcomed a project that would make a political impact and be one of the state's first.

Valesul's policy infancy was graced. It sped through viability studies and initial government approval. In May 1975, CVRD contracted RDEP to do the feasibility study, which it submitted six months later. In June 1976, Geisel approved the creation of Valesul, and two months later CONSIDER approved the project on the condition that CVRD find a private partner. In the last months of 1976, CVRD formally constituted the firm and arranged to get the technology from Reynolds. All that remained was to find financing and private partners. Here the opposition raised new obstacles.

In its quest for private partners, CVRD approached CBA/ Votorantim, several MNCs, and Brazilian aluminum consumers. The first round of contacts aroused no great interest. The president of Votorantim, Antônio Ermírio de Morães, claimed to oppose Valesul on technical and economic grounds and, anyway, preferred non-collaborative, sole ownership capitalism (Evans called him a kind of one-man conquering bourgeoisie [1982, 232]). Of the MNCs, Reynolds showed some interest, especially with the prospect of selling the technology. The idea of drawing Brazilian consumers in as partners—on the basis of the supposed common interest of guaranteed supplies and assured markets—was an interesting attempt to translate CVRD's international strategy into the domestic market. However, just as many MNCs had done before, domestic consumers lost interest when the world recession created a buyers' market in aluminum. There were rumors that the existing producers, CBA, Alcan, and Alcoa, threatened consumers with a boycott if they entered Valesul as partners (Dantas 1980, 28). Valesul would have to wait several years before finding a partner.

The opponents of Valesul looked and acted a lot like the Açominas opposition. The private sector opposed state entry into their market, and the BNDE opposed Valesul on technical grounds. Contrary to the case with steel, two of the three private producers were foreign and lacked a legitimate basis for initiating a public campaign against state entry. The battle was left to Ermírio de Morães, who spent much of the 1970s publicly criticizing government policy, especially state enterprises and their "megalomaniac" projects. Despite a strong press campaign and frequent conversations with ministers, other officials, and CVRD managers, he was unable to stop the project. That the private sector was not meeting domestic demand (as compared to private steel producers in the Açominas story) no doubt made his opposition ring somewhat hollow.

According to one of its top managers at the time, the BNDE opposed Valesul on technical grounds. He argued that the project was not economically viable on its own terms, and that a project to transform imported alumina into aluminum did not merit priority funding by the bank. However, the World Bank and Shell/Billiton later considered the project viable enough to finance it, which suggests that the motivations of BNDE managers may not have been purely technical, as former CVRD managers charge. The bank's formal and informal alliance with the national private sector could have defined Valesul out of its priorities.[20] Or it may have been predisposed to find the private sector's arguments more convincing than those of CVRD. In the end, though the private sector and BNDE could not stop Valesul, they did slow it down.

Time's Winged Chariot . . .

By late 1976, CVRD and its various partners had defined basic parameters for the three joint ventures. Through 1977 the projects slouched along. MRN continued normal construction. CVRD and Nalco negotiated endlessly the details of the Albrás agreement (Carvalho estimated that he traveled to Japan once every two months for further negotiations). Valesul progressed on paper but still lacked a private partner and financing.

Personal conflicts led Minister Ueki to fire Reis in November 1977 and call in his chief technical adviser, Joel Rennó, to act as president of CVRD for the last fifteen months of the Geisel government. Though Reis had been a moving force behind the aluminum projects, this shift did not bring new direction to them, and Rennó replaced only two of Reis's directors. Rennó's previous experience was in the electricity sector. He had neither expertise in aluminum nor an independent political base from which to launch policy initiatives. In essence, he was meant to occupy the presidency—so that other outsider groups could not take it over—and thereby allow the managers time to continue their projects. This type of ministerial confidence appointment is easier in the twilight of a government, when other political groups are less keen on gaining representation in the position.[21]

For the political entrepreneurs of the *diretoria* who had their eyes on the presidential succession of March 1979, the watchword became "point of no return." In general, the urgency of getting a project past this point co-varies with the force (or potential force) of those opposed to it and varies inversely with favorable inertia of lower-level técnicos, who circulate less. Among the projects analyzed here, there is a continuum of urgency that runs from Açominas to Carajás. In Açominas, where political opponents were strongest (private producers), and where the state enterprise técnicos (Siderbrás) harbored deep suspicion, speed was of the essence. In Carajás, which had few opponents to the basic idea, and where CVRD's strategy was geared to moving north over the longer run, speed was less relevant. Siderbrás and aluminum projects are intermediate cases, but Pratini in the first case and Carvalho in the second both felt it necessary to leave their successors the most irreversible faits accomplis possible.

MRN was slated to begin production in 1979, so it was well beyond the point of no return. Valesul and Albrás in the first months of 1978 were, however, still paper projects and incoming new managers could have scrapped them. While still trying to drum up partners and financing, CVRD began bulldozing for the Valesul plant in March 1978.[22] The negotiations were to bear fruit only in the last months of this management's term.

The turning point came when the World Bank granted a $98 million loan (one-quarter of the total investment) in November 1978, pushing Valesul beyond the point of no return. Few incoming managers would consider rejecting World Bank funding even if they had strong reservations about the particular project. The loan was even more important in providing CVRD managers leverage in other negotiations. They used this seal of approval to vindicate their proposal and rebut technical criticisms within the bureaucracy (though the BNDE was still skeptical). World Bank financing also helps overcome the reluctance of MNCs: the bank provides them with an independent technical evaluation; and more importantly, they have greater assurance that the project will go through, mostly because the bank's approval strengthens the bureaucratic hand of the project's supporters. Four months after the World Bank approval, in the succession month of March 1979, Shell/Billiton agreed to a 35 percent share of Valesul. Three years later, the new firm began producing and Brazil became self-sufficient in aluminum.

Albrás/Alunorte advanced more slowly. The negotiations finally yielded a definitive shareholders' agreement and a financial commitment from the Japanese in June 1978. However, the counterpart financing that CVRD had to come up with was still not available. The project was too big for it to finance alone, especially considering its other commitments. It had to turn to the only domestic source of long-term industrial financing, the BNDE, and the BNDE found yet another CVRD project unworthy of its support.

The BNDE's analysis found Albrás wanting on numerous counts.[23] In some of its objections the bank was merely following standard procedure (e.g., rejecting requests that lacked necessary data); however, the central objection concerned control. By the mid 1970s the bank would not fund joint ventures that were not controlled by the national partner(s), and it was not content with mere majority ownership. Certain clauses of the Albrás shareholders' agreement gave the Japanese partners veto power over critical issues such as increases in equity and future expansion. Other provisions, from the perspective of the BNDE, gave the Japanese partners undue opportunity to paralyze the project in midstream if they changed their minds.

BNDE managers were also worried about the bank as an institution. In one letter, Vianna wrote that he was particularly wary of jumping into an amorphous project that would absorb resources equivalent to those of the Inter-American Development Bank. To commit these resources would make the BNDE extremely vulnerable (as a bank) to the risks of the project and decrease the funds available for its other programs. Thus the bank's técnicos opposed Albrás on procedural and institutional grounds.

Chapter 2 argued that formal organizational and procedural issues were more likely to arise in policy battles when lower-level técnicos participate, when the agency in question is old and established, when political leaders support either the agency or technical disputes in general, and when the policy involves a zero-sum struggle over resources. In the BNDE's response to CVRD's aluminum projects, all these factors favored the bank's institutional rejection. The BNDE is one of the oldest and most respected agencies of the Brazilian state. Its refusal began with a standard rejection by its técnicos (who are more likely to defend their procedures and organizations).[24] Support for rejection from above is critical; técnicos alone would have been unable to make it stick. Under a different president, ministers, and managers (representative and confidence) the BNDE would subsequently approve a very similar Albrás project. Lastly, its managers were more willing to risk their jobs (the highest stakes) because the Albrás project constituted a zero-sum decision for the bank's resources. Albrás would have absorbed funds from other BNDE programs and jeopardized its overall financial position.

Though Vianna and the BNDE had in several other cases acceded to pressures from above to approve a loan, in this case they prevailed, and Albrás finished the Geisel government without funds from the bank. This is a prime, and rare, example of técnicos and political appointees defending the interests of their organization and winning. However, the basis for BNDE's power was not institutionalized (i.e., stable).

Unlike MRN and Valesul, Albrás had not really passed the point of no return with Figueiredo took office in March 1979; however, the project moved ahead as scheduled in the early months of the new government. Nalco disbursed the first monies in July 1979 and bulldozing began in August. If not enthused, CVRD's new president and management appeared resigned to Albrás and even invited Carvalho to stay on to complete the aluminum projects. The Figueiredo government appointed new people to head all the agencies involved in the aluminum projects. While the policy preferences of these appointees differed from those of their predecessors, the convergence of interests was still favorable to Albrás.

Batista was a CVRD engineer with a checkered political past, but he was not a political técnico in the same sense as Reis and Carvalho. He was more technical (and organizational) than political and more "visionary" than bureaucratic in his politics. He knew about all projects and in some had played an important advisory role. He supported MRN and Albrás but not Valesul. The first two fitted with his conception of a two-pole system (one in the Amazon, one in the south). And Batista knew well that much of CVRD's (and his own) success in the 1960s and 1970s resulted from close collaboration with the Japanese.

Figueiredo appointed César Cals, an electricity man and "amphibian" from the north, to MME. As a regional representative he was legitimately expected to try within limits to move government money north. His incentives to do so were strong, since his political base and future (in a more open political regime) were also in this region. As he centralized power later, superminister Delfim cut out Cals as the hierarchical intermediary and dealt directly with state enterprises, which strengthened Batista, who had good relations with Delfim.

CVRD's northern projects fitted Delfim's response to the debt crisis well: concentrate government investment in export projects, particularly if they are near completion. Neither Carajás nor Albrás were near completion, but they were for export and would not constitute a great immediate drain on government investment. Future export projects also improved Brazil's long-term ability to pay, which enhanced Brazil's ability to contract loans immediately. Furthermore, Delfim had made the Greater Carajás program a cornerstone of economic policy which favored Albrás, one of the few component projects ready to go.

The Figueiredo government changed the BNDE drastically and deinstitutionalized one of the bastions of procedure and technical rationality within the Brazilian state (see Willis 1988: 26-27 and above, chapter 2). They appointed outsider political managers and gave the bank new social spending (and thinly veiled patronage) functions. In 1979, Figueiredo shifted the bank from the Ministry of Planning to MIC but three years later moved it back to Planning (and to Delfim Netto). The administrative chaos, the outside managers, and its new patronage responsibility undermined BNDE técnicos and neutralized opponents of Albrás within the bank.

In sum the convergence of interests of Figueiredo's top appointees gave CVRD's managers the political space to push ahead with Albrás. It proceeded smoothly through the Figueiredo government and began test production in 1985.

The Politics of Industrial Success

In the last twenty years policy makers have moved Brazil from an aluminum importer with modest domestic production to a major and growing exporter of bauxite and aluminum. Brazil is currently well situated to become one of the largest producers and exporters in the world. By the late 1980s the worst fears about subsidies through low electricity prices had not materialized, and CVRD's aluminum ventures seemed to enjoy only marginally greater benefits than other Brazilian exporters. Particularly in the north, a complete accounting will have to wait until Albrás and Tucuruí are operating at full capacity.[25] In these rough terms the policies that yielded these results were effective. They also contributed to opening up the Amazon, promoting regional industrialization in one of the poorer areas of Brazil, adding value to raw material exports, and easing the balance of payments crises of the 1980s.

That Brazil developed a bauxite industry is not in itself surprising. The economic rationale was strong in the beginning, and market shifts in the 1970s strengthened it. Left to their own devices, MNCS probably would have developed the bauxite industry. However, without the pressure of committed officials, aluminum production would have atrophied because it required the integrated development of bauxite and electricity.

The "why," the economic rationale, was obvious, but how, when, and on what terms depended on political técnicos in successive governments. Dias Leite, Reis, Carvalho, and to some extent Ueki were archetypical political entrepreneurs in the way they promoted "new combinations" politically. None were CVRD careerists, nor did they have experience in aluminum, yet they were the decisive shapers of aluminum policy (and CVRD's participation in it) from the beginning through the late 1970s. When the Geisel government appointed Reis and Caravalho to CVRD, it was certainly implicit that they were to apply their dynamism to an expanding state enterprise that was flush with investable cash. Their dash into aluminum was informed by the fact that their earlier bureaucratic performance had earned them this appointment and by the possibility that success in aluminum and CVRD might mean a ministerial appointment in the next government.[26]

Of course, these political técnicos operated in a congenial environment. The organizational, market, and planning contexts were consistently favorable to their brand of entrepreneurship. First, until 1974 there was no government agency with central responsibility for aluminum, and even afterward aluminum policy was still largely up for grabs, leaving room for aggressive officials to define initial policy and bring CVRD in. An open policy area such as this attracts political entrepreneurs. Second, international markets in bauxite and aluminum improved throughout the 1970s while Brazil's balance of trade in aluminum (and in basic industrial inputs generally) continued to deteriorate. Each market development strengthened the projects and their backers within the economic bureaucracy.

Third, the general economic orientation or plan of each of the last three military governments favored (for different reasons) the three ventures. Médici's concern with the Amazon and regional inequality facilitated the approval of Dias Leite's plans for developing the Amazon. Geisel's PND II targeted the substitution of imports of basic inputs such as aluminum. The debt and balance of payments crises of the early 1980s reinforced the need to substitute for imports and promote exports and hence favored Valesul and Albrás. In sum, the context was favorable and awaited political técnicos to take advantage of it.

My analysis goes against the prevailing interpretations of CVRD's diversification into aluminum. One interpretation, favored by the official historians of the firm among others, is that it was an autonomous state enterprise with a private business or capitalist orientation: aluminum was a good investment and it leapt in.[27] Raw's (1985) case study contradicts the autonomy argument. She argues that the government, especially during the Geisel years, used CVRD as an "agent of development" against the company's will.[28] In concluding her discussion of its aluminum ventures, Raw quotes a CVRD manager who claimed that, "especially in the case of Valesul, the company 'was chosen as the victim, because it had money' " (1985, 389).

Both the autonomy and victim analyses err in treating the government and the state enterprise as distinct organizational entities. In fact, neither was a monolithic actor with distinct, identifiable interests and clear institutional boundaries. This is especially true of the 1970s, when the management of CVRD was opened to outside appointees and the various ministers of mines and energy had very diffeent relations with it. Once we accept that the firm is not a monolithic actor, we can dispense with the fiction of unitary CVRD interets.

In the Médici government, it was never clear where the Ministry of Mines and Energy ended and CVRD began. For instance, when Dias Leite became minister, he retained the same directors he had appointed when he was president of CVRD. His control of its managers was more direct than that enjoyed by most ministers because he personally had appointed them. Dias Leite also continued to act like the president of CVRD: he traveled around the world seeking partners for MRN and relied on trusted subordinates in CVRD to conduct some ministry business. The fusion of ministry and state enterprise blurred if not erased the boundaries between them. In the Geisel government it is also inappropriate to consider CVRD as an institutional participant in aluminum policy. Carvalho and Reis were managers of the company; however, they were outsiders who cared little for its interests. In fact, to call them CVRD managers obscures their true identites: they were powerful political técnicos charged briefly with developing aluminum before moving on to other policy areas.

Rather than assess the relations between CVRD and MME, it is more illuminating to search for the bases of insulation, autonomy, and coalition building in the appointment and personal relations that span organizational boundaries. Médici gave Delfim a free hand in macroeconomic policy, but he also gave sectoral ministers such as Dias Leite and Pratini freedom to make sectoral policy. Dias Leite's close control over CVRD increased his policy discretion by insulating the whole policy area from outside political forces. Dias Leite had appointed CVRD insiders and unknown técnicos who lacked outside supporters and hence could not introduce outside concerns (representation) into CVRD's management.[29]

Under Geisel, all major policies went through the president's office. Prior to 1974, Ueki had collaborated closely with Geisel in Petrobrás, and as minister he enjoyed relatively privileged access to Geisel. But he was also an unknown technocrat with no independent power base and lacked the power to appoint CVRD managers (at least through 1977). Access to Geisel plus regional support gave Reis and Carvalho significant autonomy from Ueki. In the Valesul case personal ties facilitated coalition building within the state. Before elaborating a specific project, Reis and Carvalho contacted friends and ex-colleagues in the Rio government to assess the possiblities for building a coalition that would include the then governor of Rio. The Rio officials convinced the governor, and the CVRD-Rio coalition approached Geisel and the other agencies of the federal government.

With Figueiredo, interagency personal ties again changed dramatically. Batista had an outstanding reputation and enjoyed strong support in Minas Gerais. He had free rein to name his directors and selected mostly técnicos without outside ties in order to insulate CVRD. Cals was his formal superior, but after some initial attempts to impose his authority on the firm, Cals backed off. Batista had access to and good relations with Delfim and Figueiredo himself, and therefore autonomy from Cals.

In short, CVRD was neither the primary (profit maximizing) agent in the development of aluminum nor a passive victim. Rather, consecutive generations of insider and outsider managers favored aluminum and used their varying appointment and coalition ties to develop the sector.

Part III

Comparisons and Conclusions

9

Preference and Process in
Brazilian Industrial Policy

THIS CHAPTER takes the conclusions from the four case studies and returns to the concepts and competing hypotheses in part I. The first sections evaluate the force of material, organizational, ideological, and career interests expressed by various officials in the case studies. Organizational and ideological preferences crop up in the case studies somewhat more frequently than initially hypothesized, but it is still only by considering careers that we can specify when bureaucrats will pursue these interests. Subsequent sections look at the factors—formal procedure, coalition building, circulation, and appointments—that affect the dynamics of decision making in the case studies. Formal procedure was sometimes important though secondary, but only attention to informal appointment power specifies when. Overall, the empirical reassessments of this chapter provide modified, nuanced support for the general arguments in part I. Formal elements of procedure and position sometimes do matter, but their impact cannot be understood without an examination of informal elements of careers, mobility, and appointments.

Material Urges

Direct, immediate, material self-interest was not a major factor in any of the four cases. Policy outcomes did not legally affect officials' incomes, and in all cases of investment those who originally undertook it had moved on to other agencies before the investment started yielding a return. For example, in 1979, Dias Leite was back at the Federal University of Rio de Janeiro when MRN started exporting. When Açominas came on line in 1986–87, all the major officials associated with its inception were either out of the state or out of the steel sector.

Few top Brazilian officials are selfless ascetics dedicated to the public's service regardless of remuneration. Most of those discussed in part II were earning high salaries and enjoying extensive fringe benefits such as chauffeured cars, mansions in Brasília, and expense accounts (see Macedo 1985; *Veja*, 12 August 1987). In 1976, 83 percent of sixty-six state enterprise managers earned more than thirty-nine times Brazil's minimum wage, which put them in the far upper reaches of Brazil's income distribution (L. Martins 1985, 218). And, of course, a key component in the pursuit of a career is the expectation of ever increasing material rewards. However, the policy-relevant behavior of an official who wanted to advance a career was quite different from that of one who wanted to get rich quick.[1]

While bureaucrats' preferences may vary independently of their material interests, the same is not true of the industrialists and capitalists who had an impact on policy. For example, Açominas threatened private steelmakers, and they shoved it out of their markets. Capital goods producers may have often cast their preferences in terms of their contribution to Brazilian industrialization, but they gained directly when Açominas's orders went to Brazilian firms. Thus capitalists are capitalists and officials are officials, not state capitalists.

Organizational Interest

Public policy distributes and redistributes government money, formal responsibility, and prestige. For many authors (see chapter 2), it is this zero-sum distribution that animates organizations, and their officials hence enter policy politics intent on coming out with more bureaucratic resources. In each of my cases some officials at some times acted like such organization men.

The creation of Siderbrás most clearly reveals the force of organizations in action. The holding company was to enter a policy sphere that was already densely, albeit chaotically, populated. Other organizations would have to cede the territory Siderbrás would occupy. For example, Siderbrás in any form would deprive the BNDE of policy input and capital. Officials of the bank were willing to cede influence on policy but not on money, and Siderbrás got capital, indirectly, only from the Treasury. Organizations mattered in Siderbrás, but this is hardly surprising since the policy itself was organizational. The Açomi-

nas case is a polar opposite: few policy participants acted organizationally, and organizations had little to do with the final
outcome. Ignoring formal organization altogether would not
detract much from the story of Açominas.

Carajás fitted well with CVRD's organizational interest, and
the final shape of the project bears a strong CVRD imprint.
Company careerists, and through them the organization, had a
greater impact here for several reasons. Political técnico appointees were more willing to leave iron ore to careerists. The length
of implementation gave técnicos an advantage over political técnicos, who circulated out before the project got going or circulated in too late to change it. Most importantly, Figueiredo
happened to appoint a careerist, Batista, as president when the
project was ready to roll.

Organizational interests influenced some aspects of aluminum development. Within CVRD, loyal managers were split between iron ore purists and those who favored diversification.
Was CVRD just a single-function government agency or was it to
be a diversified, profit-maximizing enterprise? Either of these
positions could be viewed as organizational, so that the firm's
entry into aluminum does not unequivocally reflect an organizational interest. That the major movers in aluminum policy
were not CVRD careerists and not dedicated to CVRD's welfare
casts further doubt on an organizational perspective. Politics
became more organizational when the BNDE entered the policy
fray and defended both its procedures and its organizational
interest in rejecting Albrás. But since the bank later funded
Albrás, it cannot be assumed that it always acts in its organizational interests.

In these four cases organizational interests sometimes enter
policy politics depending on the issue to be decided and the
participants. When the policy is one of zero-sum administrative
reform, as in the case of Siderbrás, then officials are likely to
defend organizational interests. Conversely, when a given policy
is completely positive-sum (or when no other agency is particularly concerned, as in the case of Carajás), then officials are
freer to pursue their interests, which are sometimes organizational. When the policy affects the core interests and resources
of an agency, as in the Albrás loan requests to BNDE, then the

response is likely to be organizational. When lower-level técnicos are heard in policy debates (as in the BNDE's technical evaluation of Albrás, Açominas, and Valesul) then the slant is likely to be organizational. Lastly, when the policy involves older, respected agencies and careerists tied to them, then officials' preferences are more likely to reflect those of the organization. Again, though, it bears reiterating that this kind of incipient institutionalization is dependent on outside supporters and the conjunctural constellation of political power, and it is hence reversible.

Ideology: Developmentalism and Nationalism

For the specific types of policy outcomes analyzed here, ideology was not a determining factor. In part, explicit ideology rarely formed the basis for the cleavages and coalitions in bureaucratic politics. In part, broad ideologies provided little guidance on issues such as where to locate an aluminum plant or what sort of organizational arrangement is optimal for state steel. Weber's oft-cited metaphor is apt here: "Not ideas, but material and ideal interests, directly govern men's conduct. Yet very frequently, the 'world images' that have been created by 'ideas' have, like switchmen, determined the tracks along which action has been pushed by the dynamic of interest."[2] The "tracks" of Brazil's development strategy were laid long before the 1970s; interests and preferences then clashed over how to move forward along them.

Developmentalism explains little in terms of competing preferences and potential outcomes precisely because it is so widely shared. There may have been some officials in the economic bureaucracy who believed that Brazil should forget industry and concentrate on its comparative advantage in agriculture, but I never heard about them. All officials interviewed agreed that Brazil should have steel plants, aluminum plants, and iron ore mines, though they disagreed vehemently over where, when, and how. Developmentalism cannot explain specific policy outcomes, but it merits mention in comparative terms because the first prerequisite for getting effective industrial policy is having policy makers who think industrialization desirable.[3] This basic agreement is fundamental to Brazil's early success in industrialization. Success in the Japanese case, and in developmental states more generally, depends on a prior consensus on industrialization (Johnson 1982, 22). Or, in Gerschenkron's words, "To break through the barriers of stagnation in a backward country, to ignite the imaginations of men, and to place their energies in the service of economic development, a stronger medicine is needed than the promise of better allocation of resources or even of the lower price of bread" (1962, 24).

Nationalism in some form is also widely shared; but the separate forms it takes leads to divergent policy stands and often nasty policy disputes. Until the mid 1980s import substitution in general was non-controversial; nearly everyone agreed that it was better to make a product in Brazil than import it.[4] The controversy rages over whether the local producer should be owned by state, private Brazilian, or foreign capital. Various hues of nationalism inspired some of the protagonists in my case studies, especially in those involving MNC partners (Carajás, MRN, Valesul, and Albrás). For instance, Vasconcellos in MME first held up US Steel's research requests because he worried about giving an MNC rights to such massive riches, and Dias Leite then coaxed them into a joint venture. In Albrás, the preferences of Dias Leite, Reis, and Carvalho were mildly nationalist but not as strong as those of the BNDE officials who denied it funding.

Several other ideologies were not relevant in my case studies but do arise in other policy debates. For instance, the military's national security doctrines are a specific subset of developmentalism and nationalism. Many officers feel that Brazil's military might rests ultimately on the ability of Brazilians to manufacture the implements of war.[5] Hence they favor import-substituting industrialization (ISI), but their concerns have focused on industries directly relevant to defense (see chapters 3 and 10).

The proper role of the state became a significant ideological controversy in the mid 1970s. However, it entered the policy process in the form of a political response to private sector demands rather than through the strong beliefs of policy makers (see Schneider 1987b; 1989). Few officials had an ideological attachment to state enterprise or intervention per se. For example, in 1976 only 11 percent of 107 officials (66 of whom worked in state enterprises) believed that state firms were the optimal vehicle for promoting industrialization: 46 percent favored private Brazilian firms: and another 34 percent preferred an alliance of Brazilian state and private firms (L. Martins 1985, 227–28). Developmentalism and nationalism commit officials to certain outcomes. Many preferred in principle to let the private sector achieve the outcome, but in practice they were quite willing to use the state if the private sector was unwilling or unable to deliver on their terms.

When ideological preferences did not vary across officials, as in the case of developmentalism, they are not useful in explaining policy coalitions and outcomes in Brazil, though they should help in explaining differences between Brazil and other late industrializers. When ideology did contribute to divergent preferences, it did so when the policy involved MNCs and hence raised nationalist (or national security) concerns.

Careers and the Ordering of Preferences

So far, the analysis has been disaggregate: material gain, organizational interest, and ideology motivate some actors under some circumstances. Careers provide an analytic means to reaggregate and order the myriad policy preferences that different officials have. Many theories of bureaucratic politics and policy making tend too far to one or the other end of the simplicity-complexity continuum. Some authors, often those attempting more elegant modeling of bureaucratic behavior, reduce officials to single motivations such as budget maximizing.[6] Others list the full range of possible motivations and constraints and offer a more realistic view of bureaucratic behavior (see, for example, Lynn 1987; Meltsner 1972). However, these analyses can be overly complex and unwieldy. The careerist approach steers a middle course between these extremes. It recognizes the many factors that go into bureaucratic motivation and behavior but seeks to simplify or aggregate the factors by career type and by career evolution.[7]

Presumably, officials, like most people, want some mix of income, power, and prestige, but they want primarily to secure an (increasing) flow of these things *over time*, over the course of a career. They forgo short-term gains that jeopardize the long-term flow. If you wield your current powers to the maximum you risk alienating those who may in the future be able to appoint you to better positions. For example, maximizing short-term income, licit and illicit, may taint your reputation and deny you a chair in the future at the table of the state. Such career calculus is the best way to explain why officials do not always act on immediate personal, ideological, or organizational preferences.[8]

Building on the analysis in chapter 3, the case studies suggest that the pursuit of a public career affects the generation and expression of preferences through socialization, reputation building, and the quest for advancement.[9] Socialization is most important in early careers that are often confined to one organization. Lower-level técnicos interact with only a few like-minded colleagues and tend to identify with them and their organization. To establish reputations and to advance, officials must project a persona of preferences (often genuinely held) that appointers seek. The difference between creating a reputation and seeking advancement is temporal. A bureaucrat may evince immediate preferences with an eye to a particular advancement. Establishing a reputation takes time and bears career fruit only over the longer run. Officials' preferences tend to conform to their chosen careers because of past socialization or because they seek a particular promotion or reputation.

Preferences and their expression also vary according to position in the informal hierarchy. At the bottom, reputation means less than socialization, which is probably more important than considerations of advancement because promotion is more automatic (nondiscretionary). Immediate promotion criteria are probably more important for middle-level political técnicos, who, without organizational bases and with only embryonic reputations, are more likely to secure advancement based on their present performance and preferences that should be acceptable to their superiors.

In top ministerial and state enterprise appointments, reputation becomes more important. Most of these officials will not climb any higher, and for the "terminal" appointee the key issue is reputation or place in history. Here the career patterns of the major social types have even more force. Técnicos and organization men who reach, say, the presidencies of their state enterprises know that they were appointed because of their reputations and that they should continue to act them out. They can be expected to voice strong organizational preferences (e.g., Batista). A political técnico (e.g., Ueki) at this level can give vent to subliminal preferences that were held in check during previous bureaucratic incarnations and sometimes surprise appointers and colleagues. Politicians and military officers can indulge their political desires and ideological preferences (e.g., Cals). At the top, and usually at the end of a career, officials are less likely to sacrifice reputation to promotion.

These additional factors further illuminate the expression of preferences encountered in the case studies. Table 11 is a rough attempt to typecast by career type the participants in the four cases.

This summary table first shows which types of official participated in each policy. The military was not very involved and rarely had a significant impact, and then usually through presidents and other anfíbios (military officers in electoral careers, who usually acted more like politicians). Political técnicos, in contrast, were always present and decisive. The impact of politicians and técnicos was less evenly distributed across the cases. In the creation and evolution of Siderbrás, the mix of types was fairly balanced, but the political técnicos acted more technically than one would expect from their career tracks, and few politicians were actively involved. Organizational reform seems not to inspire politicians and political técnicos to great effort and creativity. In Açominas the politicians stand out, though political técnicos Belotti and Delfim later brokered countercoalitions.

In Carajás the técnicos dominate, though the balance of politics and technical rationality changes over time. The key actors in the early years (Dias Leite and Vasconcellos) pursued nationalist, political preferences. After a lull in the mid 1970s in which técnicos and political técnicos hold sway, the técnicos reemerge forcefully after 1979 backed by the political power of Delfim. In aluminum the political técnicos have their day, but their pref-

Table 11
Social Types by Project

	Military	Politician	Técnico	Political Técnico
Siderbrás	**Américo**	**Geisel**	BNDE officials	**Vianna** (t)
			Andrade	Lopes
			Lanari	**Pratini**
Açominas	Américo	**Aureliano**	BNDE and CON-	**Belotti**
		Geisel	SIDER	Vianna (p)
		Gomes	officials	Camilo Penna
				Delfim
Carajás		Costa Cavalcanti	CVRD **insiders**	**Dias Leite**
		Figueiredo	**Batista**	Carvalho
		Cals	**Vasconcellos** (p)	**Reis**
		Pará & Mara-	Mascarenhas	Ueki
		nhão politi-		**Delfim**
		cians		
Aluminum		Cals	BNDE & CVRD	**Carvalho**
		Rio governor	insiders	**Reis**
			Batista	**Vianna** (t)
				Ueki
				Dias Leite

Note: Boldface type indicates those officials who had the greatest impact on the project. Military *anfíbios* are classified here as politicians. The (t) for "technical" and (p) for "political" indicate strong tendencies within mixed types, or a deviant tendency in the case of Vasconcellos.

erences vary over time and across agencies. In the beginning, Dias Leite is primarily motivated by political preferences, while later Vianna raises more technical objections (in part to defend his agency). It is, however, the purer political técnicos, Reis and Carvalho, who have the greatest impact.

Some policies elicited unexpected preferences. The prospect of MNCs digging up the Amazon brought a political response from técnico Vasconcellos. The threat to the organizational interests of the BNDE posed by Siderbrás and aluminum brought out the técnico, organization man in political técnico Vianna.[10] In other instances factors such as position in the bureaucracy and in one's career affected the expression of preferences. The constraints of promotion weaken as an official nears the peak or end of his career. Old officers (Américo), old técnicos (Lanari and Batista in the 1980s), and old political técnicos (Dias Leite) are more likely to push their individual preferences more forcefully because it is their last chance and the absence of further promotions might be a blessing. They also have greater discretion. Those in the middle of their careers and/or the hierarchy know that future promotion to another ministry or enterprise requires a political and entrepreneurial reputation (as well as a record of competence). Younger ministers and managers (Ueki, Pratini, Reis) are more likely to be team players and brokers than their older colleagues.

For most purposes identifying career or social type is adequate for explaining and predicting the kinds of preferences bureaucrats bring to policy making. For more detailed an nuanced analyses, the type of policy and the position of officials in their careers and the informal hierarchy further specify what types of preferences they will push and how far.

Process: Coalition, Circulation, and Appointments Revisited

Policy politics in the four cases rarely followed the formal channels for industrial planning, though at times appearances were deceptively formal. Policy making adhered to formal procedure only when officials had the informal power necessary to execute their formal responsibilities, as in Batista's implementation of Carajás. Official procedure is in many respects an extension of formal organizations (and hence of officials' commitment to them). The few officials who push organizational interests are also more likely to stick to formal procedure.

Açominas demonstrated most clearly the irrelevance of formal procedure: the major actors were either outside or marginal to the planning apparatus. Carajás and the aluminum projects seemed to follow formal channels and sometimes in fact did. US Steel and Alcan came to MME, which approved Alcan's MRN bauxite project. However, Vasconcellos and Dias Leite had no formal authority to hold up US Steel's applications in order to force it into a joint venture with CVRD. Dias Leite again overstepped his formal authority when he launched into aluminum (though he was stepping into a formal void). Carvalho and Reis followed Dias Leite's policies, without a formal mandate but with an official precedent. Valesul, however, came out of nowhere, in formal terms.

In the case of Carajás, once DNPM and MME had approved the initial project, the subsequent decisions on transportation system, buying out US Steel, and the speed of implementation were all essentially up to CVRD, though the decision on transport was so sensitive that it went to higher levels for ratification. Hence in this case CVRD managers had the formal responsibility and informal power to overcome northern politicians and US Steel in order to develop Carajás as they wanted to. One prime example of a powerless formal agency was that of the CIPGC, the council charged with integrated planning for the entire region. Despite its broad formal powers, most policies bypassed it in formulation and returned once decided for a seal of approval.

Paradoxically, even though decision making did not usually follow formal procedures (or did so only informally) the policy outputs fitted the general economic plans and sectoral priorities of the last three military governments. Brazilian planning seems convoluted; formal directives were implemented informally. That they were is, however, less a reflection of the force of official plans than of bureaucrats' use of plans in informal politics. The plan and the presumed support for it at top policy levels filtered the kinds of project that subordinates would push and strengthened coalitions that backed policies congruent with the plan.[11]

Coalitions

Policies that circumvent formal channels are made by informal coalitions (which range from tight-knit groups with articulated interests to loose convergences of officials with similar preferences). The story of Siderbrás is largely that of the coalitions opposed to it. Initially some state enterprise managers, the BNDE, and Delfim stopped Siderbrás. After the deus ex machina, Geisel, created it by fiat, state enterprise managers (and their regional backers), price control agencies, and, periodically, money ministers kept it from fulfilling its coordinating and planning functions. The pro-Açominas coalition included Aureliano, other *mineiro* elites, and Geisel. This coalition prevailed initially but later lost to managers in Siderbrás and other firms, their regional backers, and Delfim, who brought Açominas to a halt in the early 1980s.

In the case of Valesul, Carvalho wove together a new coalition with Ueki and officials in the Rio de Janeiro state government. This coalition managed to overcome the opposing convergence between BNDE and private producers. After 1979 the interests of several ministers and regional elites, and to some extent President Figueiredo himself, converged to give Carajás powerful impetus. This coalition overlapped roughly with the formal hierarchy, but it was informal to the extent that some participants pushed the project for reasons unrelated to their formal positions.

Following the organization chart will sometimes lead you to the central actors and sometimes map out the path of policy, but it will often lead you astray. When it does explain the policy, the fit is usually spurious, for the theoretical underpinnings of a formal approach do not hold. Attention to informal coalitions not only explains more policy outputs but also identifies when and why the policy process converges or diverges from its formal course.

Circulation

For most officials presidential succession set the tempo for career change and policy cycles. In the four cases this tempo subjected long-term projects to periodic revision and encouraged officials to hurry and to try to restrict possible revisions (mostly by increasing their cost). The extent to which policies suffered revision subsequent to turnover in policy positions depended on the orientations of the incoming officials, the extent of implementation, and the nature of the project itself.

Siderbrás managers had barely moved into their offices when Geisel and his new steel appointees took office. Siderbrás presented few obstacles to major reform, which is just what Geisel opted to do. Açominas was just over one-quarter implemented when the Figueiredo government took office and about half-done by the time Delfim consolidated his power at the end of

1979. In principle, this should have constrained the ability of Delfim and the anti-Açominas coalition to change the project. In fact, they could not modify the fundamentals such as size and equipment and had to settle for postponing it. Delay was difficult and costly because past investment usually compels present investment. But Delfim felt strongly and spent freely of his political capital to stem the flow of investment, though he could not scrap the project altogether.

MRN and Albrás were still on the drawing board when MME and CVRD changed officials in 1974. The projects suffered major revision, but less because of the preferences of the new bureaucrats than because of changing market and MNC positions. By the time of the Figueiredo succession in 1979, MRN was producing, and Valesul and Albrás had enough contractual obligations that changing them would have required strong preferences backed by power to match. In Carajás the type of project itself minimized the range of possible midstream tinkering. For instance, geology determined location and output.

In overcoming fragmentation, high bureaucratic mobility was instrumental in two subdecisions. Central victories over centrifugal forces were more common.[12] While lacking enormous power within the cabinet, Pratini was able to centralize sufficient power to run an increasingly fragmented state steel sector. Geisel and Delfim later had sufficient power outside steel to force coordination. Hence, in the most fragmented sector, steel, centralization made coordinated (if not particularly effective) policy possible.

The two cases of coordination that circulation facilitated were Valesul and capital goods procurement for Açominas. In the first case, Carvalho's and Reis's prior contact with colleagues who moved to the state government of Rio de Janeiro created the opportunity for rapid coalition building. In the second, Belotti's pivotal position in steel and his strategic links to the other significant policy agencies were pure circulation coincidence. Belotti came out of the BNDE in the 1960s, and by the mid 1970s his former colleagues were leading the policy of promoting domestic production of capital goods. Most central to his role as broker in Açominas, however, was that in Petroquisa he worked with Geisel, then president of Petrobrás. What is important to remember here is that Geisel appointed Belotti largely to take care of petrochemicals in MIC. By circulation lottery, Belotti found himself well positioned to make steel policy as well.

Overall, in these four cases circulation enhanced coordination less than expected. However, these cases belong to a small subset of major projects in which centralizing presidents and superministers participated. What the above comparisons show is that the effect of circulation on coordination is most evident in lesser or subsidiary decisions (which are far more numerous), precisely where fragmentation would, if unchecked, pose a greater threat to policy coordination and effectiveness.

Appointments

The appointments in my four cases illustrate the full range of power relations from complete subordination along lines of formal authority to appointments that completely bypass organizational hierarchy. Each government had its own informal hierarchy within the cabinet and between cabinet members and their subordinates. Figure 2 presents schematically the differences in the last three military governments. Although an oversimplification, it does capture the salient differences in real power within these governments.[13]

In the Médici government Delfim quickly established himself as the chief architect of overall economic policy. But Médici's was the most ministerial of the three governments, and ministers Pratini and Dias Leite were the central policy makers in their sectors. Geisel's was the most centralized and presidential government, and Geisel participated everywhere he could. By appointing subordinate officials and dealing directly with them, Geisel undercut his ministers. In the Figueiredo government, Delfim once again rose to superminister, but he also had a heavier hand in sectoral policy and thereby weakened sectoral ministers. Budget and investment crises left Delfim choosing between projects to promote his macro goals. Carajás got the green light, Açominas got the axe, Albrás limped ahead, and Siderbrás nearly went under because of Delfim's limits on investment and prices.

Figure 2
Informal Hierarchy in the Médici, Geisel, and Figueiredo Governments

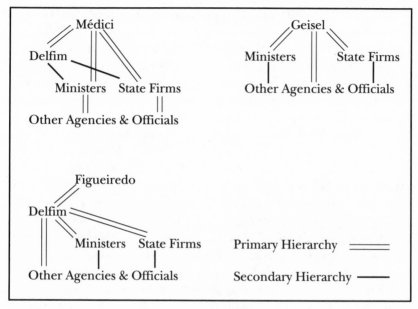

The relations between ministers and the presidents of major enterprises varied greatly within and between governments but for the most part conformed to the general pattern at the cabinet level. Ministers in the Médici government had more power over presidents of state enterprises and less in Geisel's and Figueiredo's (in part because of Delfim's intervention and in part because of the higher number of representation appointments Figueiredo made).[14] The best examples of hierarchical control are those of direct confidence appointment. For example, in the Médici government, Dias Leite appointed CVRD managers, and Pratini handpicked CONSIDER officials; and in the Geisel government, Minister Ueki appointed a trusted subordinate to CVRD in 1977. At the other extreme, in each government some officials had minimal control over mangers of subordinate enterprises. As minister of mines and energy, Dias Leite gave the Petrobrás president, Geisel, free rein. As Siderbrás presi dents, Américo and Brandão Cavalcanti had little control over some presidents of state enterprises. And Minister Cals had little say in how CVRD's president Batista implemented Carajás and Albrás.

Another set of formal hierarchical relations was more of a standoff, especially under Geisel's and Delfim's (1979–85) centralization, as in the relationships between Gomes as minister of industry and commerce and his vice minister Belotti, and between Gomes and the Siderbrás president, Américo. Both Belotti and Américo had direct dealings with Geisel, and Belotti in particular was closer to Geisel than Gomes. A similar standoff was later evident in relations between Camilo Penna as minister of industry and commerce and the Siderbrás president, Brandão Cavalcanti. Brandão Cavalcanti was appointed before Camilo Penna took over MIC; he was not a Camilo Penna appointee and therefore enjoyed some independence. But their relationship was not a critical factor in steel policy because both depended directly on Delfim, who controlled steel investment.

These examples reveal a wide range of variation over time, across governments, and across agencies. At any one time officials in different positions of formal authority will have widely differing powers and possibilities for coalition. For the second and third levels, those with direct ties to the president, whom the president appointed directly, who have personal ties to others in the policy area, and who have substantive support in society have the most independence and potential power. Confidence and technical appointees (as was discussed in chapter 4) who are unknown and appointed by their immediate formal superiors have little leeway. Overall, the first question to ask when embarking on a study of a policy or decision in Brazil is not "What is the structure of the sector?" or "What is the administrative organization?" but rather, "Who appointed the officials involved and why?"

Availability of resources also seems to affect power relations within the bureaucracy. Barzelay (1986, 115) argues that scarcity of resources centralizes policy control and forces central decision makers to choose between competing policy goals. Scarcity explains part of the difference between the ministerial government under Médici (when ministers pursued sectoral goals in a period of expanding resources) and the centralization under Figueiredo (when Delfim chose between sectoral projects).

However, the resource argument is incomplete without attention to sometimes countervailing political forces expressed through appointments. In political terms, Delfim was probably stronger during the Médici government, though he did not exercise this power to control spending. In his subsequent incarnation the debt and budget crises forced sectoral investment decisions up to Delfim; however, he had less political power to enforce the spending cuts. Successful centralization requires a concomitant shift in the power of appointment and dismissal. Many more appointees during the Figueiredo government represented outside political bases, and many were using their positions to further their political ambitions. At one time or another at least seven of Figueiredo's ministers let it be known that they would be willing to succeed him (Ames 1987, 294). Though Delfim could fire the president of Eletronorte for overspending, he could not get rid of Camilo Penna (who used his position to lobby for Açominas) or a spender like Interior Minister (and presidential candidate) Andreazza.

More generally, representation appointments can embed political cleavages, which were more likely in certain policy areas and under certain political conditions. For enterprises subordinate to MIC and MME, there were three formal levels: ministers, presidents of state enterprises, and presidents of state enterprise subsidiaries. In the case studies appointment relations between these levels ranged from great subordinate independence to near complete dependence in the case of pure confidence appointments. However, cleavages due to political representation were more likely to occur between the minister of mines and energy and his enterprises and between the president of Siderbrás and his subsidiary firms. Conversely, there were fewer significant splits between MME state enterprises and their subsidiaries and usually fewer between the minister of industry and commerce and the president of Siderbrás.

The cleavage or break in the hierarchy varied because the groups that sought representation in these policy areas did so at different levels. The three major conglomerates subordinate to the minister of mines and energy (Eletrobrás, Petrobrás, and CVRD) were first of all too large to allow one minister to appoint all their presidents. The president of the country would not want a minister of mines and energy who is as powerful as that, and hence the minister will rarely have control of "his" firms. In steel, regional groups mobilized to nominate representation appointees for the operating companies (and to oppose strong regional candidates for Siderbrás). Hence the president of Siderbrás was likely to be regionally neutral (which, in a policy area rife with regional power, is often tantamount to being powerless), while subsidiary presidents were likely to have strong outside supporters and hence greater independence.

Political representation in the bureaucracy also depends on how presidents use appointments to secure support. Over the course of *abertura*, Geisel and Figueiredo sought more support and permitted greater representation through appointments, which translated into increasing political and policy fragmentation. To the extent that the president accepts representation through appointment, it limits his choice and his discretion to dismiss later on.

Preference, Process, and Effective Industrial Policy

The comparison of the policy stories offers a more dynamic picture of the interaction of political and technical rationales and their contribution to effective policies. First, the mix of rationales manifest in an initial policy forms the basis for a sustaining coalition. Initial decisions are highly tentative, and given the turnover and lack of institutionalization in the economic bureaucracy, they require continuing political backing to reach fruition. If the mix of rationales in an initial project does not attract a broad constituency, the policy is likely to suffer over time, as in the case of Açominas.

Second, technical and political disputes of varying intensity can make policies more effective. In some projects a salutary dynamic improves policy: intense technical dispute prompts policy makers to call in political support, or intense political battle inspires greater technical debate and elaboration. Both these dynamics tend toward better policies, but when officials manage to hive off or bracket one side of the dispute, the policy result is less likely to be effective. Efforts to promote a balance, what Geisel called the *"justa medida,"* such as subjecting Açominas to technical scrutiny or politicizing Carajás can improve development projects.

Siderbrás was mostly a technical project that percolated up until Pratini created a paper company and Geisel breathed life into it. Siderbrás had some successes, but it never rationalized the administration or planning in state steel. The root of these shortcomings lies in the absence of a strong political rationale and the consequent lack of political support. Had Siderbrás been structured to ensure investment flows to steel-hungry states, had it had the power to assure low prices to consumers (or high prices to private producers), or had it otherwise facilitated the participation of powerful and interested groups, it could have built a sustaining coalition. However, at each stage the decisions avoided accommodation. The truncated debate left Siderbrás with some technical rationale but little political purpose or support and therefore relegated it to the sidelines of steel policy.

Açominas strayed in the opposite direction, though also failed over the medium run. The initial decision involved almost no political or technical debate. The initial political coalition (Geisel and Aureliano) was unstoppable albeit extremely narrow and ephemeral. Subsequent battles improved the project somewhat but did not broaden the base of support much. CONSIDER cut short possible technical debate on output by shunting Açominas into an unoccupied market niche. The political accommodation of capital goods producers improved the project and drew in more potential supporters. However, both the technical and political rationales were too feeble to survive the debt crisis and Delfim. In fact, from the opposite perspective, the anti-Açominas coalition may have incorporated a better balance of technical and political rationales, and this coalition was certainly broader.

At each step in the development of Carajás, CVRD técnicos advocated a strictly technical plan based on engineering expertise in mining and international market projections. Top managers were sensitive and flexible enough along the way to respond to political pressures in ways that usually enhanced the developmental impact of the project. The political ado over the choice between waterway and railroad intensified and improved the technical analyses and debate. Political pressures again encouraged CVRD to open up access to the railroad, first by adding a highway to the bridge over the Tocantins and then by starting passenger and cargo service ahead of schedule. Even more political pressure (say, from more powerful local governors), could have improved the project by getting it running sooner and implementing a more integrated development program simultaneously.

Though Valesul was not an unmitigated success, nor was it as big or difficult as the other projects, it nonetheless best represents the balance necessary for effective policy making.[15] Valesul had a solid economic rationale (import substitution), it made technical sense, and the clever project design incorporated a strong political rationale that elicited sufficient political support to carry the project through. The technical debate revolved around markets, electricity, and production technology, and the final project resolved most issues to everyone's satisfaction (except of course that of private producers). The political conflict pitted private producers (and the BNDE to a limited extent) against CVRD managers, top planners, and officials in the Rio de Janeiro government. The latter coalition won handily.

In sum, the consequences of political interference are not all bad, and some political rationale and support are necessary for effective policy. It is worth reiterating that the discussion has focused on only some political rationales such as nationalism, regionalism or pork barrel politics, and industrialist lobbying. These political goals deal with how and where the government should invest. Other types of politics—clientelism, electoral or populist spending, outright corruption, or, in Delfim Netto's more evocative language, self-seekers clamoring for the "teats of the state"—siphon off government investment rather than channeling it toward some larger purpose. The policy prescriptions are simple though unspecific: do not leave projects to either zealous técnicos or jaded politicians. When a policy is likely to require an injection of an opposing rationale will depend on the coalition and process for each project. Effective policy depends over the longer run on the sensitivity of officials (and regimes) who recognize the benefits of each rationale.

In sum, the case studies helped refine and extend the central concepts developed in part I. Each case study illustrated some of the impacts of circulation, careers, and appointments on policy and effectiveness. In some cases circulation was not an issue; in others several of the major social types were not protagonists. Still, circulation, social types, and appointments are the best predictors. For sectoral policy, knowing where officials have been, where they are going, and who appointed them and why is the best means for predicting the probable policy output. The model is not simple, but it is more accurate than predictions based on single motivations such as immediate self-interest or organizational goals.

10

Continuities in Brazil's Developmental State

THE FINAL TWO CHAPTERS situate the findings on the politics of discretionary economic policy: this chapter in historical perspective and chapter 11 in the political system as a whole. Despite three changes of regime and the economic and social transformation of the past half century, there are many apparent similarities in policy making across the military regime and the civilian regimes that preceded and succeeded it. Beyond expanding the historical perspective, this enquiry touches on a core theoretical concern: How much do political regimes matter? The usual point of departure is that different regimes have different policy proclivities. While recent changes of regime in Latin America have not produced uniform policy shifts, development strategies did change dramatically following such changes in Peru in 1968, in Chile in 1973, in Argentina in 1976, and to a lesser extent in Peru in 1980 and Argentina in 1983. The Brazilian development strategy by contrast is much more continuous (see Hartlyn and Morley 1986b for a comparative overview).

Determining continuity and change depends heavily on the beholder's eye: what one looks at and over what span of time. In 1967 it seemed almost appropriate for the generals to call themselves revolutionaries, and early analyses of the military regime correctly stressed the sharp discontinuities (see, for example, Mendes 1966). The first military government implemented a harsh stabilization program that no civilian predecessor would have been able to adopt.[1] The new economic team revamped the financial system, restructured government finances, initiated administrative reform, and flung open the door that had been closing on foreign direct investment. On the political front, the generals purged the left, demobilized labor, and roped politicians into a two-party straitjacket.

In the 1980s, after watching the weary generals clear out of the Presidential Palace, labeling their rule "revolutionary" seemed more an ironic device. As in all very low N comparisons, the addition of each new observation can dramatically shift the mean and the mode. Adding the Costa e Silva, Médici, Geisel, and Figueiredo governments changes the essence of military rule and makes the Castelo Branco government seem an outlier. The comparison also changes depending on how far back in time one reaches. The contrast between Goulart and Castelo Branco could not be much starker. However, in a comparison of the Geisel and Kubitschek governments, broad similarities emerge.

Assessing how much changed after 1964 also depends on the dimension. Those who concentrate on economic policies tend to perceive similarities and continuity; those who look at social and political aspects highlight the differences.[2] To workers, the difference between the 25 percent real wage compression in the first three years of military rule and the 10–20 percent real increase in the first two years of the Sarney government clearly signals that regimes (or at least regime changes) matter (Skidmore 1988, 58, 294–95). However, the basic thrust of industrial policy under military rule, state-led ISI, was not dramatically different from that of the previous civilian regime. Since the 1930s the predominant economic orientation has been developmental, nationalist, and tolerant of state intervention. The populist (Goulart 1961–64) and more free-market governments (Dutra, 1945–51; Café Filho, 1954–55; and Castelo Branco, 1964–67) represent blips in this trajectory. None of these governments succeeded in reversing more than temporarily the hegemony of ISI; the liberals at most stalled the gradual process of state intervention and nationalist protection.[3]

Within this development strategy, continuity also stands out for the types of discretionary policies and industrial projects analyzed in this research, in terms both of the desired outcomes and of the decision-making process. The 1970s witnessed the peak of huge state-sponsored projects, but this wave fitted in a tradition of intervention that began sporadically in the 1940s (CSN), and picked up in the 1950s (hydroelectricpower, Petrobrás, Programa de Metas, Brasília). Kubitschek demonstrated convincingly that a very successful political career could be built on developmentalism.[4] Goulart and Castelo Branco rejected, for very different reasons, development by state project, but Médici and Geisel vastly expanded it, and Figueiredo did what he could with more limited resources. In his analysis of the Médici government, Skidmore argues that the Amazon program resembled Kubitschek's Brasília, and that "Médici's grandiose scheme was in a mainstream political tradition that predated the 1964 Coup" (1985, 138).

Subsequent sections analyze continuities along other dimensions that were significant in the case studies. A full explanation of these enduring traits in Brazil's development strategy is beyond the scope of this chapter. The purpose is more to demonstrate that the utility of the concepts and arguments developed in this book is not limited to the second half of the military regime.

Bureaucratic Inertias

From the inside, the perspective adopted throughout most of this book, the bureaucracy seems subject to kaleidoscopic changes in personnel and organization. From the outside, the impression is one of greater continuity, if not rigidity, in such aspects as personnel, developmentalism, resistance to reform, circulation, and coalition building.

Elite bureaucrats in Brazil are highly mobile, but they also keep reappearing in different governments and different regimes (see L. Martins 1985, 196–97). Two complementary developments of the 1940s and 1950s—the expansion of technical education (engineering and economics) and the growth of the state planning and production apparatuses (which absorbed the new graduates)—created a core of new bureaucrats. As I discussed in chapter 3, most of these new officials made a career of the state and survived the changes of regime that punctuated their careers.

Even the military relied on officials who had been prominent policy makers in pre-Goulart governments (see Faucher 1979; Barros 1978, 199). Turnover was lower in the Castelo Branco government in second-and third-level positions than it had been in several previous civilian governments (W. Santos 1982, 74). Continuity was naturally higher within the military regime: nearly half of the confidence appointees in my sample served in two consecutive military governments. The transition to civilian rule in 1985 did not introduce a whole set of new faces in the upper reaches of the bureaucracy. Two-thirds of Sarney's confidence appointees ($N=125$) had served in a top position in one of the military governments.

In terms of social types, military engineers provide an example of a consistent and predictable presence in the economic bureaucracy over the last forty years, though the sectoral distribution of officer-managers has varied. Over the last four decades the military has defined successive industries as crucial for national security and helped create state enterprises and other agencies. In the 1930s and 1940s the industries were steel and to a lesser extent iron ore mining, and in the 1940s and 1950s it was petroleum. In the 1950s and 1960s military attention turned to nuclear energy, armaments, communications, aircraft, and computers.

The military supported the creation of state enterprises in these industries and trained engineers prior to the establishment of these firms. These engineers made the option of a state enterprise viable in the first place and went on to staff and run the firm. In the 1930s the military sent engineers abroad to study metallurgy and established the Instituto Militar de Engenharia. The técnicos trained under these programs later managed the CSN. In the 1960s the navy was training the computer specialists who in the 1970s would work for Cobra, the state-owned computer manufacturer. In short, only the military can afford to maintain trained but unproductive técnicos who by default staff state enterprises and policy organs in the first years.[5]

As the firms achieve their initial goals, military interest fades. The military retreats from the role of training técnicos and staffing the state enterprise, and older officer-engineers gradually drop out of the enterprises through attrition and retirement. The generation of steel engineers trained in the 1930s and 1940s had retired by the 1980s, save a few stragglers, and steel became civilian. However, the computer scientists, communications engineers, and nuclear physicists educated in the military in the 1960s and 1970s will probably be prominent in those sectors for years to come. Thus patterns of military infiltration of the civilian bureaucracy have persisted though the sectoral targets have shifted.

Despite some signs of ideological diversity, most officials (both military and civilian) since the 1950s have been nationalists and developmentalists. Leff divided economic officials in the mid 1960s into three camps: 70 percent Furtado nationalists; 15 percent Campos monetarists; and 15 percent extreme nationalists (1968, 147n). Training by the United Nations Economic Commission for Latin America (CEPAL), which strongly favored ISI, had a lasting impact on the first generation of BNDE officials (Willis 1986, 220–22), and they in turn influenced bureaucrats in other sectors. By 1976 officials still favored a nationalist development strategy: 90 percent preferred promoting industrialization through Brazilian firms ($N=107$ [L. Martins 1985, 227–28]).

Pressures from above reinforced this nationalist developmentalism. Presidents (both civilian and military) have sought popular support in high-profile development projects. Vargas discovered perhaps unintentionally the political capital hidden in these projects. However, he did not master the art. The popular mobilization over Petrobrás surprised Vargas and most other politicians (G. Carvalho 1977, 45–77). The larger lesson of Petrobrás was that development projects held great promise for those clever enough to manipulate them. Kubitschek deftly harnessed developmentalism to his presidency. His development plan and the construction of Brasília, while controversial, still redounded to his political benefit. As was discussed earlier, military presidents after 1970 seized on development projects as one of their only means of seeking legitimacy.

While bureaucrats may be individually and collectively weak, the bureaucracy, backed by outside allies, can be resistant to radical change. Few political leaders have been willing to incur the high political costs of transforming the bureaucracy. Two examples, from the two governments (Goulart and Castelo Branco) that tried hardest to change the economic bureaucracy, illustrate its latent resiliency.

In the Castelo Branco government, Planning Minister Campos wanted to transform the bureaucracy and the nature of state intervention. He succeeded on the easy side of creating new agencies (Ministry of Planning and Central Bank) and new tools such as indexation, but he failed to cut into the existing bureaucracy (Daland 1981, 70, 329–400). He favored reducing employment in the public sector by one-third of the 700,000 bureaucrats, but Castelo Branco balked at the prospect of the political outcry this could provoke (Geddes 1986, 336–37; Barros 1978, 197). In addition, Campos lost a key battle over the BNDE. He wanted to restrict the bank's developmental and planning roles. However, an enfeebled Congress came to its rescue and blocked Campos (see Willis 1986, 366, 372, 380–81).

The breakdown of the bureaucracy and economic planning under Goulart demonstrates the limits of bureaucratic transformation from a different angle, as well as illustrating some of the very high costs of meddling with traditional patterns in the bureaucracy. By appointing untrained politicians to nearly all positions, Goulart alienated the military and many industrialists and managed in some cases to provoke técnicos into organized opposition (Nunes 1984, 195).

Petrobrás is a case in point (G. Carvalho 1977, 127–57). Goulart sought the support of Petrobrás unions and strengthened their influence in management to the point where the unions were approving or rejecting nominees for top management positions. The performance of some appointees so angered middle-level técnicos that they organized to oppose them. This politicization undermined Petrobrás's performance, which greatly preoccupied some military officers. Usually jumpy on the issue of oil, the military was alarmed at its lack of influence in appointing managers (before Goulart, the first four presidents of Petrobrás had been officers). They feared that Goulart might use Petrobrás in some sort of revolutionary take over, and Petrobrás could stall even the military by withholding fuel. In August 1963 the National Security Council determined that communists had infiltrated top management and that Petrobrás could paralyze the country in forty eight hours (G. Carvalho 1977, 141). To the extent that Goulart's handling of Petrobrás encouraged officers and técnicos to support the coup, it illustrates the very high political costs of meddling in the bureaucracy, especially those parts with powerful outside backers.

These examples are ones of extreme attacks where some of the stronger organizations and their political allies resisted. The conclusion should not follow, however, that the bureaucracy is generally well stocked with institutional antibodies to change. The circulation that weakened organizational boundaries during the military regime was equally high for previous generations of officials. Those who graduated in the 1960s could expect to move every five years, just as their predecessors did who graduated in the 1930s.[6]

This continuity disconfirms one initial hypothesis that high circulation resulted from the scarcity of managerial and technical skills in Brazil. Were scarcity the cause, then officials would have become more specialized and organization-bound in the wake of the expansion in technical education over the past four decades. These career data also seem to belie W. Santos's (1979b) finding that the average tenure in top positions was much shorter in civilian governments than in military governments in that my data do not reflect this slowdown in turnover. The data sets are of course quite different, but the best explanation for the apparent discrepancy (and the disconfirmation of the scarcity hypothesis) is the constant and accelerating expansion of the state apparatus. Thus, even if Brazilian universities were turning out many more engineers and economists and even if they held their positions longer after 1964, the military also created hundreds of new councils and hundreds of new state enterprises that they staffed with people drawn from other agencies.

To summarize, despite the generally low levels of formal institutionalization (which would by definition greatly contribute to continuity) partial evidence indicates continuities in personnel, development orientations, resistance to reform, and circulation.

The Shifting Porosity of Bureaucratic Insulation

If circulation has been high throughout the postwar period (and formal organizations consequently weakened), then policy analysis should focus on informal elite coalitions that span state boundaries. This coalition basis for industrial policy appears to be fairly constant over the postwar period. During the democratic regime some industrial policies such as the creation of Petrobrás involved mass mobilization and active congressional participation (L. Martins 1976, 348). However, a small group of government officials in consultation with several other elite representatives made most other industrial policies in most other governments. Macroeconomic policy is another matter; the governments in the first half of the military regime made very different kinds of policy from those of their predecessors.

However, in industrial policy, analyses of the 1940s and 1950s identify policy actors in various agencies, Congress, the military, and the private sector who form the kinds of informal coalitions found in the 1970s. In steel, petroleum, hydroelectric power, and automobiles, officials, officers, politicians, and industrialists successfully pressured the president (and sometimes lobbied Congress) to create agencies and firms, provide finance, and close off domestic markets.[7] In these informal coalitions, the military maintained a consistent interest in heavy and high-technology industry; industrialists sought protection and promotion; and regional politicians lobbied for government investment.

These policy coalitions raise again the issue of bureaucratic insulation, which chapter 4 argued depended in turn on appointment patterns. Other analyses usually focus on bureaucratic insulation against one type of actor—distribution-bent, clientelistic politicians or "purely self-serving political" groups, in Hirschman's terms (1967, 53)—but many others would like to penetrate the insulation. The broader question should be: How insulated are officials from military, capitalist, industrialist, clientelist, and regional demands? This disaggregate approach permits a more nuanced appreciation of the changing types and degrees of insulation (illustrated above in part II) that shelter or expose policy makers over time and across agencies and policy concerns. At times different parts of the state are hermetically sealed to some groups, wide open to others.

Standard anticlientelist insulation has varied widely over the last half-century. In the 1940s and 1950s, Vargas used appointments to insulate some parts of the emerging economic bureaucracy.[8] Kubitschek maintained partial insulation by hiving off core planning officials. Goulart seemingly dispensed with insulation altogether and transformed the executive "into a deck of cards available for use only in the game of political influence" (W. Santos 1979a, 17). Castelo Branco, Costa e Silva, and especially Médici appeared to reinsulate with a vengeance.[9] Then Geisel and Figueiredo again appointed some clientelistic politicians to positions with spending power.

After the electoral scare of 1974, the military by some accounts came to rely more heavily on clientelism, more so even than previous civilian governments had because it had eliminated class and programmatic electoral appeals (Cammack 1982). However, this return to clientelism was more pronounced at the state and local levels than in top federal positions in the economic bureaucracy (see also Hagopian 1986). Sarney's appointments initially returned to the earlier pattern of insulating some parts of the bureaucracy, though fewer and fewer over the course of his term. Overall, partial insulation from clientelistic politicians is a fairly continuous practice that Goulart disrupts in the early 1960s and that Geisel begins to reestablish in the mid 1970s.

The early military governments caulked up some patronage leaks or at least initially shifted them from the economic bureaucracy to other parts of the state. However, politicians also sought to penetrate the bureaucracy to increase the flow of resources to their states.[10] These pressures and this type of penetration suffered less interruption from the military regime and became increasingly important as the states became ever more dependent on federal funds. Moreover, when the regime lost support at the polls and in opinion surveys in the mid 1970s, the government turned to conservative regional elites for help.[11] In the end, the regional elites who backed Açominas in the 1970s and 1980s were much like those who pushed Usiminas and Cosipa in the 1950s.

Industrialists also attempt to perforate insulation. The state has favored them throughout the postwar period, but the puzzle is that this outcome is not the manifestation of bourgeois hegemony or predominance, because industrialists have never modeled lasting paths of access to policy-making circles.[12] If politically active officers are amphibians, their counterparts in business are chameleons. Industrialists lobby Congress, organize sectoral associations, run for Congress, mount press campaigns, enter governments as ministers, sit on formal policy councils, and establish informal links to lower-level officials— whatever seems to work at the time. Throughout the postwar period they have had some influence in industrial policy, but their access and impact have varied greatly.

Both civilian and military presidents appointed industrialists or financiers to head economic ministries (as non-responsible representatives). Before 1964 presidents often asked prominent businessmen to run the Ministry of Finance (Leff 1968, 124). The Castelo Branco government attempted to institutionalize business input by seating representatives on government policy councils. Under succeeding presidents, Delfim phased out official representation but remained open to informal contacts with leading industrialists. Geisel attempted to reinstitute formal dialogue with industrialists, but though consulted, they felt excluded from his very centralized decision making (Diniz and Boschi 1978, 164–65). After 1980, Delfim again opened informal channels.

When denied top-level input into policy formulation, industrialists turned to middle-level, informal links that Cardoso calls "bureaucratic rings" to influence policy implementation.[13] Managers in the private sector forge these personal links to mid-level officials to influence the details of implementation such as licensing, exchange controls, and subcontracting. The relations are informal and personal and change dramatically as bureaucrats circulate through pivotal positions.

When industrial policy affected a whole sector or range of producers, then industrialists sometimes mobilized publicly using the press and business associations to influence policy. Though industrial associations were generally weak, new dynamic associations emerged in the 1960s and 1970s often in new sectors and outside the cumbersome corporatist framework (Schmitter 1971; Boschi 1979). These sectoral associations often became influential participants (as in the case of Açominas) because they spoke for the sector, were publicly quite visible, and often conducted more thorough data collection and analysis than the government.

Industrialists' influence also varied according to their position in officials' vision of Brazil (Barzelay 1986, 78–82). Policy makers were more likely to be indifferent to retrograde commercial interests than to producers of capital goods and petrochemicals, who were at the heart of the military's attempt to mold a modern bourgeoisie and substitute for increasingly sophisticated imports (Diniz and Boschi 1978, 168). Industrialist pressure was most effective when it could speak in the interests of Brazil's future industrialization rather than merely in favor of individual or collective greed. Investing heavily in a priority sector greatly amplified industrialists' voices. The fact that private steel producers were investing to meet demand while aluminum producers were not helps explain why the government pulled Açominas out of nonflat steel but went ahead with Valesul.

Overall, industrialists have a greater impact and greater likelihood of penetrating insulation if they are autonomously organized, invest in a target sector, and have access through bureaucratic rings to sympathetic officials. These factors, as well as the president's policy style and economic program, influence industrialists' penetration throughout the postwar period and do so more than regime change.

As I discussed in the previous section, the military's influence on, or penetration of, economic policy making has been fairly constant since the 1940s.[14] One of the lasting consequences of the revolution of 1930 and the *Estado Novo* was the incorporation of the military into parts of the civilian state. Because of the constant fear of a military coup (of which five were attempted in the 1945–64 period) civilian presidents were understandably willing to accommodate the strong preferences of the military on industrial policy, which throughout the postwar period have centered on evolving national security industries.

Ironically, some military governments *increased* the exclusion of some military interests. Those close to Castelo Branco *(cast-*

elistas) who supported Campos's internationalist orientation were a minority in an officer corps where economic nationalism predominated (Stepan 1971, 236–53). Castelo Branco insulated policy makers from the majority opinion in the military and hence was more exclusionary than some previous civilian governments. Other anomalies arose in the 1970s. A civilian government would have been less likely to spend as much on a nuclear program, though it would probably have acceded to military demands for some sort of program. However, at the same time as military governments redirected civilian spending toward such paramilitary goals, they *cut* the direct military budget. The Brazilian military regime is one of the only ones on record to have reduced military spending (Stepan 1988, 80). In fact, some officers favored a return to civilian rule precisely because they knew they could wring more money out of a civilian president (which was initially the case in the Sarney government). The apparent increase in military influence after 1964 should not be exaggerated; some military presidents were more successful in excluding military influences than most civilian governments.

Up close, it is difficult to generalize about insulation. Different agencies are insulated from different actors in different periods. There are few, if any, watersheds; the change of regime in 1964 did not completely exclude politicians and industrialists, nor did it completely accommodate the military. Insulation is not institutional but rather the result of political battles among groups that seek to control the agency. When one group wins, it insulates the agency from the others (see Nunes 1984, 39). Presidents are the final arbiters in these struggles, and insulation depends primarily on the appointments they make. Kubitschek gave the Ministry of Labor to populist politicians, gave Petrobrás to the military, and kept the BNDE for himself and the técnicos. Castelo Branco insulated policy makers from military nationalists and clientelistic politicians. Geisel accommodated some regional demands made by politicians but cut military spending. Insulation is a highly political and contingent outcome, and successful presidents have wielded it carefully and selectively.

Familiar Faces in the Nova República

A full consideration of the Sarney government is beyond the scope of this chapter, but it is worth pausing to assess briefly the initial effect of the most recent transition of regime on the critical variables in previous chapters (see Schneider 1987b for a broader analysis). The Sarney government attempted and achieved little change in personnel, policy processes, and appointment politics. In the first years of the New Republic, top policy makers were familiar to close observers of the military regime.

Continuity in industrial policy is not a major issue largely because it was rarely at the top of the agenda in the Nova República. What is striking in the Sarney government is not change in industrial policy but rather the lack of one. Macroeconomic stabilization dominated policy making, and many in the economic bureaucracy had no time or resources for sectoral policy and development projects, which, in the rare moments when the government had money to invest, continued along previous lines. The Sarney government promised liberalization of trade and privatization, which could have transformed the developmental state, but these reforms were stillborn.[15]

Before his untimely death in April 1985, president-elect Tancredo Neves nominated the first cabinet in the civilian regime. His major criteria for selection for ministerial appointments were party affiliation and regional background, as well as an accommodation with the outgoing regime through the incorporation through appointment of many of its prominent members (see Schneider (1987a, 610–22) for more extensive coverage). Beyond the distribution of five ministries to the Partido da Frente Liberal (PFL) and PDS in return for their votes in the electoral college and continuing congressional support, the cabinet was solidly rooted in the PMDB. Within the PMDB, Tancredo also attempted to include representatives from the major internal factions, but as a PMDB cabinet it was to the right of the party's center.[16] Nearly half of the civilian ministers emerged from the core of Tancredo's regional base (Minas Gerais and São Paulo), and the northeast and its political factions were also well represented. In part because of the difficulties in pleasing all his supporters, Tancredo opted to create six new permanent ministries.[17]

That 12 of 21 civilian ministers participated in the military regime (affiliated with Arena/PDS and/or appointed to confidence positions in federal or state government during the military regime) is the most surprising and significant trait of the cabinet. Of course, the coalition with the PFL meant necessarily that some of the ministers would have participated in the military regime, since PDS dissidents formed the PFL. This distribution reveals how Tancredo and his congressional coalition, the Aliança Democrática, viewed the transition. It was not to be a complete transfer of power and renovation of the elite, but rather the substitution of a civilian for a military president and the inclusion of some political elites hitherto excluded. At lower levels continuity was even higher. Two-thirds of 125 top officials of the New Republic in 1985–86 had served in high positions in one or more military governments. In this respect succession to civilian rule resembled the last transition from authoritarian rule in Brazil in that the democracy "established in 1945 was dominated by the same political actors who had held power during the preceding dictatorship" (Nunes and Geddes 1987, 7).

The center of gravity of the top twenty appointees in the economic bureaucracy is farther to the right and more technocratic than the civilian cabinet.[18] The inclusion of the most powerful appointees in the second formal echelon raises the number of appointees who participated in the military regime (fourteen of twenty) and who lacked strong party identifications (eight of twenty). Tancredo was not afraid of giving top economic posts to people who were likely to pursue conservative, "continuationist," and "technocratic" policies. In the case of the four largest state enterprises (whose budgets dwarf that of the federal government proper), Tancredo apparently wanted to hive them off from party politics. None of the four presidents had strong links to party or electoral politics.[19]

For the first year after Tancredo's death, Sarney opted to govern with Tancredo's cabinet in order not to upset the delicate balance he had pieced together and to avoid unleashing the intense infighting that accompanies ministerial appointments. In February 1986, Sarney reshuffled the cabinet and did so frequently thereafter, but most of its essential features survived. He maintained a rough balance between the

PMDB and the PFL. The proportion of appointees who participated in the military regime remained high, betraying both Sarney's lack of interest in renovating the policy elite and the ties
he forged as a past member and president of the PDS. As was to
be expected, the number of ministers from Tancredo's state
(Minas Gerais) fell while Sarney appointed more colleagues
from the northeast. Thus a high degree of continuity within the
political elite and within the state characterized the initial transition to civilian rule.

The executive bureaucracy was still the focal point of the
Brazilian political system, and within it técnicos, the military,
the former governing party, and the PMDB elites were all
strongly represented. The position of politicians improved
markedly, though their direct penetration of the bureaucracy
was initially similar to that before 1985 and before 1964.
Through mid 1986 the number of politicians appointed to top
positions in the economic bureaucracy was about the same as
during the Geisel and Figueiredo governments: about 14 percent of top officials had electoral experience ($N=123$). Subsequent turnover among Sarney's confidence appointees was very
high, and politicians gained ground at the expense of more
technical officials, especially at middle levels.[20] Congressional
votes became a far more valuable currency, and some legislators
traded them freely for the opportunity to appoint officials and
to influence administrative decisions.

The military remained very active and influential in all
realms of civilian policy (Stepan 1988). Sarney considered this
perfectly legitimate. His spokesman stated, "The military ministers can talk about politics because they occupy political posts"
(*New York Times*, 23 January 1986). The Presidential Palace remained thoroughly militarized. The head of the National Information Service was active in formulating the government
response to strikes and in revising the labor code, and the minister for military liaison (Casa Militar) helped revise and atten-
uate the land reform program. Also the military's budget
increased in the first two years of the Sarney government
(Stepan 1988, 80). Continuing military power shows little
change from both the previous *dictablanda* and *democradura*.

The Sarney government evolved into a textbook case of the "politicized state" (Chalmers 1977). Sarney's mandate was ultra-tentative. He began his term without much legitimacy, and after the collapse of the Plano Cruzado in late 1986, his popularity sank to new lows. Calls for direct presidential elections became louder and more frequent. That low popularity translates into calls for replacing the president is one of the endemic features of the politicized state. Worse, Sarney even lacked a clear constitutional term and had to bargain with Congress for a five-year term.

One of the few political resources Sarney had was his power to appoint, and he made it the major currency of exchange with other political leaders. Using cabinet appointments to represent one's support coalition is standard procedure the world over. Although such representation appointments at a ministerial level limit presidential power (as I argued in chapter 4), they do not necessarily undermine administration. However, swapping lower-level positions for congressional support can quickly immobilize the bureaucracy. To govern, Sarney needed congressional support; but the price of that support was the loss of executive control and governability. Not surprisingly, public employment grew by about fifty thousand, and the Sarney government was never able to restrain government spending.[21]

In short, the Nova República held fewer surprises in terms of industrial policy and personnel than have accompanied transitions to civilian rule in other countries. Most striking were the increasing politicization of the economic bureaucracy and the apparent willingness to trade almost any appointment for short-term congressional support.

Conclusion

This brief consideration of change and continuity over a half-century, several regimes, and almost a dozen presidents was necessarily selective. Sharp discontinuities abound, and many of them have not received much attention here (though several receive more in chapter 11). The stress on continuities was designed in part to counter the more common overemphasis on discontinuity. The evidence suggests that it is still worth asking whether and how much regimes matter. The patterns of policy making highlighted in this chapter are enduring but not immutable. However, the focus on continuous dimensions and previous failed attempts at change should serve as a warning that reform is likely to be arduous and costly.

The advantages of hindsight make 1964 and the governments of Goulart and Castelo Branco stand out in relief. The revolutionary fervor of the first military governments faded and the last military governments began to look more and more like civilian governments. In terms of ruling coalitions, 1964 is the sharpest alternation in government since 1937 and perhaps before. The other changes of regime in 1945 and 1985 (or 1990) and other presidential successions manifest much more of a shifting of the elite coalition to exclude some groups on the margin and incorporate some others.

As was noted at the beginning of this chapter, the degree of change depends on what one examines. The concentration on discretionary industrial policy and state projects promotes a perspective of continuity because many of the actors (and their preferences) in these policy areas do not change and manage to make themselves heard in a variety of macropolitical contexts. A focus on macroeconomic policy would produce starker contrasts between regimes, although the inability to control inflation, cut government spending, and manage the balance of payments is a long-standing tradition, and after Geisel and Figueiredo it appears common to both (relatively open) military and civilian governments.

The focus has also been on elites. In Brazil's usually accommodationist politics most elites in most periods have done fine. Change of regime has a more profound impact on the vast nonelite majority who lack the independent wealth and privileged access that survive political change in Brazil. The types of policy that change most radically and consistently from authoritarian to competitive (even semicompetitive) regimes—such as the minimum wage, freedom of speech and assembly, habeas corpus, and other civil liberties—can be the most important events in the lives of the middle classes and the urban and rural poor.

The emphasis has been on continuities, but it is important to note that the time frame is limited to the last half-century, and that the subject of analysis is restricted to patterns of recruitment and policy making in the developmental state. As such, my interpretation is not of the historical (Veliz 1980), cultural (Wiarda 1974), or patrimonialist (Roett 1978) schools. My interpretation differs from the cultural or historical schools in several respects. First, the analysis is restricted to the developmental state, which, despite some apparent roots in previous periods, is essentially a postwar phenomenon. Second, as I noted in part I, the patterns in circulation, career paths, and appointments are rational responses to the noninstitutionalized and uncertain environment of the economic bureaucracy in Brazil rather than vestiges of tradition.

Patrimonialism has similar limitations. Weber's formulation may well have held in the state prior to the twentieth century but can hardly be applied to contemporary economic policy makers. Some recent attempts to apply it to the Brazilian bureaucracy have used patrimonialism to emphasize continuity or encompass a grab bag of cultural practices and bureaucratic dysfunctions.[22] Roett, for instance, uses patrimonialism to connote the survival of stable patterns of elite politics throughout at least this century, patterns that the changes of regime in 1930 and 1964 affected only marginally (1978, 25, 42–46). He defines the patrimonial order "as a composite term for many of the attributes noted by other students of Brazilian politics," including clientelism and the many forms of personalized, politicized traditions in public employment and regulation (*cabide de emprego, empreguismo,* and *estado cartorial*) (Roett 1978, 27). Beyond the impossibility of operationalizing such an all-encompassing term, such a characterization again misses the immediate, rational motives for personalized exchange and politics and gives an exaggerated sense of continuity across the centuries.

The primary goal of this chapter was to evaluate the utility of concepts such as informal coalition building and careers for the analysis of industrial policy before and after military rule. A by-product of an evaluation favoring a perspective of continuity is a conclusion that authoritarianism was neither necessary nor inherently superior. To the extent that policy making manifests continuities throughout the postwar period, then neither the successes nor the failures observed in part II can be attributed primarily to peculiarities of the military regime.

11

Politics by Appointment and the Bureaucratic Political Economy

IN THE LATE 1960s, Schmitter's research did not reveal the changes in formal associational behavior that he expected, and he concluded his book with an analysis of Brazil's underlying, informal "*sistema*":

> Despite the substantial, accelerated, and asynchronous structural transformations, the extreme range of internal variance, the frequency of unscheduled executive changes, and of course the omnipresent confusion and seeming aimlessness of the political process, the patterns of attitudinal predisposition, group interaction, and policy-making in Brazil have remained quite regular, consistent, and predictable. In sum, beneath the obviously (and often superficially) kaleidoscopic aspects of Brazilian politics lies a system . . . "*o sistema*," in the local jargon. (Schmitter 1971, 376–77)

Though Schmitter does not highlight them, circulation, careerism, and appointments constitute central elements of this informal *sistema*. The term *system* is appropriate in that it captures the interaction among the elements and between economics and politics. It is also apt in that it conveys the persistence discussed in chapter 10.

Throughout this book institutionalization has denoted the strength of formal organizations and the attachment of employees to them. However, by Huntington's standards of "stable, valued, recurring patterns of behavior" (1968, 12), the informal *sistema* is institutionalized. The formal organizations in the state are weak, but the overall patterns of circulation, career building, and appointments are stable, recurring, and often valued. It is to this system and its larger political ramifications that this conclusion turns.

237

Appointments, Succession, and Authoritarian Rule

Discussions of appointments in previous chapters concentrated on their impact on power and policy making in the economic bureaucracy. But, if appointments distribute power throughout the government, then they become central as well to political recruitment, representation, presidential succession, and ultimately stability and change of regimes.[1]

One of the the key mechanisms for representing elite, pro-regime interests during military rule was the appointment. Authoritarian exclusion was not complete, and politics continued under the guise of limited, elite pluralism. Because the military closed down many open channels such as the press, parties, and elections, elite politicking focused even more on getting sympathizers appointed to relevant policy positions. Furthermore, the military vastly expanded the scope of power by appointment. After the elections of 1965, Institutional Act no. 2 made subsequent gubernatorial elections indirect, which meant in effect that central authorities nominated the governors because the government party Arena controlled most of the state assemblies, which formally elected the governors. The military government also appointed mayors in cities deemed important for national security, which included all state capitals and hundreds of other cities and hence covered most city dwellers in Brazil.

By narrowing the avenues to power to appointment, the military also modified previous patterns of political recruitment. As mentioned in chapter 10, clientelistic politicians were excluded from early military governments, and electoral and legislative performance ceased to be the predominant path to the very top (though it became more significant for rising Arena politicians during the *abertura*). From 1947 through 1962, 70 percent of the governors and 60 percent of the ministers had prior legislative experience. After 1964 (through 1974) only 40 percent of governors and 29 percent of ministers had passed through the legislature. Conversely, prior to 1964, 26 percent of the ministers and 1 percent of governors had prior technical careers, while the proportions rise after the coup to 52 percent and 40 percent respectively.[2]

Within the military, appointment has always been the route to the top. Though political criteria mattered in military promotions before 1964, they became more important afterward. Promotions determined which generals and factions would be in positions to influence policy and succession. Military presidents juggled promotions to advance their protégés in order to sustain the power of their faction. For instance, Castelo Branco in 1966–67 was so worried about Costa e Silva and the incoming "authoritarian nationalists" that he forced the early retirement of many top officers, which allowed him to promote an "exceptionally large number" of officers and nominate seven new full generals (Flynn 1978, 381). He also passed over two senior generals to promote sympathizers, including Ernesto Geisel. Geisel later had to promote Figueiredo out of turn to give him the rank necessary to become president. However, after 1974 military promotions lost importance because the military as government succeeded in distancing itself from the military as institution (see Stepan 1988; Viola and Mainwaring 1984, 211).

Appointments in the military differ from civilian ones, and parts of the argument in chapter 4 that appointments determine informal power and hierarchy do not extend to the military. Objective performance and academic achievement govern many more military promotions (Stepan 1971, 50–51). The military takeover politicized promotions, but less so than civilian appointments. The critical difference is that it is almost impossible to fire a general. Civilian appointees may have backers who make dismissal costly, but they are clearly removable at any moment. In the military, the leaders of the coup for the first time in the postwar period purged suspect officers. The dismissals were very costly to military unity and posed a serious obstacle to a rapid return to civilian rule.[3] After Castelo Branco dismissals were rare.

Stripping the appointment relation of the power to dismiss means that those promoted are less dependent on their promoters, and the strong ties of informal hierarchy that structure the civilian bureaucracy are superseded by formal military hierarchy. Nonetheless, military promotions determine the resentation and force of political coalitions within the officer corps. The appointment of officers to civilian posts (the military as government) conformed much more to civilian patterns. Military appointees fulfilled the same political functions (such as representing factions within the military institution), and entered into the informal hierarchy because they were as easily dismissed from their government posts as their civilian colleagues.

Military rulers used representation through appointment to bolster support from economic and political elites. Chapter 4 discussed criteria for appointment and limited pluralism in some detail. Suffice it to reiterate that military presidents tried to maintain regional balance, especially in the formal cabinet, to incorporate promising politicians into the government, and to nominate some representatives from the major civilian support groups. These appointees were generally non-responsible representatives, that is, able to promote the interests of the sectors or regions from which they came but removable by the president (and easily replaced by another "representative").

Turnover in the bureaucracy is critical in authoritarian regimes, where politics occurs within the state and through appointments. Other political systems have alternative means, usually parties, that channel pluralism and representation and recruit new political elites. Most authoritarian regimes have primarily the bureaucracy. In Brazil it is particularly central because the incoming government appoints tens of thousands of officials. This turnover determined the nature of limited pluralism in authoritarian Brazil.

If appointment is the road to power and representation, then presidential succession becomes one of the few means for renewing the ruling elite and incorporating previously excluded elites. In this regard, regular presidential succession, a peculiar feature of Brazilian authoritarianism, widened the opportunities for representation and thereby contributed to the stability of the military regime and facilitated its goal of a gradual return to civilian rule. Of the five military presidents, the last three left office on the day set before they took office. The second, Costa e Silva, suffered a stroke midway through his term, and only the first military president, Castelo Branco, extended his term once by a year and a half in the first fluid months of the new regime. Although the process of succession was turbulent and several presidents feared internal coups, contending factions ultimately respected presidential terms and the rules of succession (see Chagas 1985; Góes and Camargo 1985).

Why did the military adhere to its rules of succession, especially since it felt little compunction in breaking most of the other rules it made? Attitudes were a factor. Many officers considered the military a modernizing force and personalized *caudillos* retrograde. Officers went out of their way to publicize their view that Brazil was not another "banana republic" (*republiqueta*). Castelo Branco resisted pressures to stay in office "on the grounds that the greatest evil in Brazilian politics was that of *continuismo*" (Stepan 1971, 248). His convictions along these lines were especially relevant since, as the first military president to leave office as scheduled, he set a strong precedent. Furthermore, the military was sufficiently divided that the factions excluded from any one administration would want to make sure the president stepped down on the appointed day. Disaffected officers usually concentrate on internal coups, but regular succession redirected their mobilization to supporting their candidate for the next president.[4]

Regular presidential succession distinguishes the Brazilian military regime from other authoritarian regimes the world over. Few authoritarian or Communist regimes have accomplished regular and institutionalized succession (authoritarian Mexico is a striking exception to this rule). Among recent military regimes in Latin America, only Uruguay managed a regular presidential succession. A whole string of authoritarian regimes are coterminous with one dictator—a *generalíssimo* who personalizes power. Recent specimens in Latin America include Pinochet, Stroesner, and Somoza. Other military regimes such as the last one in Argentina do not produce *generalíssimos* but fail to institutionalize succession.[5] In the absence of mechanisms to decide which generals will rule, the internal coup becomes the only way to change presidents.

The turnover following succession in Brazil renovated the political elite by recruiting new, young officials and politicians, allowing the regime to escape the tendency of authoritarianism to ossify for lack of new blood.[6] Other authoritarian regimes may periodically shuffle ministers or remake their cabinets to accommodate new forces. What distinguishes authoritarian Brazil is that change in the top echelons of government was scheduled and widespread.[7] Regular presidential succession and subsequent turnover gave excluded but sympathetic elites the opportunity to mobilize to secure better representation in the next government. High turnover and the hope of future representation presumably allowed supporters of the regime who were alienated by specific governments to maintain overall support for military rule. As has often been noted in Mexico, the possibility of future participation keeps elites from embarking on regime-threatening opposition and thereby enhances stability (Smith 1979, 159).

Presidential succession helped the military to initiate and control the return to civilian rule. Regular succession affected the lengthy transition in three important ways. First, it allowed the regime the flexibility to initiate its own withdrawal. A president with a fixed term is more likely to consider alternative future regimes (after his departure), because he does not necessarily have a personal stake in the survival of the regime. Second, it helped the military to keep the process gradual while keeping the opposition in. An opposition is more likely to go on the offensive if a president-for-life reneges on promised reform. In constrast, Geisel could close Congress in 1977 and jury-rig the upcoming elections without completely alienating the opposition, who could wait out Geisel and hope the incoming president would be different.[8] Lastly, succession allowed the military president and the military a graceful exit. Figueiredo could sponsor an amnesty because he had not presided (as president) over the worst abuses of human rights. For the same reason he could leave office without having to leave the country and join Marcos, Baby Doc, and others in the tyrants' diaspora. Thus keeping the opposition in and allowing the military a graceful exit greatly facilitated a slow, negotiated transition.

Limiting Pluralism through Politics by Appointment

Appointments are also major events outside the civilian bureaucracy. In the elitist politics of twentieth-century Brazil, it is not a gross oversimplification to narrow the significant types of political event to three: coups, elections, and appointments. Academics have devoted far more effort to analyzing the first two. Of course, coups and elections determine who, by and large, is in a position to appoint and be appointed. However, appointments affect elections and coups. Some elections are by appointment only, and military promotions determine who is in a position to join a conspiracy. The political machines in the northeast are extreme cases of election by appointment. For regional and local elections the *coronel* (the local political boss and usually a large landowner) appoints the candidate that his machine will run.[9] Hélio Garcia (governor of Minas Gerais, 1984–86 and 1991–) claimed in an interview during the campaign to succeed him in 1986, "If I wanted to, I could get this cup elected" (*Veja*, 31 December 1986). His candidate won the election.

Administrative careers can be generally useful springboards into electoral politics, particularly if the career involves significant positions in state and local branches of the federal bureaucracy. These positions introduce the bureaucrat to the world of the local elite, which can in turn ensure the bureaucrat's election should he choose to run. This pattern is fairly common for heads of local agencies of the Banco do Brasil (which has resources for patronage), enterprises owned by individual states, and (especially for the military) regional security and road-building authorities (Nunes 1984, 140). Historically, the largest mass movement from appointed office to legislative seat came when Vargas created the Partido Social Democrático (PSD) and the Partido Trabalhista Brasileiro (Brazilian Labor Party, PTB) out of the officials he had appointed to local government and the labor administration. The core electoral coalition during most of the postwar democratic regime started as appointees in the Estado Novo (see Nunes 1984, 96–98; Souza 1983, 41, 87–88, 143).

At the national level, ambitious politicians covet ministerial appointments as stepping stones to senatorial, gubernatorial, or presidential elections. As in most polities, prominence in the media is crucial, but where clientelism attracts voters, an appointment to a "spending" ministry can secure more support than press coverage.[10] Also, since the founding of the Republic, the blessing (read "appointment") of the outgoing president has weighed heavily in presidential elections (see Góes and Camargo 1985, 43–44).

Skillful juggling of military appointments can discombobulate coup conspirators. Wobbly civilian presidents have attempted with varying success to appoint sympathizers to high commands in order to forestall coup coalitions. However, the military's semiautomatic procedures for promotion normally leave presidents (and politically active generals) less leeway to pursue their political interests through military appointments. In most cases the president, minister, or general can appoint one of a handful of candidates deemed eligible by institutional criteria. Nonetheless, within the formal procedures pre 1964 military careers often moved to a political rhythm. Unsuccessful conspirators were not purged (though advancement stalled), but if later a politically sympathetic president took office, their careers took off again (Stepan 1971, 222).

The general point is that under normal, noncoup conditions three avenues to positions of power exist: promotion by impersonal rules, political appointment, and election. Each process permits a different degree and type of outside participation. Promotion by regulation allows the least, except for those in a position to change the rules. Political appointment allows pressuring, lobbying, and bargaining by small groups of relevant elites. In principle, elections allow the expression of all (unequally endowed) interests and groups. Compared to more or less free elections, personal appointment is secretive, exclusionary, and elitist; it severely limits participation in selecting legislators and administrators.

The power of appointees depends in part on the power of other actors to constrain them. In other polities, rules, laws, interest groups, parties, legislatures, and local governments all constrain top appointees in the central government. From 1945 to 1990 few of these factors had much force in Brazil. Rules and laws were flexibly applied, the executive dominated the legislature, parties were unstructured and fluid, interests were largely unorganized, and the states became ever weaker. All of these weaknesses translated into power for executive appointees (who were still of course dependent on the president). Furthermore, parties, unions, and other organized groups were highly dependent on the state. Far from challenging appointees, social groups more often come under their control through either formal corporatist arrangements, as in the unions, or informal patronage, as in some parties.

These exclusionary aspects of politics by appointment fit in the mainstream of analyses of postwar Brazilian politics. Typical characterizations include: semicompetitive, centralized, *democradura*, top-down, state-centered, and "modernized from above." Appointment politics also flesh out neglected aspects of centralizing mechanisms such as clientelism and corporatism. The basic mechanism of control in both "isms" is that political elites manipulate the distribution of resources to client groups.

This manipulation requires an intermediate set of brokers who ensure that those at the bottom of the hierarchy such as workers, peasants, small landholders, and the urban poor do not organize autonomously. The careers of these brokers— union leaders (*pelegos*), ward bosses, and low-level government appointees—are controlled by the central patrons or ministries. That is, the career interests of those closest to the ultimate clients (and those hence in the best position to detect, block, or destroy alternative forms of organization) are tied directly to their superiors. Channeling careers is a powerful tool in political as well as economic organization.

Clientelism as a strategy of central, elite control requires a large number of dependent intermediaries or gatekeepers in patron-client pyramids or, in current terminology, appointment chains.[11] Since clientelistic ties are in most definitions personal, ascriptive, and informal, the broker has no legal or organizational base and is therefore more dependent on and attentive to the appointment relation, probably more so than most confidence appointees in the economic bureaucracy.

Corporatism usually involves an elaborate legal system and formal administration backed up by periodic doses of coercion designed to limit mobilization by workers. Over the longer term, effective corporatist systems come to rely on coopting or excluding alternative leadership and rewarding collaborative leaders. That is, to maintain a corporatist structure, state elites must wield their appointment powers effectively. In Brazil, the legal framework governing union leadership and labor administration provides those in control of the labor ministry with many inducements and constraints to use in manipulating union elections. For instance, the list of characteristics that makes candidates for union leadership ineligible is sufficiently long and vague to provide ministry officials great discretion in disqualifying those deemed undesirable. On the inducement side, a career at the head of a union does not allow for much upward mobility, but hundreds of positions in the labor courts and the ministry allow top officials to reward loyal leaders with stable and lucrative employment.[12]

Schwartzman (1982) develops one of the more systematic analyses of semicompetitive, elite politics in his theory of neopatrimonialism. His inspiration is Weberian, but he uses the term *neopatrimonial* to denote modern political practice in Brazil, as opposed to *patrimonial*, which is usually associated with "traditional" society. The distinctive feature of neopatrimonial systems is that state-society relations are characterized more by cooptation than by representation (Schwartzman 1982, 23). All polities have a mix of cooptation and representation, but, in those where the former predominates, social groups are disorganized, dependent, and hierarchically controlled.[13]

Representation politics revolve around policies; cooptation politics concentrate on positions. In the former, autonomous interest groups (and the politicians who represent them) mobilize to force policy decisions favorable to these interests. In contrast, coopted groups and the more independent "political class" concentrate on capturing positions in the government. Groups mobilize to get sympathizers appointed, and politicians use their appointed positions to coopt. Political appointment is a central process in a neopatrimonial system.

General political analysis, like research in policy making, stands to benefit a great deal from closer attention to appointments. First, political appointees in political economies such as Brazil enjoy enormous power because of the dominant position of the executive bureaucracy and because of the weakness of potential counterweights in society. Second, appointments are more significant building blocks in successful political careers. Lastly, though they rarely receive the attention they deserve, appointment relations are key elements in corporatism, clientelism, and cooptation. Also, considering the antidemocratic consequences of political appointments, these lacunae and linkages have more than purely analytic import.

The Web of Compromise: Weak Governments in Strong States

Clientelism, cooptation, and corporatism are designed to contain mobilization, reduce conflict, and limit pluralism. Appointees control positions, funds, and regulations on which social groups depend. Hence appointees need not represent or respond to the groups that ostensibly support them. Such concepts fit well with the prevailing notions about Brazilian politics in the twentieth century: civil society is relatively weak and dependent, the state dominates society, the center controls the periphery, the *classe política* is autonomous from its electoral base, and the president enjoys great independence from parties and Congress.

The anomaly is that even with such a concentration of power, individual governments are often fragile and tentative, and the state has never brought its massive, unfettered power to the task of direct social transformation. How do we square this consensus on central power with a separate consensus that social and political change has almost always occurred in increments, by accretion, through accommodation, and with a minimum of conflict and violence?[14] Why has no government used its power to expropriate unproductive and politically marginal landowners in the northeast? Why has no government attempted a massive direct transfer of resources from agriculture to industry? Why have so few governments, civilian or military, been able to control government deficits and inflation? Why has no president succeeded in overhauling the bureaucracy?

Schwartzman provides a partial answer and notes how volatile this type of policy is: "Cooptation weakens the center, but at the same time it undermines the autonomy and independence of those coopted. . . . The consequence is the formation of a leaden political system . . . that becomes imprisoned in an ever greater and more complex web of compromise and accommodation, until it implodes."[15] Chalmers's politicized state has similar qualities. In it political institutions (and electoral mandates) are tentative (Chalmers 1977). Political actors are not committed to institutions such as the legislature or procedures such as elections, and with good reason since power bypasses them. However, without institutional guarantees, presidents do not know how long they can expect to stay in office and strive continually to recreate or maintain their support coalitions. Worse, the support is uncertain (it too lacks institutionalization), and presidents hence seek "maximum coalitions." In other words, governments that cannot count on solid support are unlikely to embark on an attack on a political minority such as retrograde landowners.

These insights illuminate part of the paradox. Many of the very factors that centralize power also increase uncertainty at the center. Clientelism, personalism, and appointments all weaken support institutions such as parties, organized social groups, and to a lesser extent the military. The flip side of neo-patrimonialist autonomy from civil society is extreme uncertainty in how much support the president and the center can really count on.

An analysis of different types of appointment helps to disaggregate state strength and weakness and to illustrate Schwartzman's "web of compromise." The terms of an appointment can give the president enormous power, as was seen in some of the case studies. But if the appointer trades a position for political support, the appointee is free to exploit the office. To gain votes in Congress, presidents have every incentive to auction off administrative positions.[16] Over time, legislators come to expect payment in this political currency. For presidents the trade-off is unappetizing: win in Congress but lose control of your bureaucracy. The predicament can only be worse if you seek a maximum coalition. Staying in power is a prerequisite for, and hence takes precedence over, governing. Fretful presidents such as Sarney can quickly trade away the power and autonomy of their office.

They can, however, still insulate parts of the bureaucracy and impose isolated sacrifices that demonstrate the latent power of the state. Appointees without outside support are responsive to central wishes and deaf to outside pressures. Hence some groups in society can feel excluded, manipulated, and unfairly taxed (i.e., feel the force of a strong state) at the same time that political "representatives" in other agencies make fiscal restraint impossible (i.e., exploit the weakness of the government).

The Bureaucratic Political Economy

This research began with a puzzle of a bureaucracy that suffered from supposedly debilitating pathologies—including short tenure in office, mismatched expertise, weak institutions, and a web of informal personal ties—but nonetheless made policies that contributed to industrialization. A primary goal was therefore to explain how some of these pathologies in fact improved policy making and to highlight elements of careers and appointments that gave officials incentives to perform effectively.

In concluding, it is worth noting some of the limitations of the Brazilian economic bureaucracy. The focus has been on discretionary industrial policy geared mostly to substituting for imported goods. In this type of policy the technology is generally well understood, and policy coordination, though difficult within the bureaucracy, still involves relatively few participants. It is an elitist policy process requiring bureaucratic and organizational entrepreneurship.

The factors that promote success in industrial policy may ruin other types of policy. It is one thing to build a coalition among a handful of officials, cajole financing out of national and international banks, and start bulldozing for an industrial plant. It is another thing altogether to weave together a broad political consensus on the quality of education (or health care or nutrition) a society's children are to have, and to design a vast bureaucracy of teachers and administrators to deliver it to millions of students. In other words, Brazil's economic bureaucracy and policy style may be up to the challenge of industrialization but may be ill suited for or may even impede effective social spending. This inadequacy could prolong the tragedy of the vast minority of the Brazilian population that still lives nasty, brutish, and short lives.

The politics in sectoral policy may also be inappropriate for macro policy. The plan-rational, developmental state is particularly effective in promoting specific outcomes, whereas the market-rational state is effective in setting the rules governing interaction among economic agents (Johnson 1982). In other words, it may not be possible to determine the rules of macro policy with rulings. The Plano Cruzado of 1986 attempted to regulate market interaction by prolonged rulings. The government attempted to set nearly all relative prices and determine inflation by decree or ruling. The Plano Cruzado and successive heterodox stabilization programs did stem inertial inflation, but over time they so disrupted, distorted, and disarticulated markets that it may be some time before stable rules can be reestablished. These plans approached, if they did not exceed, the limits of what a government can achieve by discretionary policy in an economy where markets still function.

States like Brazil's appear to pass a threshold of intervention that gives them a qualitatively different political economy: a bureaucratic political economy comprised of a highly politicized form of capitalism and a highly politicized bureaucracy. Weber argued that in political capitalism "opportunities for profit are dependent upon the preparation for and the exploitation of warfare, conquest, and the prerogative power of political administration" (Gerth and Mills 1946, 66). In Brazil opportunities for profit depend primarily on the "power of political administration."[17] Capitalists make investment decisions based on market and strategic (political) calculations (Barzelay 1986). When the latter predominate, capitalism is political. Many companies in many countries live in a world of political capitalism, and of course monetary and fiscal policies affect almost all private investment decisions. What makes the bureaucratic political economy different is that most (not some) capitalists are primarily dependent on discretionary public policies, and these policies are short-lived and almost always negotiable.

This dependence on the state and the volatility of its policies mobilize all political actors to seek influence in the economic bureaucracy. Capitalists naturally mobilize to influence the decisions that most affect them. Politicians and other political actors recognize that the normal functions of a weak legislature (or even the traditional functions of a liberal state) are less relevant than the enormous discretionary powers the economic bureaucracy wields. These actors seek power in this bureaucracy and thereby politicize administration, which in turn makes it more likely that policies will be temporary and negotiable.

Adding in the critical economic functions of the bureaucracy clarifies the immediate and constant pressures that promote the continuities observed in appointment politics. To the extent that the term *neopatrimonial* suggests that the politics of cooptation and appointment derive their staying power from tradition or culture, it should be discarded in favor of labels that capture the driving force behind appointment politics. This force is the rational attempt by capitalists and others to insure their interests by influencing access to those in the bureaucratic positions that affect economic outcomes. If the economic bureaucracy maintains discretion directly or indirectly over the allocation of resources in the economy—that is, if capitalism remains political—then political actors will flock to this bureaucracy. And, since widespread participation cannot be channeled through the executive bureaucracy, political capitalism acts to inhibit fuller democracy. In this sense privatization and pulling the state out of the economy can facilitate subsequent democratic reforms (see Schneider 1989; 1991).

The breadth and depth of state intervention in the bureaucratic political economy necessarily fragment the state, at least in functional terms. For example, it is one thing to set the interest rate for the whole economy, and a single monetary authority can be responsible. However, when the state sets different rates for different financial instruments, for different sectors, and even for individual firms, it requires an enormous functionally differentiated bureaucracy. The fragmentation opens up avenues for outside political actors to influence policy and makes policy coordination one of the most urgent political tasks.

Understanding the bureaucratic political economy requires a focus on the politics of administration. Bureaucratic politics determine major economic policies (and to the extent that outside social actors have an impact, they are usually represented within the bureaucracy rather than organized against it). Because other political actors are drawn to, and represented in, the economic bureaucracy, the normal business of politics is superimposed on the administrative structure and its economic functions. In this sort of structure—which is both weakly institutionalized because it is politicized and politicized because institutions are weak—an analysis of careers and appointments best illuminates the preferences that policy actors have and the relative powers that they will have to pursue them.

While this focus is essential for understanding the bureaucratic political economy, it is also useful in analyzing more institutionalized, less politicized bureaucracies that intervene much less in the economy. First, a sizable amount of power in all polities is distributed by appointment. This arena of politics may not be rich in powerful generalizations or elegant theory (which may explain in part the neglect it has suffered), but if we are interested in power, we are obliged to study it. Second, bureaucracy has been the growth industry of the twentieth century. While under attack from all sides, the bureaucracy is likely to retain a substantial measure of power. Unless we focus on the careers of bureaucrats, we are unlikely to know how they will use their power and responsibility.

Appendices
Notes
Bibliography
Index

Appendix A

The Survey of the Careers of Elite Bureaucrats

Sampling and Data Collection

The quantitative basis for my analysis of career patterns and bureaucratic mobility is a sample of 281 careers of individuals who held high administrative office during the military regime (1964–85) or the first year of the Sarney government (1985). Data collection first concentrated on all top officials active in the sectors and periods of my case studies. For all four case studies the relevant time span stretches from the officials who first came up with ideas for the projects in the late 1960s (beginning in 1967 with the Costa e Silva government) to those who were completing the projects in the 1980s.

The agencies covered include most of those listed at the outset of the chronology of each project in appendix B. In steel the core agencies were Siderbrás and its three major (later five) operating enterprises, and the MIC and its relevant agencies such as CONSIDER (and its predecessor GCIS). In the case of aluminum and iron ore, the survey covered CVRD and some of its major subsidiaries, and MME and some of its mining agencies such as DNPM (and CIPGC in the case of Carajás). The universe includes the presidents and directors of the largest enterprises, the ministers and their general secretaries (vice ministers), the presidents of some minor state enterprises (e.g., Acesita), and the heads of ministry agencies.

It was fairly easy to construct a complete list and to compile mostly complete biographies for almost all the officials in the core agencies for the period 1967–85. The career information sought from each individual was basic and easy to collect from either resumés or published biographies. The usual biography included: date of birth; state of residence through the age of eighteen; undergraduate university, date of graduation, and specialization; graduate university, date of graduation, and specialization; and then employer, title of position, and length of time in the position for all subsequent jobs.

Once I had data on the core survey, I added information from other sectors and previous governments. Since they move around so

255

much, locating officials is very time consuming, and expanding the size and coverage of the sample meant turning to simpler techniques for collecting data. For agencies outside steel and mining, I began by writing to the incumbents of top positions in ministries and enterprises. For these agencies most of the officials in my sample served in either the Figueiredo or Sarney governments. This may introduce some bias, but for most of my findings the general career patterns are quite stable across agencies and over time. A standard curriculum vitae contained the necessary information, and I sent letters to over 150 officials requesting a copy. A felicitous combination of vanity and ease of response contributed to a response rate of over 80 percent.

To expand my sample back in time, I consulted *Who's Who*, newspapers, magazines, government publications (e.g., *Ministros da Fazenda*), state enterprise periodicals and special publications (e.g., *História da Faculdade de Economia e Administração da Universidade de São Paulo*). The best single source was the monumental undertaking of CPDOC, *Dicionário Histórico-Biográfico Brasiliero, 1930–1983*. Unfortunately its definition of elite differs from mine. It covers mostly elected and military officials and includes only the presidents of selected state enterprises such as Petrobrás, BNDE, Banco Nacional de Habitação, and the Banco Central. Hence for earlier governments my sample has more military officers and politicians who served in the civilian bureaucracy, though not so many as to skew the overall distribution of social types. Moreover, the sample for earlier periods is more concentrated on the highest levels of the bureaucracies because only the famous make it into published sources. The distribution of officials by agency and top position attained is presented in tables A1 and A2.

The difficulties of data collection introduced biases in my sample in terms of distribution over time, across agencies, and by top position attained. However, these biases should not greatly affect my general conclusions about circulation and career patterns which are not particularly sensitive to variations across agencies, governments, and positions. When they are, I have noted so in the text. In any case, the fact that the sample is not representative recommends caution, and I thereby report in rough proportions only the most consistent results from simple calculations.

Table A1
Distribution of Officials by Enterprise and Ministry

	Number	Percentage
State enterprises (including subsidiaries)		
Siderbrás	77	21.8
CVRD	55	15.5
Petrobrás	23	6.5
Eletrobrás	39	11.0
BNDE	39	11.0
Other enterprises	120	33.9
Total enterprise	353	100.0
Ministries		
Sectoral ministry	107	
Money ministry	51	
Total ministry	158	

Note: The sum exceeds the sample size of 281 officials because almost all worked for several agencies.

Table A2
Top Position Attained by Decade of Graduation
(percentage)

	1930s	1940s	1950s	1960s	All
Minister	27	21	13	4	15
President of a major firm	21	16	10	6	11
Secretary general		2	11	18	10
President of a minor firm	9	11	13	7	10
Director of a major firm	24	20	35	31	29
Department head	6	11	2	2	5
Director of a minor firm	9	8	12	22	14
Other	3	3	4	9	5
Number	33	61	93	94	281

Coding

Years in the Public Sector

Years in the public sector include all years that an official worked in federal, state, or municipal administration (including state enterprises). Legislative terms and military service were not included. Though these positions are clearly public, including them would have artificially reduced and understated the rates of circulation for officials in the civilian executive bureaucracy. Legislators often make a habit of reelection, and military service is usually a career in itself.

Number of Agencies for Which an Official Worked

The principle for counting the number of agencies in which bureaucrats worked was to assess how many times they had entered new hierarchies in their careers; that is, to capture lateral movement but exclude normal vertical ascension. For example, moving from one Siderbrás subsidiary to another or to Siderbrás itself constituted an agency shift, whereas moving from a Petrobrás subsidiary to Petrobrás did not because Petrobrás has direct control over its firms but Siderbrás never did. Moving from one major ministry department to another (under a different minister) also counts as an organizational change. I did not count movement back to an agency that an official had worked for earlier, even though reentry could well constitute moving into a very different hierarchy. Hence the rates of circulation reported in the text are understated.

Number of Moves Between the Public and Private Sectors

Each change either from the public to the private sector or vice versa counts as one move. Moves within the private sector were not included.

Highest Job Attained

Each official is coded according to the highest job attained in the administrative hierarchy as of 1986. In rough descending order the hierarchy is as follows: minister, president of major state enterprise, secretary general (vice minister), director of a major enterprise, head of a ministry department, president of a minor state enterprise, and director of a minor firm. The coding was mutually exclusive. Officials who served as directors, presidents of enterprises, and ministers were coded as ministers. Hence the sample in fact includes many more subministerial positions.

Regional Background

The questionnaire asked respondents to specify where they had lived for their first eighteen years. In cases where this information was unavailable, place of birth serves as a proxy. The goal was to identify regional loyalties a bureaucrat might have, and place of birth is not always an adequate indicator.

Politician

Any official who had held electoral office at any level either before or after appointment to high executive office was coded as a politician. The goal was to distinguish social types, and I assumed that high administrators who went on to run for electoral office usually had a fairly clear idea of the career track that they were on. In other words, an official who is contemplating running for a legislative seat after his term in the bureaucracy will tend to act like a politician rather than a técnico. This coding scheme inflates the number of politicians who served in executive posts during the military regime because many of them ran for elected office after serving in appointed positions. Hence my results are higher than those of Nunes (1978), who covers only previous electoral experience.

Firm and Type of Ministry

Anyone who worked for Siderbrás, Eletrobrás, Petrobrás, CVRD, BNDE, a money ministry, and/or a sectoral ministry at any level was so coded. Hence an official who worked for three or four of these agencies shows up in the subtotals for each one. Positions in subsidiary firms were coded by the parent company.

Confidence Appointee

This category includes about two hundred top officials in the federal administration, as well as a few top officials in Arena/PDS and in the governments of the largest states. According to the generic definition used in the text the Brazilian bureaucracy has thousands of lower-level confidence positions, but the goal in coding was to capture the level of continuity between governments and between the military regime and the Sarney government. All these positions required personal approval by either the president or the minister responsible for the sector. The definition hence includes all the positions listed above in the section on highest position attained: that is, from the director of a minor enterprise or department head on up to the minister. The inclusion of several state secretaries, presidents of major state government firms, and Arena/PDS politicians may seem overly broad. But under authoritarian rule, those achieving these positions were for the most part dependent on approval from above.

Appendix B

Chronologies and Background Information for the Case Studies

Siderbrás

Major Organizations

Government Agencies: MIC, GCIS, CONSIDER, ministries of Finance and Planning.
State Enterprises: Cosipa, Usiminas, CSN, BNDE, Banco do Brasil.

Key Individuals (* indicates interview)

*Américo da Silva, Alfredo (General). President of CSN (1966–73); president of Siderbrás (1973–78).

*Andrade, Benedito Martins. Executive secretary of GCIS (1967–70).

Calmon de Sá, Angelo. President of Banco do Brasil (1973–77); Minister of industry and commerce (1977–79).

Brandão Calvalcanti, Henrique. Industrial director of Siderbrás (1975–78); president Siderbrás (1978–85).

*Delfim Netto, Antônio. Minister of finance (1967–74); minister of planning (1979–85).

*Gomes, Severo. Minister of industry and commerce (1974–77).

*Lanari, Amaro, Jr. President of Usiminas (1957–74); president of Siderbrás (1985–87).

Leão, Mário Lopes. President of Cosipa (1967–73).

Macedo Soares, Edmundo (General). Minister of industry and commerce (1967–69).

Magrassi Sá, Jayme. President of BNDE (1967–69).

*Pratini de Morães, Marcus Vinicius. Minister of industry and commerce (1970–74).

*Sarcinelli Garcia, Luiz Fernando. Executive secretary of CONSIDER (1970–73); superintendent of Siderbrás (1974).

*Velloso, João Paulo dos Reis. Minister of planning (1969–79).

*Vianna, Marcos Pereira. President of BNDE (1970–79).

Chronology

1966   BAHINT report.

1967 Costa e Silva becomes president and appoints Macedo Soares (MIC) and Delfim (Finance).
GCIS established.
GCIS publishes PSN I.

1968 CONSIDER established.

1969 Médici becomes president.

1970 Pratini de Morães appointed minister of industry and commerce.
CONSIDER reorganized and given greater powers.
Vianna appointed president of BNDE.

1973 Decree creates Siderbrás.

1974 Américo sends new minister of industry and commerce, Gomes, a proposal to change Siderbrás legislation.
CONSIDER changed so that only ministers are full members.
Siderbrás gets control of CST and USIBA.
CONSIDER takes on policy for nonferrous metals as well.

1975 Siderbrás capital increased.
Siderbrás gets CSN, Cosipa, Usiminas, and three small firms.

1976 Siderbrás gets Açominas.

1978 Brandão Cavalcanti replaces Américo in presidency of Siderbrás.

1985 Amaro Lanari, Jr., appointed president of Siderbrás.

1990 President Collor abolishes Siderbrás.

Açominas

Major Organizations

Agencies and Enterprises: MIC, Siderbrás, CST, government of Minas Gerais, CONSIDER, BNDE, Usiminas.

Key Individuals (* indicates interview)

*Américo da Silva, Alfredo. President of CSN; president of Siderbrás (1973–78).

Belotti, Paulo. Secretary general of MIC (1974–79).

Brandão Calvalcanti, Henrique. Industrial director (1975–78) and president of Siderbrás (1978–85).

Calmon de Sá, Angelo. Minister of industry and commerce (1977–79).

*Camilo Penna, João. Secretary of finance in Minas Gerais (1975–78); minister of industry and commerce (1979–84).

*Campos, Roberto. Ambassador to Great Britain (1974–79).

Chaves, Aureliano. Governor of Minas Gerais (1975–79); vice president (1979–85).

*Gomes, Severo. Minister of industry and commerce (1974–77).

*Lanari, Amaro, Jr. President of Usiminas (1957–75); president of Siderbrás (1985–87).

*Marins, Aluísio. Executive secretary of CONSIDER (1974–85).

*Mendes, Moacélio. President of Açominas (1975–84).

*Pacheco, Rondon. Governor of Minas Gerais (1970–75).

*Sarcinelli Garcia, Luiz Fernando. Executive secretary of CONSIDER (1970–73).

Souza, Miguel Augusto Gonçalves de. President of Açominas (1984).

*Velloso, João Paulo dos Reis. Minister of planning (1969–79).

*Vianna, Marcos. President of BNDE (1970–79).

Chronology

1962 Minas Gerais Governor Magalhães Pinto commissions study for an integrated steel plant.

1966 Açominas founded.

1969 Médici becomes president.

1970 Pratini appointed minister of industry and commerce.

1972 CONSIDER Resolution no. 15 calls for proposals for new plants in nonflat and semifinished steel.

1973 Açominas delivers proposal for 3.5 million ton per year plant in nonflat steel to CONSIDER, which rejects it.

1974 Geisel assumes presidency and appoints Simonsen to Finance and Gomes to MIC.

1975 Aureliano Chaves inaugurated as governor of Minas Gerais.
CONSIDER Resolution no. 31/75 gives Usiminas ninety days to come up with plan for new plant.
Usiminas presents viability study for 2 million ton plant in semifinished and nonflat steel. Study proposes 30 percent of equipment be bought from Brazilian producers.

1976 CONSIDER approves of Açominas in Resolution no. 37/76. Resolution sets nationalization index of 50 percent.
Geisel officially breaks ground for construction of Açominas.
Minas Gerais government gives Açominas 32 percent tax refund for ten years.
Geisel goes to Great Britain to sign $1.1 billion financial package
CONSIDER Resolution no. 41/76 defines production lines of medium and heavy shapes, rails and semifinished steel.
Açominas passes to Siderbrás's control.
Bulldozing begins.
Agreement between Açominas and industry associations on nationalization index of 60 percent (ratified by CDE).

1977 Geisel replaces Gomes in MIC with Angelo Calmon de Sá.
Final project approved.

1978 First components of blast furnance shipped.
All European contracts finished.
Prince Charles visits Açominas.
Açominas 25 percent done.

1979 Figueiredo assumes office and appoints Camilo Penna to MIC.
Schedule revised: plant to come on line mid 1981.
Delfim takes over Planning.
Açominas 50 percent done.

1981 Siderbrás reschedules Açominas's completion: plant to come on line mid 1983.
Plant 75 percent done.

1983 Construction nearly paralyzed.

1984 Schedule revised: plant to come on line 1985.

1985 Figueiredo inagurates Açominas, which begins partial operation.

Carajás

Major Organizations

Agencies: CIPGC, MME, DNPM, state governments of Pará and Maranhão.

State enterprises: CVRD, and subsidiaries Amza, DOCEGEO, RDEP. MNCS: US Steel.

Key Individuals (* indicates interview)

*Batista, Eliezer. President of CVRD (1979–86).
Cals, César. Minister of mines and energy (1979–85).
*Carneiro, Oziel. Executive secretary of CIPGC (1980–82).
*Carvalho, Eduardo Pereira de. Director of CVRD (1975–79).
*Delfim Netto, Antônio. Minister of finance (1967–74); minister of planning (1979–85).
*Dias Leite, Antônio. Minister of mines and energy (1969–74); president of CVRD (1967–69).
Jost, Nestor. Executive secretary of CIPGC (1984).
*Mascarenhas, Raimundo. President of CVRD (1970–74, 1986–87).
Reis, Fernando Roquette. President of CVRD (1974–77). (Note: He is known by the last name of either Reis or Roquette Reis.)
*Rennó, Joel Mendes. President of CVRD (1977–79).
Ueki, Shigeaki. Minister of mines and energy (1974–79).
Vasconcellos, Francisco Moacyr de. General Director of DNPM (1967–70).

Chronology

1967 Dias Leite Jr. becomes president of CVRD.
US Steel finds iron ore in Serra dos Carajás.

1969 Dias Leite appointed minister of mines and energy. Mascarenhas becomes president of CVRD.
DNPM grants CVRD and Meridional (US Steel) joint prospecting rights.

1970 US Steel and CVRD (51%) create Amza to exploit Carajás.

1971 CVRD creates DOCEGEO for research and exploration.
CVRD establishes RDEP for engineering contracting.

1972 Amza begins first feasibility study of Carajás.

1973 Japan Steel Corporation and Siderbrás studying joint production (Itaqui) in São Luis, Maranhão.
CVRD becomes largest single mining complex in world.

1974 Geisel takes office and appoints Simonsen (Finance), Ueki (MME), and Reis (CVRD); Velloso stays on in Planning.
Amza completes port study.

1975   Railroad approved for Carajás.
1977   US Steel pulls out of Amza and is paid $50 million. Rennó becomes president of CVRD.
1978   CVRD begins constructing Carajás railroad.
1979   Figueiredo assumes presidency and appoints Cals (MME), Delfim (Planning), and Batista (CVRD).
1980   Federal government announces Greater Carajás program and creates CIPGC.
1985   Railroad completed, and pilot production begins.

CVRD Aluminum Projects
Major Organizations

Government Agency: MME.
State Enterprises: Eletronorte, BNDE, CVRD, RDEP, DOCEGEO.

Joint Ventures

Albrás (CVRD 51 percent; Nalco 49 percent). Aluminum plant in the Amazon.
Alunorte (CVRD 60 percent, Nalco 40 percent). Alumina venture to supply Albrás.
Valesul (CVRD, Billiton (Shell), and Reynolds). Aluminum plant in the state of Rio de Janeiro.
Mineração Rio do Norte (MRN) (CVRD 46 percent, Alcan 19 percent, CBA 10 percent, Billiton and others). Bauxite mine in the Amazon.

Private Firms

CBA (of the huge Brazilian conglomerate Votorantim), Alcoa (US), Billinton/Shell, Nalco, Reynolds Aluminum (U.S.), Alcan, Alumar (Alcoa 60 percent; Billiton 40 percent, aluminum joint venture in Maranhão).

Key Individuals (*indicates interview)

*Azevedo, Gilvan de Oliveira. Director of BNDE (1974–78).
*Batista, Eliezer. President of CVRD (1979–86).
Cals, César. Minister of mines and energy (1979–85).
*Carneiro, Oziel. Director of CIPGC (1980–82).

*Carvalho, Eduardo Pereira de. Director of CVRD (1975–79) in charge of aluminum projects.
*Delfim Netto, Antônio. Minister of finance (1967–74) and of planning (1979–85).
*Dias Leite, Antônio. Minister of mines and energy (1969–74).
Ermírio de Morães, Antônio. President of Votorantim and CBA.
Reis, Fernando Roquette. President of CVRD (1974–77).
*Rennó, Joel Mendes. President of CVRD (1977–79).
Ueki, Shigeaki. Minister of mines and energy (1974–79).
*Velloso, João Paulo dos Reis. Minister of planning (1970–79).
*Vianna, Marcos. President of BNDE (1970–79).

Chronology

1967   Alcan discovers Trombetas bauxite deposits in eastern Amazon.
Dias Leite becomes president of CVRD.
Alcan creates MRN for mineral exploration.

1969   Dias Leite appointed minister of mines and energy. Raymundo Mascarenhas becomes president of CVRD.
Alcan decides to go ahead with Trombetas and reorganizes MRN to start construction.
Médici assumes presidency.

1971   Government tells Alcan it wants bigger MRN and national partners.

1972   CBA agrees to 10 percent of MRN.
Studies on Tucuruí, a major dam in the Amazon, begin.
Alcan drops Trombetas/MRN project.
Alcan offers CVRD 51 percent of MRN.
CVRD and Alcan sign protocol to study Trombetas bauxite and alumina production.

1973   Japanese aluminum committee comes to Brazil.
Eletronorte established.
Law of Participation allows aluminum producers to have energy at cost if they invest in hydro electric plant.

1974   CVRD associates with LMSA (Japan) for viability studies of Albrás.
Geisel takes office and appoints Ueki to MME and Reis to presidency of CVRD.

IBA established.

Alcan, 6 other MNCS, CVRD, and CBA join MRN.

RDEP presents Albrás viability study for 640,000 ton aluminum plant.

Japanese Prime Minister Tanaka signs accords in Brazil creating Albrás.

Tucuruí decided.

1975 CVRD and LMSA meet in Rio and decide that 640,000 ton plant would not be viable because of market and infrastructure investment.

CVRD restructured (CVRD 46 percent, Alcan 19 percent, CBA 10 percent).

CVRD contracts RDEP to do viability study for Valesul.

Tucuruí begun.

Albrás I split into Albrás II (320,000 tons) and Alunorte.

RDEP presents Valesul study.

1976 Albrás protocol ties electricity price to aluminum price.

Resumption of MRN construction.

RDEP presents new viability study for a smaller Albrás.

President Geisel goes to Japan. Brazilian aluminum projects declared of national interest to the two countries.

CVRD creates Valesul.

1977 Joel Rennó appointed president of CVRD.

1978 Definitive Albrás/Alunorte accords signed.

World Bank agrees to loan Valesul $98 million.

1979 Figueiredo assumes presidency and appoints Cals to MME and Batista to presidency of CVRD.

Shell/Billiton signs accord to buy into Valesul (35 percent).

MME offers aluminum producers 15 percent discount and twenty-year guarantee that electricity will not exceed 20 percent of international aluminum price.

Albrás bulldozing begun.

MRN begins operation.

1980 BNDE finally forced to concede financing to Albrás/Alunorte.

1981 MRN venture renegotiated; three MNCs drop out.

Alcoa (60 percent) and Billiton (40 percent) create Alumar.

1982 BNDES and Japanese banks sign Albrás finance agreements.
      Valesul begins operation.
      Brazil becomes net exporter of aluminum.

1983 Alunorte delayed because of excess world alumina supply.

1984 Alumar begins production.
      Tucuruí inaugurated.

1985 Albrás begins production.

Notes

Chapter 1. Studying the Brazilian State

1. *Democracy in America* (New York: Random House, 1945), 2:352.

2. The narrative is Carvalho's reconstruction of events (interview, 5 September 1985). Chapter 8 gives the full story of aluminum policy.

3. A survey of seventy-four developing countries in the 1960s gave Brazil a B- for administrative efficiency and ranked it in the bottom third of the sample. Yet Brazil earned an A (top quarter of the sample) for its success in industrializing since 1950 (Adelman and Morris 1967, 78, 100).

4. For the most part I use the terms *state* and *bureaucracy* interchangeably. State intervention in most economies is the responsibility of the bureaucracy, and in authoritarian Brazil the legislature and judiciary were not relevant for policy.

5. *Técnico* is probably best translated directly as technician. However, its usage in the Brazilian context is much broader where it is used for those people with university education in technical fields. Chapter 3 analyzes a more specific técnico social type.

6. Other authors who rely at least partially on career concepts include Becker (1983), Doig and Hargrove (1987), Grindle (1977), Heclo (1977), Smith (1979), and Suleiman (1974). See chapter 3 for further discussion of previous uses of career analysis.

7. Part of this disjuncture may be attributable to a lack of interdisciplinary dialogue, especially among Latin Americanists. Those who study organizations and institutions are likely to be political scientists and organization theorists. Those who study industrial policy and state enterprises are mostly economists.

8. Schneider (1989) applies this comparative method to an analysis of Brazil, Mexico, France, Japan, and the United States.

9. This methodology has illustrious though controversial precedents. Weber's argument in *The Protestant Ethic* (1958) is that Protestantism induced new behaviors, such as a drive to accumulate, which in turn favored the rise of industrial capitalism. Weber devotes most of the work to the first relationship between religion and appropriate

271

capitalist behavior without providing much data on its industrial impact. Stinchcombe further elaborates this methodology (1974, 3–4).

10. See Moe (1985), Nechemias (1986), and Aberbach and Rockman (1987) for recent updates on the continuing split.

11. The major works on dependent development include Cardoso (1973), Cardoso and Falletto (1979), and Evans (1979). The best-known works in the patrimonialist/cultural school are Roett (1978) and Véliz (1980). Classic works in bureaucratic authoritarianism include O'Donnell (1973) and the Collier (1979) collection. Bureaucracy was of course conceptually central to *bureaucratic* authoritarianism: "The term 'bureaucratic' suggests the crucial features that are specific to authoritarian systems of high modernization: the growth of organizational strength of many social sectors, the governmental attempts at control by 'encapsulation,' the career patterns and power-bases of most incumbents of technocratic roles, and the pivotal role played by large (public and private) bureaucracies" (O'Donnell 1973, 91). However, most work on the theory of bureaucratic authoritarianism focused on the "deepening" hypothesis. I know of no empirical studies of bureaucracy that assesses this theory.

12. Sources: Itaipú (*Folha de São Paulo*, 12 July 1989), Tucuruí (*Estado de São Paulo*, 7 May 1989), Açominas (*Jornal do Brasil*, 25 July 1986), Carajás (*Folha de São Paulo*, 24 March 1985), nuclear reactors (*Folha de São Paulo*, 3 May 1987 [this article further estimates that the parallel paramilitary nuclear program cost an additional $13 billion], cst, Companhia Siderúrgica de Tubarão (*Folha de São Paulo*, 18 March 1983), and Pró-álcool (*Folha de São Paulo*, 25 December 1989).

13. The case study method used here follows an intellectual tradition in the analysis of economic policy making in Brazil. First Leff (1968) studied four policy areas in pre-1964 Brazil: coffee, industry, foreign investment, and exports. Wirth (1970) used a similar technique to understand economic policy and industrialization in the Vargas era. Wirth studied steel, petroleum, and trade policy. L. Martins (1976) reapplied this method to a longer period in his study of Petrobrás, steel, the BNDE, and the auto industry. Abranches (1978) extended the methodology to policy making under the military. He studied steel, foreign trade, and industrial policy. Partly on the basis of research conducted in collaboration with Abranches, L. Martins (1985) later published an analysis of CDI, Cacex, and the BNDE under military rule.

14. These interviews serve as the basis for reconstructing the inside political history of each project. Where it is possible, I cite the interviewee by name, though in most cases I exchanged a promise of anonymity for the promise of a more candid interview. Limitations of space and patience preclude a full explanation of how I resolved the inevitable conflicts in testimony. Sometimes I chose the majority opinion; in other cases I weighted the testimony by how closely the person had been involved in the decision. Where it was possible, I confirmed oral accounts with written evidence: newspapers, magazines, government documents, company reports, internal government memos, and published studies.

Chapter 2. Mobile Bureaucrats and Weak Institutions

1. Cited in Richardson 1905, 448–49. I have edited out Jackson's main argument that his proposal would make the bureaucracy more democratic. I am indebted to Russell Murphy for the reference.

2. Polsby 1968, 145. Polsby's definition is incomplete, but I use it here because it applies most directly to the formal organization of government. My purpose here is to discuss the weakness of formal organization in economic policy making, and I use the term *noninstitutionalized* to denote this. The following section pursues institutionalization in greater depth.

3. See especially Roett 1978; Daland 1981; Monteiro and Cunha 1973; Schmitter 1971; Schwartzman 1982; and Geddes 1986.

4. *Jeito* has almost as many meanings as the contexts and intonations with which it is used. In this context it means circumventing formal procedures to get something done.

5. See O'Donnell 1973, and especially Oszlak 1980; 1984; 1986.

6. Others have also noted the persistence of personalism under military rule. See for example Ames 1973; Nunberg 1978.

7. Huntington 1968, 12. Selznick was one of the first to define *institution* as a function of values and commitment, and to distinguish between organizations and institutions (1957; 1980). There are many other definitions of institutions and institutionalization (see Perrow 1986, 157–77), but Huntington's is simple and captures the essence of commitment in institutions. Stinchcombe defines an institution as "a structure in which powerful people are committed to some value or interest" (1968, 107).

8. Toffler 1970, 119–34. Few empirical studies relate circulation to institutionalization or bureaucratic politics. Tenure in top bureaucratic positions is simple to investigate and document. On Brazil see W. Santos 1979b. On the United States see Stanley, Mann, and Doig 1967; Mann 1965; Warner et al. 1963; and Lowi 1964a. Such studies often relate average periods of tenure to issues of expertise, familiarity with the policy machinery, and ability to control the bureaucracy. But tenure is an incomplete measure because it excludes the officials' prior and subsequent career, which may or may not have been tied to the same organization.

9. I counted agencies only once, which underestimates the number of shifts because managers often moved in and out of the same agency several times. See appendix A.

10. For example, Mexican officials circulate as fast as their Brazilian counterparts. Smith's career data on 708 Mexican officials (1946–71) yield an average of 4.7 organization changes per career (Smith 1979, 150–51). I calculated this average, which is not strictly equivalent to my figures because Smith uses a different definition of organizational change. The Korean bureaucracy, in contrast, may conform more to lower patterns of circulation prevalent in industrial countries (Kim 1987, 97–131).

11. McGregor 1974, 24. Some types of top corporate executive in the United States probably move more often. For example, Toffler cites a "survey of 450 American advertising men [which] found that 70 percent had changed their jobs within the last two years" (1970, 101). The rate has probably increased in recent decades. In the early 1950s business leaders averaged 2.9 different companies by the age of fifty-four, or roughly one move every eight years ($N=7,476$) (calculated from table 62 in Warner and Abegglen 1955, 127).

12. In his study of entrepreneurship in the Zambian bureaucracy, Dresang also concludes that highly ascriptive societies do not rule out advancement by achievement: "The entrepreneurial bureaucrat assumes that merit and achievement are criteria for promotion. This assumption does not deny the existence and significance of other criteria. . . . Within the framework of particularistic prejudices, however, achievement and merit as a standard for personal advancement are operative. Members of advantaged groups can distinguish themselves from their peers through identification with productive efforts" (Dresang 1973, 78).

13. In the Forest Service, high rates of circulation help control deviance (and in Brazil, perhaps corruption) because replacements check over their predecessors' performance and will not want to take blame for their mistakes (Kaufman 1960, 156).

14. For example, Dias Leite criticizes the creation of "countless organs to exercise functions of debatable priority, organs which, for the most part, do not have either human or material resources to execute functions for which they were created. They compete . . . with the essential organs of Public Administration to the detriment of these organs. . . . There are innumerable examples of sectors . . . that are subject simultaneously to regulation and oversight by various different areas of Public Administration" (Dias Leite 1984, 29–30).

15. See also Rezende 1983; L. Martins 1985, 81; and Ames 1987, 295 for similar critiques.

16. Barzelay (1986) argues that under normal conditions centrifugal institutional conflict can thwart policy coordination, but severe resource constraints allow top decision makers to recentralize policy. This works for explaining changes in the alcohol program between the Geisel and Figueiredo governments but does not stretch well to other policies and periods. See below, chapters 4 and 9.

17. See also chapter 3. Abranches (1978), Baer, Trebat and Newfarmer (1981), Bresser Pereira (1981), and others use variations on this theme. The most extreme version is Duvall and Freeman's (1983) caricature of technocratic behavior. Cardoso is not completely comfortable with the notion of state bourgeoisie, but he argues that state managers are different from traditional officials and that they share an interest in state expansion (1975, 16–17).

18. After 1982 the government tacked an S on to make it the BNDES (Banco Nacional de Desenvolvimento Econômico e Social) to signal the bank's new role in social development. This section relies on Willis 1986; L. Martins 1985; and interviews with Marcos Vianna (president of BNDE, 1971–79), four ex-directors, and several other former employees.

19. For more on the evolution of the BNDE's personnel practices, see Willis 1986, passim; and L. Martins 1985: 104–05.

20. The bank did of course fund several highly dubious projects that no técnico would have approved (and without losing many técnicos), but for the most part top managers stood by their técnicos. When superior political force prevailed, managers asked for written notice

from above that they were being forced to fund a project that their técnicos had rejected (Willis 1986, 127).

21. These are the major factors encountered in the analysis of development projects. Organizational factors may figure more prominently in macroeconomic policy and in long-term programs that involve a large target population such as education or the land settlement programs that Bunker (1985) studied.

22. Interviewees in a wide range of sectors and periods bore out this hypothesis. On any given policy issue, those at lower levels at the time perceived the policy process as a conflict between organizations. Ministers and others at the top of the hierarchy would, however, dismiss these struggles and maintain that relations at the top were very congenial.

23. In Brazilian firms a director is not necessarily a member of the board of directors, but rather a second-level manager or the equivalent of a vice-president in a U.S. corporation. The *diretoria* is the top management of a firm.

24. The case of Açominas (chapter 6) provides a clear illustration. Lowi argues that policy making is distinct in positive-sum distributive or pork-barrel arenas in contrast to zero-sum redistributive or regulatory policy arenas (1964b: 692ff). However, general scarcity of resources can make even distributive policy zero-sum and contentious.

25. In the cases of Açominas and aluminum (chapters 6 and 8), organizational opposition forced revisions that improved both projects. In the early stages of the alcohol program, sectoral authorities directed government banks to give alcohol producers subsidized loans. The banks opposed the policy and stalled the distribution of credit. The producers invested anyway. The dilatory actions of the banks improved the policy by reducing unnecessary government subsidy (Barzelay 1986, 259).

26. Hence, "by forcing the project's promoter to 'sell his product' many times, financial uncertainties necessitate the invocation of performance standards throughout the whole period of construction— precisely the period when the discipline of these standards is most needed" (Tendler 1968: 151).

27. L. Martins argues that the personal characteristics (such as charisma) "of a President (or a 'strong' minister) are sufficient to reorganize . . . all the internal relations of an administration that was meant to be efficient and modernizing" (1985, 199).

Chapter 3. Careers in the State

1. Research on bureaucratic elites in Brazil is still incipient. After a brief flourish in the 1960s, only a few narrowly focused studies followed in the 1970s, even though this was the height of bureaucratic power. The pioneers were C. Martins (1974), Daland (1967, 1981), Graham (1968), and Motta (1972). Excellent studies by L. Martins (1985), McDonough (1981a, 1981b, 1981c), Sarmento (1978), Santos (1979), Coelho (1977), and Nunes (1978) followed.

2. On bureaucrats' views see C. Martins 1974; L. Martins 1985; Sarmento 1978; McDonough 1981c.

3. Evans 1979, 46. In private firms it makes more sense to lump professional managers in with owners or capitalists because they share a common interest in *private* accumulation and partake in the surplus value generated in a private firm.

4. *Gazeta Mercantil,* 2 February 1984; and *Jornal do Brasil,* 9 March 1984. In her study of electricity policy in the 1960s, Tendler found "no camraderie among state power interests, based on the common cause of state capitalism or dislike of the foreign utility" (1968, 145).

5. João Paulo dos Reis Velloso, often considered a prime example of a post-1964 technocrat, argues that no such "animal exists," nor is there a technocracy with its "own ideology and objectives" (1977, 52).

6. Downs 1967, 89. Downs includes another (reality) factor: the probability that individuals can achieve the goals in their predisposition.

7. For John Van Maanen, a rare student of careers, "organizations cannot be understood unless we first have at least a rudimentary conception of the values, beliefs, and behavior styles of the people located in various positions within the organization. And these values, beliefs, and behavior styles are related most clearly to the training and subsequent careers of individuals. Unfortunately, a concern for the careers of people—particularly power holders—is a key missing feature in all but a few organizational studies" (Van Maanen 1977a, 4).

8. Van Maanen (1977c, 161). Writing early in this century, Michels was repelled by a similar phenomenon: "In every bureaucracy we may observe place-hunting, a mania for promotion, and obsequiousness towards those upon whom promotion depends; there is arrogance towards inferiors and servility towards superiors" (cited in Etzioni-Halevy 1983, 19).

9. The supposed obsession bureaucrats have over the size of their budgets has spawned a whole subliterature. See Tullock 1965, 134–37ff.; Niskanen 1971.

10. In the U.S. Forest Service, "a classic illustration of a career system," "it does not take most men long to learn there are attributes rewarded by the organization, and those who yearn to rise deliberately cultivate these attributes" (Kaufman 1960, 179, 182). Kaufman further argues that "even those who profess to be indifferent to promotion cannot help picking up many of the traits of the culture in which they work." Other insightful uses of careers include Stinchcombe (1974, especially 125–27) and Sabel, whose analysis of labor politics in Europe "turns on the idea of a 'career at work,' another name for a worker's world view" (1982, 80).

11. A full career analysis would cover three facets or stages: 1) personality and early psychological predisposition; 2) socialization through formal education and on the job; and 3) the behavior required to advance in a career track. My analysis and data focus primarily on the second and third stages because they have a more immediate impact on preferences, and because extensive psychological and personality data are not readily available. The analysis that follows assumes the prior existence of this internal predisposition to adopt the values and preferences of the chosen career. Verifying this assumption would require a separate empirical study beyond the scope of this research. For one such in-depth study of twelve individuals and their predispositions, careers, and political views, see Reinarman 1987.

12. Kelly (1982, 108). Downs gives a similar justification: "admittedly, these 'ideal types' are oversimplified. Every man pursues a great many goals. . . . No small number of 'ideal types' can encompass the bewildering variety of personalities . . . encountered in the real world. Nevertheless, we believe use of these five abstractions will provide significant insights into the way bureaus actually behave" (Downs 1967, 88).

13. Nunes (1984) goes farthest in adopting from the analytic outset a set of "grammars" that orient the behavior of different officials in the Brazilian state.

14. Often engineers work for a private company for a few years after graduation before entering the state for good. In other cases, of-

ficials at the very top retire from the state and spend their golden years in the private sector. See Schneider 1989.

15. The basic data for classifying officials by these four career tracks comes from the career biographies or resumés of the bureaucrats in my sample. The discussion of the preferences of each social type is based on a combination of deduction, secondary literature, and interviews with each type in the course of my research on the case studies in part II.

16. Military organizations such as the National Security Council (CSN) and the National Information Service (SNI) had little effect on industrial policies examined in part II (see Schneider 1987a). The council was more involved in policies affecting areas such as nuclear energy and computer technologies. The military also influenced civilian officials who attended military schools. To propagate its brand of developmentalism, the military invited civilians to matriculate in the Military Institute of Engineering (IME), the Instituto Tecnológico da Aeronáutica (ITA), and the Superior War College (ESG).

17. This is one instance of an important division within the military. The "internationalists" in the Castelo Branco government went to great lengths to attract foreign investment. Subsequent governments and policy makers were cooler in dealing with MNCs. Stepan shows that the internationalists (also knows as *castelistas* or supporters of Castelo Branco) were in fact a minority faction in the military (1971, 237–49). See Coelho (1976) for the history of developmentalism within the military.

18. The 1964 coup encouraged a great deal of empirical work on military careers: Stepan 1971; Barros 1978; Rouquié 1980; Silva 1984; Coelho 1976.

19. Stepan also focuses on mid-careers (especially participation in the Brazilian Expeditionary Force, which fought in Italy in World War II, and training in the United States) to explain the cleavage between the *castelistas* and the opposing majority of the officer corps (1971: chapter 11).

20. See chapter 10. Most observers consider the golden parachute a creation of military rule. The practice was most popular in the late 1960s and early 1970s, when state and private firms courted retiring officers, thinking they would give the firms an edge in political capitalism. The practice generated resentment among poorly paid offi-

cers who stayed in active service (Barros 1978, 249–50, 267) and ultimately did not help much in dealings with the policy bureaucracy. Extreme *pantouflage* (hiring an ex-officer purely to exploit his personal contacts) appears very limited. Nearly all of the officers in my sample who were appointed to top policy positions had either appropriate technical training, previous non-military experience in management, and/or political clout.

21. For the period 1964–74, Nunes claims that the military occupied only 11 percent (8 of 75) of the civilian ministries (1978, 61 and table 5). Barros finds officers in 13 of 51 or one-quarter of the civilian cabinet positions between 1964 and 1976 (1978, 218). The discrepancies in their calculations probably arise from different classifications of civilian ministries and of anfíbios (Nunes counts them as civilian, Barros as military).

22. The average for the military regime is calculated from table 10 (Barros 1978, 221). This is the average of the rates for each government, which varied from 9.8 percent for Castelo Branco, to 11.8 percent for Costa e Silva, to 11.9 percent for Médici, to 8.6 percent for the first years of the Geisel government. Schmitter cites a much smaller survey, which found in 1970 that 28 of 60 top administrative offices were occupied by military officers (1971, 223). Góes claims that as late as 1979 former military officers occupied 28 percent of 300 top bureaucratic positions (1983, 7). He does not describe his methodology, so it is impossible to explain the discrepancy. Barros, and perhaps Góes, include SNI representatives, who inflate their figures. I exclude them because they had little impact on economic policy.

23. (N=450). The N represents the number of confidence appointees over the last five governments and hence double counts many of the 281 individuals in my sample who served in two or more governments. In fact, only thirty-two officers, including eight anfíbios, served in sixty-nine confidence positions over the course of the military regime. See appendix A.

24. Ex-officers stay in touch with their uniformed colleagues. One important informal factor is that of the military *turma* (graduating class). The graduates from the military academies maintain close contact with their classmates. At least some *turmas* have class reunions. These and other personal ties hold together the diverse military subtypes in the state.

25. O'Donnell qualifies this description as perhaps oversimplified

but one that "corresponds quite closely to the position taken by many technocratic role-incumbents in their appraisal of the pre-coup Argentine and Brazilian social contexts" (1973, 81).

26. This percentage also includes a handful of anfíbios. My definition of *politician* includes appointees who held elective office either before or after serving in the bureaucracy. Some of the politicians had not run for elected office prior to their appointments. See appendix A.

27. See Ames (1987) for a general analysis of the political goals of public spending in the last three military governments.

28. Even at this stage a political técnico's career can start to diverge from that of a técnico by virtue of participation in student politics or because of ties to professors, such as Delfim Netto and Simonsen, who would later occupy central ministries.

29. For Schumpeter the entrepreneurial "function does not essentially consist in either inventing anything or otherwise creating the conditions which the enterprise exploits. It consists in getting things done" (Schumpeter 1975, 132).

30. Even Brazil's political geography contributes to interaction among officials who fly regularly between their homes in Rio de Janeiro and São Paulo, and their offices in Brasília. A plane crash on a Friday afternoon or a Monday morning could leave parts of the economic bureaucracy severely understaffed.

31. "A regulatory, or market-rational, state concerns itself with the forms and procedures—the rules if you will—of economic competition, but does not concern itself with substantive matters. For example, the United States government has many regulations . . . but it does not concern itself with what industries ought to exist and what industries are no longer needed. The developmental, or plan-rational, state, by contrast, has as its dominant feature precisely the setting of such substantive social and economic goals" (Johnson 1982, 19).

32. Heclo also argues that the interaction between these rationales or social types (politicians and bureaucrats in his terms) is critical, though his arithmetic is more ambitious: "Government performance . . . can be thought of as the product of political leadership times bureaucratic power. A product rather than merely a sum is at stake because, depending on how politicians and bureaucrats are linked, either one can diminish or magnify the impact of the other on total performance" (Heclo 1977, 7).

33. Technical rationality should be subdivided into its engineering and economic variants. Both are concerned with efficiency, but the engineer thinks in physical terms—the greatest amount of output for a given quantity of inputs—while the economist brings in prices—maximize the value added using inputs of a given cost. However, for Brazilian técnicos these technical rationalities are limited or bounded in that their internal "laws" do not cover their assumptions nor future uncertainties.

34. A politician may argue publicly that a railroad should pass through his town to benefit his constituency. But the politician cannot argue publicly that the railroad should take a particular route requiring many tunnels to be built by the construction firms from his district.

35. Interview with Joel Rennó, ex-president of cvrd, 2 June 1989.

Chapter 4. Appointments and Bureaucratic Politics

1. Former federal deputy from Minas Gerais, cited in *Veja*, 13 March 1985.

2. Mackenzie 1981, 272–75. For a rich empirical history of appointments in the Johnson administration, see Schott and Hamilton 1983.

3. "The men who come to power reflecting the views of various groups and institutions do not derive their position from the support of these groups alone, but from the trust placed in them by the leader, monarch, or 'junta,' who certainly takes into account their prestige and influence. They have a kind of constituency, . . . a potential constituency, but this is not solely or even principally the source of their power" (Linz 1964, 300).

4. Leff 1968; Wirth 1970, 8; Nunes 1984; Geddes 1986. Hirschman may have been the first to use the term *bureaucratic insulation* in his general discussion of development projects (1968, 52).

5. Tendler interviewed a manager in a state electricity company who wanted *not* to be promoted to president and preferred "to have the state governor assign the position as political spoils. . . . Having a politician in the company who knew nothing about electric power and at the same time occupied the managerial position most sensitive to political pressure was a kind of preemptive maneuver. The company became politically well-connected and at the same time ensured that it would not be meddled with. The new enterprise might feel

safer with the politician in its midst rather than on the outside" (Tendler 1968, 179).

6. The Mexican bureaucracy suffers from many of the same pathologies that afflict Brazilian administration: high turnover, short tenure in office, weak formal controls, and risk-prone careers that subordinates can torpedo. Grindle argues that these factors make confidence one of the four critical elements in Mexican public careers. For top officials it is "imperative to surround oneself with subordinates one can trust, in whom one has *confianza*." Further, "from the point of view of the individual administrator, this is the most efficient way to ensure that orders are executed, that mistakes are avoided or covered up discretely if made, . . . and that subordinates fulfill their responsibilities, even when not directly supervised" (Grindle 1977, 59).

7. Smith finds that kinship, school ties, and other personal relations help advance careers in the Mexican bureaucracy. These ties in fact appear to be stronger in Mexico than in Brazil. Smith however reaches a conclusion similar to mine. Culture is "only a secondary causal agent." The primary explanation is that "Mexico's office-seekers and officeholders have adopted functional, and in this sense entirely rational, modes of responding to the structure of opportunities that they confront" (Smith 1979, 275–76).

8. Furthermore, career data show little group movement from one part of the bureaucracy to another. Such movement would be similar to the Mexican *camarillas* and might have helped confirm the existence of *panelinhas.* The *Delfim Boys* are the major exception. See chapter 3.

9. Van Maanen argues that in general "an emerging trend in large, bureaucratic organizations seems to be decreasing reliance on control through the fixed chain of command and an increasing tendency to rely more on indirect or remote kinds of control. . . . Even more significant is the emphasis upon control through recruitment, promotion, and transfer. Using the career as an unobtrusive form of control has the advantage of seeming more legitimate than a system based on fist or fiat. Not only is such a system likely to excite less resistance from organizational members, it may work more smoothly" (Van Maanen 1977a, 4).

10. An oft noted problem in controlling state enterprises is the firm's monopoly on information on its performance and sometimes a near monopoly on the expertise necessary to evaluate the

information. Beyond this, top policy makers lack the time to monitor state enterprises (Aharoni 1981, 190–91). The power of appointment (and dismissal) cannot really overcome these asymmetries except, as was frequently the case in Brazil, when an appointer nominates both the president of the firm *and* a trusted subordinate to a lower level. Multiple appointments open up multiple flows of information.

11. Saraiva makes the size argument most directly: "The degree of autonomy of Brazilian public enterprises exists in direct proportion to their relative size" (1977, 73). G. Carvalho claims that "the political influence of large government enterprises reaches even greater proportions when they demonstrate the capacity to finance their own expansion programs" (1977, 116). Aharoni stresses self-financing as the "first and foremost" factor enhancing managerial discretion (1981, 189).

12. See Story (1986, 168) for a similar tale of conflicts between PE-MEX and ministerial "superiors."

13. Interviews with Mário Henrique Simonsen, 13 November 1984; Moacélio Mendes, 13 June 1989; Alfredo Américo da Silva, 13 June 1985; and numerous other managers in state steel. See chapters 5 and 6.

14. In her study of electricity development, Tendler interviewed a técnico who said, "To my mind, that which we in Brazil call a 'mixed company' is nothing more than a government office. Through its majority stockholding participation, the government holds *de facto* control of the state company. Because of its power to hire and fire directors at will, the government exerts pressures on the management" (Tendler 1968, 184).

15. Confidential memo from Heitor Ferreira to Ernesto Geisel, January 1973, from the personal archives of Heitor Ferreira and Golbery do Couto e Silva.

16. The following description of presidential and ministerial appointments draws heavily on interviews with nine ex-ministers.

17. Senado 1981, 64. I cite Carneiro's response not so much to counter the critics by showing that Pará was effectively represented but to relate this response to the notion of representation through appointment. Carneiro's response illustrates clearly Linz's idea of *non-responsible* representation. Carneiro did not say that he represented the Pará majority. It is enough that he is from Pará, but he is not responsible to that constituency.

18. Delfim Netto and Galveas, ministers of planning and finance respectively in the Figueiredo government, each tried to fill vacancies in their ministries from suggestions made by the other. Delfim felt that close coordination between these ministries was critical, and when a vacancy opened up in Planning he would first ask Galveas to suggest a candidate from Finance (interview, 3 September 1985).

19. This is a composite picture reconstructed from interviews (from 1984 to 1989) with thirteen presidents of state enterprises.

20. The military, the president, and his close advisers do not usually participate in these lower-level appointments, but they do have veto power. If a governor feels slighted, or if sectors of the military are ruffled by the appointment of a poorly qualified official, they can appeal the decision to a higher veto power.

21. Interviews with Delfim Netto (3 September 1985) and six of his ex-advisers and subordinates.

22. When Delfim's popularity hit new lows in 1983 (60 percent of 643 businessmen disapproved of his performance and nearly one-third of all political cartoons included him), one of his close subordinates got into a scuffle in a Brasília restaurant with patrons at another table who were making indecorous comments about Delfim (*Veja*, 31 August 1983).

23. For example, pre-1964 civilian governments had been unable to create a central bank and central monetary authority. They could not strip the Banco do Brasil, a public commercial bank, of its monetary authority because it had too many allies in Congress (see Nunes 1984). The Castelo Branco government broke the deadlock, created the Central Bank and the National Monetary Council. But subsequent governments deinstitutionalized this rational structure (see Vianna 1987; and above, chapter 2).

Chapter 5. Siderbrás

1. It should be noted, however, that Brazil's 15 million tons in 1983 accounted for only about 2 percent of world production (CONSIDER 1984, 9).

2. The president of the Republic, in consultation with regional elites, appointed the presidents of the three large plants. MIC appointed the directors of CSN, and the BNDE those of Cosipa and Usiminas. The choice of the president of Acesita was usually a compromise

between the Banco do Brasil and Usiminas. Interviews with ex-directors of Usiminas and Cosipa, 23–24 October 1984.

3. See Dutra and Salles (1975, 43–62, 88–124) for an overview of state steel in the 1960s and for a fairly favorable evaluation of administrative reform in it. This recognition came at a time of increasing efforts to promote central planning throughout the economy. The military had published an economic program in 1964, set up a planning council in March 1965, and created the Ministry of Planning (see B. Lafer 1970).

4. BAHINT 1966; Dutra and Salles 1975, 85–87. Planning Minister Campos recommended the study, the World Bank and the BNDE funded it, and a multinational team of U.S. consultants and BNDE técnicos executed it (Naves 1977, 15).

5. The minister of MIC, Edmundo Macedo Soares, presided over the GCIS, which included as members the presidents of CSN, BNDE, Banco do Brasil, CVRD, and representatives from the ministries of Planning and Mines and Energy. GCIS requisitioned technical staff from the BNDE, CSN, and MIC. The BNDE seemed to dominate GCIS. Thirteen of its twenty-three técnicos came from the bank, and the technical staff worked out of its offices (Siderbrás 1983a).

6. EPEA 1967, 49. The Italian experience inspired the EPEA técnicos, some of whom had worked in Europe. The preliminary EPEA plan cites Finsider (EPEA 1966, 79).

7. While insisting on centralizing state ownership in one holding company, it discussed means of compensating the BNDE for the shares it would have to surrender (GCIS 1967, 5/29). Moreover, while it proposed a separate fund just for steel, the plan went out of its way to note that it might be acceptable to leave the BNDE in the role of financier (GCIS 1967, 5/17).

8. An ex-manager of Siderbrás told the story of the approval of CSN's *Plano D* expansion. The members of CONSIDER were presented with two-inch thick plans, which they rubber-stamped without the time or competence to evaluate them (interview, October 1984).

9. For example, CDI, another bureau in MIC, already had authority to grant import tax exemptions, and it was its metallurgy group that lost power through the reorganization of CONSIDER in 1970 (interviews with former CONSIDER técnicos, 1984).

10. World Bank officials were favorably impressed by CONSIDER's early attempts to coordinate and plan (World Bank 1972, 6).

11. According to Amaro Lanari Jr., the president of Usiminas, Pratini "had two options—either resolve the delay in the National Steel Plan using existing means, or create Brassider and give it this task. The minister preferred the first solution" (*Visão* 13 March 1972). Pratini confirmed Lanari's view (interview, 5 February 1985).

12. Pratini enjoyed close personal ties with Médici and with the political elite in Médici's home state of Rio Grande do Sul.

13. In their study of the Inter-ministerial Price Council (CIP), Diniz and Boschi found that "time spent in CIP tends to be seen as a form of accumulating experience and establishing contacts that can facilitate entry into new positions inside or outside the bureaucracy." Working in CIP helps técnicos create "a network of relations, [and] functions as a trampoline in their careers" (Diniz and Boschi 1987, 29 [page number from their 1983 ms]).

14. Beyond issues of access and loyalty, there is also the charge that state enterprises attempt to withhold data. The small world of top técnicos in state steel is laced with informal school, military, and previous career ties that crosscut hierarchies, thereby opening myriad channels for information flows. In at least one case, a CONSIDER técnico relied on a classmate in a state enterprise to complement data received through formal channels. The manager of the state enterprise (who wished to remain anonymous) was later promoted partly in compensation for these services.

15. Itaqui (with US Steel), CST (with Finsider, Kawasaki and CVRD), and Mendes Jr. (with Mendes Jr.).

16. Furthermore, Lopes was a friend of Pratini's father and may have owed his appointment in part to Pratini. Prior to becoming minister of industry and commerce, Pratini was a special adviser to President Costa e Silva and recommended approving Lopes's nomination.

17. Several interviewees stressed that the joint venture had created a distinct managerial subculture. Usiminas managers were not enthusiastic about being lumped together with the others in Siderbrás. Interview with a former BNDE functionary responsible for Usiminas, 9 November 1984.

18. *Visão*, 13 March 1972. Ironically, Sarney appointed Lanari president of Siderbrás in 1985, ten years after he resigned from Usiminas in protest over Siderbrás. His plan, though, was to dismantle many Siderbrás controls and turn it into a loose financial holding (interview, 25 June 1985).

19. Pratini, Vianna (president of BNDE) and Sarcinelli Garcia (executive secretary of CONSIDER) claimed they enjoyed excellent relations and that there was no conflict between CONSIDER and BNDE. However, lower-level técnicos claimed that the battle between the two was constant and fierce at lower levels. The different perceptions support the argument in chapter 2 on residual organizational conflict; the lower the hierarchical position of officials, the more likely they are to fight to defend their agency's interests.

20. It is important to remember that for every project undertaken, the technical bureaucracy produces hundreds of others. Most interviewees related stories of projects they worked on that never took off. This constant production gives incoming political técnicos the wherewithal rapidly to splice together projects.

21. Trebat also reports that Usiminas had the best management (1983, 229). The *Estado de São Paulo* wrote that Usiminas had the highest productivity of steel firms (28 April 1973).

22. The press charged that Delfim opposed Siderbrás because he felt it would create a new layer of administration and thereby raise the overhead costs (and hence prices); because he did not want BNDE's shares transferred to Siderbrás (*Estado de São Paulo*, 28 April 1973); and because he opposed the special tax for steel included in the Siderbrás proposal.

23. Siderbrás "was not successful in lobbying for tax mechanisms to generate investment resources for steel or in developing a budget of its own out of which it could loan to the companies" (Trebat 1983, 229). For a comparison with Eletrobrás, which did control earmarked funds, see Dutra and Salles 1975.

24. In 1975, Dutra and Salles concluded that the administrative centralization had had a beneficial impact (1975, conclusion, p. 4).

25. Brown and McKern 1987, 74. The misconception that steel is a motor of growth that attracts other industry is also widespread. Several interviewees pointed out the fallacy of this argument—transport adds little to the final cost of steel, and consumers prefer proximity to their final markets. It is easier to ship steel than cars or appliances. Yet regional elites continue to view steel as the locomotive for regional industrialization.

26. One measure of the political *lack* of importance of CONSIDER after Pratini is the tenure of its executive secretary. Aluísio Marins was promoted to executive secretary from within the council in 1974.

This technical, insider solution is already an indication that the position had ceased to be politically sensitive. From 1974 to 1985, Marins survived four ministers. That Marins could survive without a particularly strong outside power base demonstrates CONSIDER's political insignificance.

Chapter 6. Açominas

1. Then president of Usiminas, cited in *Estado de São Paulo*, 23 October 1973.

2. *Mineiro* refers to someone from the state of Minas Gerais, where the mineral tradition runs deep. Minas Gerais translates as "General Mines," and *mineiro* also means "miner."

3. For instance, Açominas was to make steel for construction. Various engineers informed me that buildings can be made largely of steel or largely of cement. Since Brazil manufactured little building steel, most construction relied on cement. Açominas was therefore to provide the steel option.

4. Açominas published its official history in commemoration of the formal inauguration of the as yet incomplete mill. The book, entitled *Açominas: Aspiration of Many Generations of Mineiros* (my translation), provides evidence that the eighteenth-century *Inconfidente* rebels included in their list of grievances the prohibition of iron making in their iron-rich province (Souza 1985, 29). The history proceeds to recount the many attempts to establish an iron and steel industry in Minas Gerais during the nineteenth and early twentieth centuries. The highway signpost for the plant reads: "Açominas: The Dream of the *Inconfidentes*." One CONSIDER official called Açominas a twentieth-century "inconfidência mineira" in steel.

5. The BAHINT study mentioned Açominas as a long-term possibility but rejected it as a short-term option (1966, 1:41–42). The PSN also favored expanding existing firms in the immediate run but suggested building a future plant where Açominas now stands.

6. Cited in Souza (1985: 94). For the state government, mineiro love for steel is not just a matter of cultural affinity. Even before Açominas, steel provided 29 percent of the *imposto sobre circulação de mercadorias*, a sales tax, which provides most of the state government's revenues (*Perfil Açominas*, no. 98, August 1984). Initial projections

estimated that, operating at full capacity, Açominas would contribute another $58 million in steel taxes to the state government (Souza 1985, 110).

7. Interviews with CONSIDER and Ministry of Finance officials and with a very open director of one of the four largest construction companies.

8. This discussion lumps together many individuals and associations under the generic label of Açominas backers or *mineiro* elite. This coalition includes federal- and state-level politicians, the industrial and commercial associations of Minas Gerais, and major *mineiro* newspapers. See Souza's commemorative history for a list of the people and organizations he thanks for their support (1985, 79 and passim).

9. Some interviewees casually attributed Açominas's success in the bureaucracy to the large *mineiro clique* or *panelinha* in the bureaucracy responsible for steel policy. In fact, at that time top officials in MIC, CONSIDER, and Siderbrás were from Rio or São Paulo. In general, though, *mineiros* are overrepresented in the economic bureaucracy, especially in steel. Over the last decade and a half of military rule, one-quarter of all officials ($N=260$) and more than one-third of officials in steel policy ($N=68$) came from Minas Gerais. That state produces more steel and more bureaucrats than any other.

10. Américo was not completely satisfied. He left Siderbrás in 1978 in part because of his annoyance with Açominas and its negative impact on his preferred projects, Stage III and CST.

11. These various tasks are usually undertaken sequentially. Mendes (1979) describes how this pattern usually takes 8.5 years and then sketches out Açominas's innovative scheme to telescope construction to meet a five-year deadline, which also meant that the technical and political timetables would coincide.

12. One subhypothesis of this research is that the more politically vulnerable a project, the sooner the bulldozers come into action (see chapter 8).

13. *Estatização*, "statization," denotes in Brazil the process of increasing state intervention in the economy, especially the expansion and diversification of state enterprises. See Cruz (1984) for a detailed account of the origins and evolution of the campaign to reverse this process. See also Boschi 1979; Schneider 1987b.

14. Brown and McKern (1987, 60) cite the "commonly accepted" figure of 1 million tons per year but suggest that in the 1980s econ-

omies of scale are possible up to 5 million tons per year. Technical clarification: an integrated plant turns iron ore into finished steel products. It includes blast furnaces for transforming ore into pig iron, further processing to make steel out of pig iron, and mills to roll steel into final products. Non-integrated plants lack one of these processes and usually roll steel slabs produced elsewhere. The size of the blast furnace establishes the minimum scale requirements, and non-integrated plants can be much smaller.

15. See Barzelay (1986) for a general discussion of the political force of targeted or privileged investors. The relative economic weight of this group also enhanced their visibility and power. In 1980, members of the Brazilian Association for the Development of Basic Industries (ABDIB) employed about 300,000 workers (interview with an economist employed by the association, November 1984). On its history and organization see Boschi and Diniz 1978; Boschi 1979.

16. CONSIDER Resolution no. 37/76, 18 February 1976.

17. *Estado de São Paulo*, 3 and 4 December 1976, cited in Klein 1980, 20. Vianna went public after the CDE had approved the 60 percent nationalization index but, according to Klein, had withdrawn from the producers' coalition earlier and was not an active participant in the fourteen months leading up to the CDE resolution.

18. The press battle at one point took on regional overtones. Gomes, the minister of industry and commerce, was a São Paulo industrialist and businessman, and nearly all producers of capital goods were located in that state. Açominas was a *mineiro* project. After one attack by the producers, the Açominas management clarified that it was not their intention to hurt São Paulo interests (*Estado de São Paulo*, 18 November 1976, cited in Klein 1980, 18). See also *Veja*, 8 September 1976, which recounts more verbal jousting between São Paulo industrial associations and government officials in Minas Gerais.

19. See *Veja*, 8 December 1976 for a blow-by-blow account of Belotti's brokering, which included at least one marathon eight-hour meeting in his office with representatives of producers of capital goods. This personalized interaction between the state and industrialists illustrates clearly Cardoso's concept of bureaucratic rings (1975, 206–09). See also Schneider (1987b) for an elaboration of bureaucratic rings in the Açominas case.

20. For Açominas, one of his most important innovations was SEST. In principle all state enterprises had to get approval from SEST for

total spending, investment, and foreign and domestic borrowing. In effect, this took remaining Açominas decisions away from Açominas, Siderbrás, CONSIDER, and MIC.

21. Interview with João Camilo Penna, former minister of industry and commerce, in *Isto É*, 6 March 1985. Many of my interviewees stressed that Delfim undercut Camilo Penna's power. One of the indications of this shift in power is that Delfim transferred the BNDE from MIC back to Seplan.

22. *Gazeta Mercantil*, 3 May 1984. In the same interview, Mendes availed himself of the opportunity to take a parting shot at Delfim. He claimed that an international loan of $300 million had been taken from Açominas and diverted to agencies of the Ministry of Transport.

23. Souza held his state government appointments in the 1960s and served in Fiat from 1979 to 1982. He was also very active in the politically influential commercial and industrial associations of Minas Gerais.

24. Mendes's ire is understandable. Siderbrás president, Brandão Cavalcanti, informed him of his dismissal the night before the shareholders' meeting that Mendes would chair and in which the major shareholder, Siderbrás, would fire him, though Brandão Cavalcanti had been planning the move for six months.

25. See *Veja*, 31 August 1983, p. 39. Politically, Camilo Penna was closely tied to Chaves. Hence, in mid 1984, when Chaves split with the pro-regime PDS, both of them fell out of favor, but Figueiredo could not fire his vice president. Camilo Penna went on to the presidency of a major electricity firm, Furnas, in the Sarney government.

26. Badaró was, like all *mineiro* politicians, a long-standing supporter of Açominas, and he considered its completion a central political task. On the occasion of his visit to Açominas in 1981, he wrote in the visitor's book, "It is lamentable that the project has suffered such delays in its execution, delays motivated by incomprehensible obstacles that will certainly be removed by the determination and ability of *mineiros*" (*Perfil Açominas*, no. 97, August 1984).

27. Brown and McKern 1987, 64–65. Their calculations of investment per ton of installed capacity are based on a plant with 3 million tons annual capacity. The Açominas viability study projected total investment of $2.2 billion or about $4.7 billion in 1984 dollars (Souza 1985, 176).

28. For instance, had Açominas been rendered palatable to the BNDE, the struggle in the 1980s for domestic counterpart financing would not have been so desperate.

29. For example, using a model of domestic resource costs, Braga (1984) finds, not surprisingly, that Brazil's Stage III investment in steel fails a strict test of comparative advantage.

30. Tendler 1968, 154. She further argues that "multicompany development of power was beneficial to the extent that the highly local nature of each company appealed to specific interest groups, which in turn generated pressures in favor of project completion. One of the most important specific interests that could be served by locally executed projects was precisely that of the state governor" (Tendler 1968, 167).

Chapter 7. Carajás

1. Federal deputy and future governor of Minas Gerais, 1973, cited in Chagas 1985, 219. "To tecnicos goes the valid task of studying and proposing viable solutions; to politicians, that of choosing those closest to the legitimate wishes of the people. This is not to say that the construction of nations is the exclusive work of politicians, but, without them, it would not be possible."

2. Sá and Marques 1987a, 76. Joel Rennó, adviser to Minister of Mines and Energy Ueki (1975–77) and president of CVRD (1977–79), read earlier versions of these two chapters and agreed with my interpretations.

3. *Gazeta Mercantil* (1984, 94, 98). CVRD's 13 billion shares account for 80 percent of the turnover on Rio de Janeiro's stock exchange and 43 percent of the total number of shares listed (*Jornal da Vale*, July 1985).

4. For further background on CVRD consult CVRD 1982; Raw 1985; Strasser 1981; F. Fernandes 1982; Pimenta 1981.

5. CVRD did benefit from a nationalist surge against foreign mining in general and in particular against the way British firms had handled iron ore over the three decades prior to 1942.

6. For many employees, the company is a lifetime career. One-fifth of its managers in my sample worked only for CVRD in their public ca-

reers. On the whole its employees seem to circulate somewhat less than average. They average 3.5 agencies per career and move every 5.6 years ($N=55$) compared with the average of 4 agencies or 1 every 5 years for the whole economic bureaucracy ($N=281$). cvrd has roughly the same shares of high- and low-mobility officials as the bureaucracy as a whole, though those company officials who circulate the most do so more between the public and private sectors than within the state.

7. The "discoverer" of Carajás, Breno Augusto dos Santos, recounted in his congressional testimony how the team arrived at Carajás (B. Santos 1984). In the first place, US Steel moved its base of operations several times to avoid overlapping with, and potential spying by, Union Carbide, which was working in roughly the same area. When they settled on a base camp, an Indian told them of an uncharted landing strip on a plantation inland. When they got to it, they ended up within helicopter range of Carajás. Santos called the discovery of Carajás the last of the "romantic phase" of mineral exploration. Later, systematic use of more sophisticated technologies made such dramatic, happenstance discoveries ever less likely.

8. From a facsimile exhibited in the Carajás museum. The accompanying Portuguese translation explains that the message was in code, apparently referring to the last phrase, which seems to be an estimate of when the news of the discovery would break in the press.

9. Dias Leite calls this appointment an accident (interview, 11 June 1985). Factional infighting (with Delfim and with other military factions) led to the resignation of the minister of the interior, Albuquerque Lima in 1969. Costa e Silva wanted to replace him the same day with a confidence appointee with ties to the northeast. Costa Cavalcanti, then minister of mines and energy, was the only such candidate. Moving him to Interior left mme vacant, and Dias Leite became the choice of least resistance because he was already participating in mining policy. Dias Leite claimed it all happened so quickly (within twenty-four hours) that "his wife learned [of the appointment] on the radio" (*Jornal da Vale*, 1982).

10. Castelo Branco reversed the prohibition on foreign participation in iron ore mining (Stepan 1971, 233). See also Flynn 1978, 372.

11. That the US Steel man in charge of Carajás had been its buyer of cvrd's ore facilitated negotiations. He was favorably impressed with cvrd and disposed to consider a joint venture (interview with Dias Leite, 11 June 1985).

12. Interviews with Mário Claudio Costa Braga, 1 February and 14 June 1985; and Antônio Dias Leite, 11 June 1985. Congress had very little influence in economic and industrial policy. One of the few powers left to it was to call in officials from the executive to provide it with information. Legislators could use this power to influence policy indirectly by publicizing it.

13. Senado 1981, 99. Some CVRD managers claimed that US Steel preferred the waterway precisely to make Carajás production captive. Others claimed that it wanted the railroad because it hoped to provide the rails and equipment (Accioly 1975, 10–11; Senado 1981, 99). Triches pointed out that no firm invests $2 billion in a faulty transportation system just to be able to supply a few million dollars' worth of supplies and equipment (Senado 1981, 99). In general the perception of US Steel's interest varied inversely with the preference of the interviewee. US Steel was always on the wrong side using its illegitimate influence to promote the wrong option. One's position is more legitimate if a MNC opposes it.

14. The magazine *Portos e Navios* waged an untiring campaign in favor of the waterway throughout the 1970s. Several interviewees, especially those from Pará such as Oziel Carneiro, ex-secretary of CIPGC, made similar arguments (interview, 14 May 1985).

15. Jarbas Passarinho, from Pará, was the minister of social security in the Costa e Silva government and minister of education and culture in the Médici government (1969–74) when the controversy took off. However, his power in the economic area seems to have been limited, and in the end he admitted publicly the technical superiority of the railroad option, which cost him political support in Pará.

16. CPDOC 1984, 348, citing Sérgio Quintella in *Jornal do Brasil,* 23 July 1981. Quintella was the president of one of the engineering firms that worked on Carajás.

17. See Seplan 1981. Note that CVRD began distinguishing between its Carajás Iron Project and *Greater* Carajás, which refers to the whole region and early government plans for integrated development.

18. Interview, 14 May 1985. Some councils never met, and in others ministers sent low-level representatives. In both cases council staff cannot count on support from ministers (see Schneider 1987a, 57–62). The ministers who were members in 1980 were from: Seplan (president), MME, Transport, MIC, Finance, Interior, Agriculture, and Labor. In September 1982 the extraordinary minister for land matters joined the CIPGC.

19. See Rodrigues (1986, 421) for a similar assessment of CIPGC's planning.

20. CVRD calculated total investment for a mine producing 35 million tons per annum at $3.6 billion (in 1981 dollars). As of 1987, when the mine reached 25 million tons per annum, the total invested was over $2.8 billion (CVRD, *Relatório 1987*, 13). Several interviewees suggested that, because state enterprises are subject to so much criticism about delays and cost overruns, CVRD purposely overestimates the budget and time required, knowing it will be able to do better and thereby reap the benefits of positive press coverage. Nineteen eighty-four was a particularly good year for such coverage: CVRD announced cost reductions on at least three occasions (*Gazeta Mercantil*, 12 April and 9 August 1984; *Jornal do Brasil*, 23 August 1984).

21. In 1988, CVRD in collaboration with Seplan drew up the Plano Diretor do Corredor da Estrada de Ferro Carajás, which targeted industry as the "priority sector for the promotion of social and economic development . . . because of its multiplier effect on employment and income" (CVRD, *Relatório 1988*, 25).

22. Interview with an engineer who worked on the railroad design in the early 1970s (4 December 1990). This engineer claimed that the bridge pylons had always been designed to be able to carry road and railroad traffic, but the specific design for the road part was delayed until political pressure made it a high priority.

23. IBASE 1983, 87. The *Gazeta Mercantil* calculated the delay at five years (9 March 1985).

24. CVRD ore production in southern mines dropped by 17 million tons from 1985 to 1987 while it rose to 25 million tons in Carajás (CVRD, *Relatório 1987*, 10–11).

25. Planners usually calculate the "Amazon factor" into projects because of uncertainty. If major construction work has never been done in the region, no one knows what to expect. Unexpectedly high rainfall, "the waters of March," delayed the Tucuruí dam by a year and added $355 million to the total cost (*Gazeta Mercantil*, 22 October 1984).

Chapter 8. Bauxite and Aluminum

1. Cited in Skidmore 1985, 137.

2. Technical note: Bauxite is untreated aluminum oxide ore, which

a thermochemical process reduces into alumina. Electrolysis transforms alumina into primary aluminum.

3. See appendix B for lists of the institutions and people involved in bauxite and aluminum and a brief chronology.

4. See CONSIDER 1984 on the 1970s and *Gazeta Mercantil,* 26 September 1990 on 1988. The method for breaking down production by capital ownership is subject to some controversy. Many Brazilian analysts divide the production of joint ventures according to shares of each partner; others calculate "effective" control where majority ownership is not sufficient. My calculation here is based on majority control as "effective" control.

5. World markets were in such turmoil in the late 1980s that it made more economic sense to export bauxite, import alumina, and export aluminum (see Brown and McKern 1987, 23, 34; Paine Webber 1986, 54).

6. Alcan's new managers had several good motives for this decision: aluminum prices had entered a slump in 1971, while new sources of bauxite were becoming available (e.g., Guinea Bissau) and old sources (including the newly nationalized mines in Guiana) continued to supply Alcan. The Amazon factor was also increasingly discouraging, and estimates of total investment continued to rise past the break-even point. Lastly, Alcan had suffered a traumatic decade of nationalizations. Memories of political turmoil in Brazil were still fresh, and nationalism (especially in mining) was not weak, even during the military regime.

7. Many of the major projects of Médici's government were oriented toward these areas: Carajás, the aluminum projects, Tucuruí, the petrochemical complex in Bahia, and of course the Transamazon highway (see Skidmore 1985, 134–38).

8. Dias Leite later traveled (with the CVRD financial director) to visit various MNCs in Japan, the United States, and Europe to drum up partners for MRN. In this case he went beyond his duties as minister to conduct state enterprise affairs, or in his case continued on as president of CRVD.

9. In addition, even before initiating discussions on aluminum, Dias Leite had taken steps to fill the electricity gap in the north. In April 1972 studies for a major dam at Tucuruí were begun, and in July 1973, Dias Leite created a special Eletrobrás subsidiary, Eletronorte, to build and run generating plants in the north.

10. In June 1973 a group from the Japanese aluminum industry visited Brazil (at the government's invitation), and later that year Dias Leite went to Japan. Japanese MNCs made potentially good partners. They were outside the oligopolistic Sisterhood, which would in principle make them more compromising bargainers. Also, Japanese MNCs in Brazil have a history of entering ventures as minority partners. CVRD also had every interest in strengthening ties to Japan, which passed from an insignificant client in the 1960s to the company's largest single market by 1970. Given CVRD's time-tested strategy of entering joint ventures with consuming firms, and given the willingness of Japanese firms to enter long-term purchase contracts, the courtship was very strong. This is an instance in which the commercial interests of CVRD may have contributed to the initial MME policy of seeking out Japanese partners.

11. Samuels 1983, 496. The second oil shock finished off the industry. Japanese aluminum production dropped from over 1 million tons in 1979 to 41,000 tons in 1987 (ABAL 1989, 21).

12. It also meant that Geisel spent hours going over the projects in minute detail. Geisel negotiated with Vianna the exact price at which BNDE would transfer shares in steel firms to Siderbrás (interviews, 19 July 1984; 8 April 1985). Geisel reviewed the engineering specifications of the Alunorte project, specifications that Carvalho—four hierarchical levels below him—thought too trivial to merit his attention (interview, 5 September 1985).

13. Batista asked Carvalho to stay on in CVRD in 1979, but Delfim had other jobs in mind for him. Carvalho went first to the Ministry of Agriculture with Delfim, then in 1980 to be secretary general of the finance ministry, then to the presidency of the São Paulo state bank, before abandoning his career as a political técnico to return to the private sector.

14. See Schneider 1987a, table 9.3; P. Cruz 1983, 61, 73; Reichstul and Coutinho 1983, 45, table 2.

15. One gets a mistaken impression by looking at the end points of the MRN project. Alcan created MRN in 1967, and the latter began exporting bauxite in 1979. This view gives the impression of a firm struggling to overcome investment, partner, and market obstacles. While the name stuck and the location remained the same, MRN was not one firm but a series of quite different firms and projects. It began

as an Alcan subsidiary for research in 1967. In 1971 it became a mine construction firm. In 1972 it could have become an integrated alumina plant or a bauxite mine with capacity ranging from 1 million to 6 million tons. After 1974 the fluctuations were within more clearly bounded limits, but its ultimate realization was in serious jeopardy several times. See Machado 1985, 417–38 for a description of five major aluminum projects that never materialized.

16. CVRD was also overextended. Over the five-year period 1971–75 it was involved in projects slated to absorb $10 billion, a tall order for a company that had $717 million in total revenues in 1976 (CVRD 1982, 89).

17. CVRD managers described one two-week negotiating session in Brazil where CVRD and Nalco representatives talked through the day and in the evening telexed draft ideas to Tokyo, where the day was about to begin. The following morning a new set of instructions from Japan awaited Nalco's team.

18. Paine Webber estimated the long-run average price of aluminum at 58 cents per pound and Brazil's variable production costs at 40 cents per pound. Brazil's costs were the lowest (tied with those of Australia and Norway) of eight countries (Paine Webber 1986, 53–54).

19. CVRD's previous expansion and diversification had been premised on moving into new activities in old areas or old activities in new areas. In most cases the expansion fitted rationally into the company's integrated production or marketing. Carajás was an old activity in a new place, pelletization was forward integration, bauxite was another mineral, and aluminum was just more forward integration within the emerging "northern system." Valesul did not fit anywhere in the CVRD *system,* and some traditionalists in the firm opposed it, though they could not block it. CVRD's outside managers tried to sell Valesul as a pilot plant, which is also a company tradition when entering unknown sectors. Valesul was to be a vast training school for CVRD's engineers and workers.

20. Formally, BNDE had been charged with redirecting financing to private Brazilian firms, which by 1977 received 82 percent of its funds (Willis 1986). Informally, as I explored in greater detail in chapter 6, the bank had assumed the role of champion of the Brazilian private sector within the state. In a confidential memo (22 March 1976) to Velloso, in favor of limiting state intervention, Vianna cites Valesul

and MRN as examples of unnecessary state activities and recommends they be transferred to the private sector (published in *Jornal de Brasília*, 26 May 1976).

21. That Rennó was a confidence appointee is borne out by his subsequent career. Ueki took Rennó with him to Petrobrás in 1979 to head several subsidiaries before appointing him director in 1983.

22. Like Açominas, Valesul shows that the more politically vulnerable the project, the sooner its backers will want to bring on the bulldozers.

23. According to the specifications, Albrás would not earn an adequate return; it would sell aluminum to the Japanese at lower prices than those charged Brazilian consumers; the proposal was incomplete and out of date; and the shareholders' accord gave the minority Japanese partners effective control of the joint venture (letter from BNDE president Vianna to CVRD president Rennó, 6 November 1978).

24. The director in charge of the department that analyzed Albrás never overturned his técnicos' recommendations and claimed that if he did, they would resign. Vianna, for the most part, did the same thing. Officials above Vianna also held the *opinão do técnico* in high regard. Velloso had a reputation as one of the most technical and technocratic of Geisel's (and Médici's) ministers (interviews with Vianna, 19 July 1984 and 8 April 1985, and BNDE managers).

25. Complete data are not available even now. Calculating the potential subsidy in electricity pricing is exceedingly difficult, especially when (as in the case of Albrás) it is linked to the wildly fluctuating international price of aluminum. Aluminum producers throughout the world pay lower rates than others because they are steady, high-volume consumers. Unforeseeable factors, such as floods, epidemics, and the debt crisis, vastly inflated the construction costs of Tucuruí, and it is unlikely that the price Albrás pays will ever be able to cover the dam's average costs. However, none of its clients will, since they all pay the same national prices. The National Energy Commission of the Congress calculated an annual subsidy for the whole aluminum industry of $52 million (*Gazeta Mercantil*, 7–9 April 1990). Even at this rate ($60 per ton produced or 4 percent of the value exported in 1988) the subsidy is small. The benefits (in terms of industrialization and regional development) outweigh the costs, especially if these costs are temporary as the new additions to the industry get established. However, prices will likely change, and a full accounting will not be possi-

ble for several years. See Machado (1985, 1988) for a full analysis of prices, costs, and subsidies and a similar overall positive evaluation of CVRD's aluminum ventures. For a more critical view, see Sá and Marques 1987b.

26. Several interviewees (including Rennó) related the rumors that these two were shooting for ministries or top state enterprises in the next government. Reis had in fact been considered for appointment as finance minister in the Geisel government (memo from 1973 from Heitor Ferreira listing potential candidates, Golbery do Couto e Silva and Heitor Ferreira personal archives). From past patterns, they had reason to hope that the next president would include several young, political técnicos in his cabinet.

27. CVRD's official history claimed the company wanted to get into bauxite to compensate for declining demand for iron ore (CVRD 1982, 81). CVRD was acting like any private firm by forecasting demand and using its expertise to move into growth sectors to minimize vulnerability to market shifts. Moreover, the company moved into aluminum production because the "determination to add the greatest possible value to [its] products . . . is a constant preoccupation in the history of CVRD" (CVRD 1982, 90). It moved into aluminum just like any firm pursuing a normal strategy of vertical integration. See also Evans 1979, 252; Abranches 1983; Abranches and Dain 1978.

28. Some CVRD managers whom Raw interviewed were dissatisfied with the MRN agreement and blamed the "government" for forcing them into a subordinate relationship (because they lacked expertise to stand up to MNCs) (Raw 1985, 382–83). Other managers disliked Valesul because it was "completely outside [CVRD's] region of influence and area of expertise. The constitution of the company was a result of a government decision further illustrating the use of CVRD as an agent of development in the mid-seventies" (Raw 1985, 386).

29. At the same time their lack of outside contacts was not a major liability for coordination, because aluminum policy did not require much collaboration from other agencies.

Chapter 9. Preference and Process in Brazilian Industrial Policy

1. Charges of corruption in the economic bureaucracy were legion in the 1970s and 1980s (see Assis 1984a; 1984b). It did not come up in

my interviews as a major factor in decision making. At least half of those interviewed had retired from government service, and none of them was living in remarkable luxury. A director of one of the five top construction firms (that do virtually all the contracting for major development projects) told me that his company paid out about 3 percent of the project's value in bribes: 2 percent in Brasília (mostly in Congress, even during military rule) and 1 percent in the field. Even this director thought that these contributions had little impact since the construction firms supported only projects that already had strong technical or political rationales. They spent the money to speed projects along rather than to decide winners and losers.

2. Gerth and Mills 1946, 280. I am grateful to John Ikenberry for this citation.

3. See Adler 1987 and Sikkink 1988 for analyses of developmentalism in Brazil in comparison to less successful Argentina; and Bielschowsky 1988 on different forms of developmentalism in Brazil.

4. Leff argues that the ideological attachment before the 1960s to import substitution blinded policy makers to the merits of export promotion as a complementary (and necessary, considering the import intensity of ISI) policy to promote industrialization (1968, chapter 5 and passim).

5. On the national security and other ideologies in the military, see Stepan 1971; Alves 1985; Coelho 1976.

6. Niskanen (1971) offers a general argument of this type. Duvall and Freeman (1983) make a similar reductionist argument for state managers in developing countries.

7. Other analyses that effectively balance empirical complexity and theoretical simplicity in the study of bureaucratic politics include Crozier 1964; Kaufman 1960; Grindle 1977; Leonard 1977; Smith 1979; Suleiman 1974. These authors use elements of a careerist framework but without developing it fully.

8. Here, as in chapter 3, much of the analysis is deductive. Beyond impressions and anecdotes, I lack systematic interview data on "internal" elements of careers such as the force of socialization and the private career calculations. The goal is to provide a deductive analysis that fits the behaviors observed in the case studies and does so better than other deductive theories of bureaucratic politics.

9. Officials whose careers prior and subsequent to public service lie outside the state are not subject to the same pressures. The analysis

developed here is less relevant to bureaucracies such as that of the United States, where top officials come from the private sector and return there after a few years. See Mackenzie 1987; Mann 1965; Stanley, Mann, and Doig 1967.

10. For an example of Vianna's political técnico behavior, see the history of the computer industry in Helena 1984; Adler 1987.

11. In Western democracies, Aberbach, Putnam, and Rockman find that "policymaking is . . . a kind of dialectic, in which the 'law of anticipated reactions' normally governs the behavior of bureaucrats. Consequently, in broad political and ideological terms most major policies reflect the preferences of party and parliamentary majorities" (Aberbach, Putnam, and Rockman 1981, 248).

12. In the other cases either there was no fragmentation or officials shared common preferences, which rendered formal fragmentation moot. The clearest case of no fragmentation was Dias Leite's aluminum policy. No one in particular was responsible for aluminum, so he could decide without coordinating. Carajás was in some respects similar; it was an iron ore mine and hence CVRD's natural responsibility in sectoral terms. In the first Carajás decision to stall US Steel, coordination was important, but here it hinged on the convergence of the nationalist preferences of Vasconcellos in DNPM and Dias Leite in CVRD.

13. For an overview of policy making and the internal power relations of all three governments, see Skidmore 1988; on Médici see especially Vianna 1987; on Geisel see Vianna 1987, Ames 1987, and Lessa 1978; on Figueiredo see Ames 1987, Castro and Souza 1985, and Fishlow 1989.

14. Médici claimed that his ministers "had the power to choose their subordinates" (*Veja*, 16 May 1984, as cited in Skidmore 1988, 335).

15. A World Bank official who had followed the project closely also felt it was doing quite well (interview, 5 February 1987).

Chapter 10. Continuities in Brazil's Developmental State

1. Skidmore 1988, 31, 59. See Skidmore (1973) and Collier (1982) for a general discussion of stabilization in the postwar period.

2. Soares 1978, 278. Some political analyses also highlight continuities: see, for example, Hagopian (1986) on the persistence of

traditional political elites; Ames (1973, 46–48) on the politics of social policy; Cammack (1982, 64) on the military's reliance on clientelism.

3. For example, G. Carvalho concludes: "Although the postwar period witnessed a renaissance in liberal economic ideas . . . in certain economic and social sectors the legislation elaborated in the first Vargas government proved to be ineradicable" (1977, 205).

4. See Lafer (1970) and Sikkink (1988) on Kubitschek's economic program; and see Leff (1968, 155ff.) on pressures before 1964 to undertake developmental projects.

5. Barros gives an interesting labor market analysis of this phenomenon in the case of the telecommunications industry: "For a long period . . . the attitude of civilians . . . was that it was not worthwhile to specialize in a professional area which did not offer much employment potential. Military officers, on the other hand, could afford to specialize in this area, and actually had to do it as a result of professional needs. They did so as part of their own military career training at the expense of the Armed Forces. This may be one of the reasons why . . . the number of military who appeared both in the telecommunications ministry, as well as in private—both national and multinational—corporations was far greater than that of civilians. The Armed Forces were the largest—and perhaps the only—pool of talent in that area" (Barros 1978, 251).

6. The average for all 281 officials is 5 years between moves. For those who graduated before 1940, the average was 4.6 years ($N=33$); for the 1940s cohort, 5.4 years ($N=61$); for the 1950s, 5.0 ($N=93$); and for the 1960s (including 9 from the 1970s), 4.9 ($N=85$).

7. On steel see above, chapters 5 and 6, Wirth 1970, L. Martins 1976, and Abranches 1978; on petroleum, Wirth 1970, L. Martins 1976, and G. Carvalho 1977; on electricity, Tendler 1968; on automobiles, Shapiro 1988 and C. Lafer 1970b.

8. See Nunes and Geddes 1987. The BNDE, one of the major examples in the 1950s of the new insulated agencies, started off as a highly penetrated organ. Vargas's nominee for the top post was a close personal and political friend who had every intention of using the BNDE's resources for patronage (Willis 1986, 200–203).

9. See Skidmore 1988. These governments used a technocratic discourse to legitimate their rule, though policy studies reveal that even in the 1960s the process was not as technical and apolitical as the military liked to believe and portray (see Ames 1973; Fishlow 1973). Mé-

dici claims to have chosen his ministers while "immune to pressures of any kind . . . whether political, military, or economic" (cited in Skidmore 1988, 106). In practice, though, some of his appointees in military and economic positions were more open, less insulated, than some predecessors and successors.

10. Leff argues that "the state governments and the regional *bancadas* (delegations in the Congress) have been among the few participants with an independent bargaining position in Brazilian politics" (1968, 124).

11. Ames 1987, 227–97. Roett argues that "regionalism has been and remains an important factor in political life because the internal dynamics of the authoritarian state revolve around the economic and political rivalries and alliances of the nation's five regions, particularly the Northeast, the Southeast and the South" (1978, 53).

12. The comparative weakness of the bourgeoisie has been a major and continuing controversy in Brazilian social science. See, among others, Leff 1968, especially 113–17; Schmitter 1971; Diniz and Boschi 1978; Martins 1976; Cardoso 1972; Bresser Pereira 1978; Dreifuss 1981; Payne 1990.

13. Cardoso 1975: 206–09. See Schneider (1987b, 230–32) for an application of the concept of bureaucratic rings to the politics of supplying capital goods to Açominas.

14. See, for example, Benevides (1979) on military influence in the Kubitschek government.

15. On privatization see Schneider 1988–89, 1991. For a firsthand account of the overwhelming demands of stabilization and debt renegotiation, see Bresser Pereira 1988. For more on industrial policy under Sarney, see Suzigan 1988; Faucher 1989.

16. Five of ten PMDB ministers, and Tancredo himself, were from the extinct Popular party (a short-lived centrist party that merged with the PMDB in 1981), and only one minister (Pires) was considered a representative of the left wing of the PMDB.

17. Urban Development and Environment (new ministry split off from the Ministry of Interior), Culture (split off from the old Ministry of Education and Culture), Science and Technology (new), Administration (new ministry based on a previous department), Debureaucratization (formerly an extraordinary ministry), and Agrarian Reform and Development (formerly an extraordinary ministry).

18. This economic "cabinet" includes eleven ministers in the eco-

nomic area and the presidents of the major state enterprises: Banco do Brasil, Banco Nacional de Habitação (BNH), BNDE, Caixa Econômica Federal, Siderbrás, Eletrobrás, CVRD, Petrobrás, and Cacex.

19. Hélio Beltrão, the president of Petrobrás, was also the president of the Rio de Janeiro chapter of the PFL. However, shortly after arriving at Petrobrás, he resigned the PFL-Rio presidency.

20. By the end of his first four years, Sarney had set a new record for the most ministers in a single government: sixty-eight. Only one civilian ministry had a single minister for the full period; most of the others had three or four (*Jornal do Brasil,* 16 January 1989).

21. Figures on Sarney's expansion of public employment are usually estimated at about 150,000, but this number includes about 100,000 employees who had been working for the government, often for many years, on service contracts, and who were converted to regular employees during Sarney's term (interview with Marcus Vinicius Brei, director, Departamento de Modernização Administrativa, Secretaria de Administração Federal, 30 August 1990).

22. See Uricoechea 1980; Faoro 1984; and Schwartzman 1982 for authors who use Weber, patrimonialism, or neopatrimonialism to analyze Brazilian politics. Chapter 11 considers Schwartzman's formulation at greater length.

Chapter 11. Politics by Appointment and the Bureaucratic Political Economy

1. Decades ago, Eisenstadt noted the political consequences of "precocious" bureaucratic expansion in developing countries: "A major aspect of the bureaucracy's involvement in the political process . . . is its tendency to develop as one of the main instruments of political regulation. It is one of the main channels of political struggle in which and through which different interests are regulated and aggregated. Its role . . . may be not only important but predominant." Eisenstadt further notes that "the bureaucracy may tend to fulfill different types of political functions and, like parties, legislatures, and executives, become the center of different types of political activity" (1963, 112).

2. Nunes 1978, 55–61. I cite these figures to demonstrate the shift in recruitment from civilian to military rule. These data reveal greater discontinuity in terms of politicians and técnicos in the cabinet than

those presented in chapter 10. The discrepancy arises largely because of Nunes's distinction based soley on prior electoral competition. My definition of *politician* includes postministerial electoral activity. This definition is based on the assumption that future career plans affect behavior as much as and usually more than past experience (see appendix A). Focusing exclusively on prior careers gives an exaggerated impression of a defeat of politics and a triumph of technocracy.

3. Stepan 1971, 222–25. Junior officers investigated and passed sentence on superiors, hence "the possible return of the purged officers in the future presented a built-in institutional obstacle to amnesty" (Stepan 1971, 225).

4. In the crisis of October 1965, War Minister Costa e Silva mediated between President Castelo Branco and the rebellious officers. He closed off the possibility of Castelo Branco's continuation and virtually assured the selection of himself as president (see Stepan 1971, 254–57).

5. The 1981 succession from Videla to Viola was more or less programmed, though long overdue. Videla had been initially selected in 1976 for a three-year term. Difficulties in reaching an agreement on his successor lengthened his term (Ricci and Fitch 1990).

6. See Linz 1964, 327. In this sense the Figueiredo government stagnated. Many top officials had participated in the Médici and Geisel governments, and this ossification contributed to the near universal repudiation of the Figueiredo government. Delfim Netto may have appeared new, young, and cherubic in 1967, but by 1980 he was aging, jowled, and far too familiar. However, the Figueiredo government is the exception; previous successions were more successful in promoting the incorporation of new elites.

7. Though succession entailed wholesale change, midterm turnover was lower. Military presidents were loath to fire ministers. The military wished to distinguish their governments from the ministerial musical chairs that characterized previous civilian governments, especially Goulart's. So, appointees could reasonably expect to serve out the president's term, which gave them greater freedom to pursue their preferences and to represent interests. Stable tenure coupled with high and regular turnover gave Brazilian authoritarianism a defined political cycle and informal rules that other authoritarian regimes lack.

8. See Kinzo (1988, especially 181–82), for an analysis of the decision by the MDB (as the PMDB was known before 1979) not to dissolve itself despite its disappointment with these measures (though she does not argue that its members were hoping Figueiredo would be different).

9. Purcell makes a similar argument for Mexico: "Just about all positions in Mexico are appointive, even those that are supposedly elective. . . . In a political system in which a single party is dominant, nomination is tantamount to election" (Purcell 1981, 201).

10. For example, Figueiredo appointed Andreazza to the Ministry of Interior (which has the most federal funds for regional and social spending), and the latter built his (unsuccessful) presidential campaign on his ministry. So prevalent is this practice that the military decreed that candidates for elected office must resign executive positions six to nine months (depending on the position) before the election.

11. In their overviews of clientelism, Flynn (1974) stresses control and coercion, Powell analyses gatekeeping and intermediation (1977, 149), and Scott uses the term *pyramid* (1977, 128).

12. Cohen 1989, 102–03. See also Erickson 1977; Mericle 1977; Collier and Collier 1979.

13. Schwartzman 1982, 123. He argues that the emergence of neopatrimonial systems depends on the timing of industrialization relative to the expansion and strength of the state. When the economy develops independently with little interference from a weak state, then social groups organize autonomously to represent their interests. When the emergence of a strong state predates industrialization, the state tends to lead development and to attempt to control or incorporate on its terms the new social groups that arise (Schwartzman 1982, 22).

14. Nunes 1984, 21. Schmitter concludes: "This nonantagonistic, nonrevolutionary, externally penetrated pattern [of development] has had a number of political consequences. Most critically, there has been no dramatic confrontation between the *ancien* and the *nouveau régimes;* no single 'modernizing elite' has succeeded in capturing the political apparatus and imposing its distinctive model of society. Instead there has been a process of continuous accommodation whereby previous power holders have made concessions to new power contenders

without losing the original privileges and perquisites" (Schmitter 1971, 369).

15. The original Portuguese is more felicitous: "Ao cooptar, o centro se enfraquece, mas ao mesmo tempo tira a autonomia e independência dos cooptados, que de constituintes se transformam em clientes. A conseqüência é a formação de um sistema político pesado, irracional em suas decisões, que se torna presa de uma teia cada vez maior e mais complexa de compromissos e acomodações, até o ponto de ruptura" (Schwartzman 1982, 144).

16. Kaufman noted that U.S. presidents quickly discovered that patronage appointments can be more a curse than a boon. "The spoils system had its uses for chief executives, but, as it operated in this country, it never really gave these officers control of the administrative hierarchy. As a source of inducements to persuade legislators to support executive-sponsored measures, it was quite helpful at times. It was also valuable in providing incentives to attract workers for the parties. But it never furnished the executives with loyal, enthusiastic, capable, disciplined administrative machines; it did not make them chief administrators" (Kaufman 1956, 1068).

17. See Guimarães (1977) for a more extensive discussion of political capitalism in Brazil.

Bibliography

Aberbach, Joel D., Robert D. Putnam, and Bert A. Rockman. 1981. *Bureaucrats and Politicians in Western Democracies.* Cambridge, Mass.: Harvard University Press.

Aberbach, Joel D., and Bert A. Rockman. 1987. "Mandates or Mandarins? Control and Discretion in the Modern Administrative State." Paper prepared for delivery at the Western Political Science Association meeting, Anaheim, California (March).

Abranches, Sérgio Henrique. 1977. "Governo, Empresa Estatal e Política Siderúrgica no Brasil." FINEP, Rio de Janeiro (January).

———. 1978. "The Divided Leviathan: The State and Economic Policy Formation in Authoritarian Brazil." Ph.D. dissertation, Department of Political Science, Cornell University.

———. 1983. "O Sector Produtivo Estatal e a Crise." IUPERJ, Rio de Janeiro (July).

Abranches, Sérgio Henrique, and Sulamis Dain. 1978. "A Empresa Estatal no Brasil: Padrões Estruturais e Estratégias de Ação." FINEP, Rio de Janeiro.

Accioly, Brasilo. 1975. "Os Interesses e as Pressões que Asfixiam o Desenvolvimento." *Portos e Navios,* no. 196 (dezembro): 10–12.

Adelman, Irma, and Cynthia Taft Morris. 1967. *Society, Politics and Economic Development: A Quantitative Approach.* Baltimore, Md.: Johns Hopkins Press.

Adler, Emanuel. 1987. *The Power of Ideology: The Quest for Technological Autonomy in Argentina and Brazil.* Berkeley & Los Angeles: University of California Press.

Aharoni, Yair. 1982. "State-Owned Enterprise: An Agent without a Principal." In Leroy Jones, ed., *Public Enterprise in Less-Developed Countries.* Cambridge: Cambridge University Press.

Allison, Graham. 1969. "Conceptual Models and the Cuban Missile Crisis." *American Political Science Review 63,* no. 3 (September): 689–718.

Alves, Maria Helena Moreira. 1985. *State and Opposition in Military Brazil.* Austin: University of Texas Press.

Ames, Barry. 1973. *Rhetoric and Reality in a Militarized Regime: Brazil*

311

since 1964. Beverly Hills, Calif.: Sage Publications.

————. 1987. *Political Survival: Politicians and Public Policy in Latin America.* Berkeley & Los Angeles: University of California.

Assis, J. Carlos de. 1984a. *Os Mandarins da República: Anatomia dos Escândolos da Administração Pública.* Rio de Janeiro: Paz e Terra.

————. 1984b. *A Dupla Face da Corrupção.* Rio de Janeiro: Paz e Terra.

Baer, Werner. 1983. *The Brazilian Economy: Growth and Development.* New York: Praeger.

Baer, Werner, Richard Newfarmer, and Thomas Trebat. 1976. "On State Capitalism in Brazil: Some New Issues and Questions." *Inter-American Economic Affairs 30,* no. 3 (Winter): 69–91.

BAHINT (Booz, Allen & Hamilton International). 1966. "Brazilian Steel Industry Survey" (August).

Barros, Alexandre. 1978. "The Brazilian Military: Professional Socialization, Political Performance, and State Building." Ph.D. dissertation, Department of Political Science, University of Chicago.

Barzelay, Michael. 1986. *The Politicized Market Economy: Alcohol in Brazil's Energy Strategy.* Berkeley & Los Angeles: University of California Press.

Becker, David G. 1983. *The New Bourgeoisie and the Limits of Dependency: Mining, Class, and Power in "Revolutionary" Peru.* Princeton, N.J.: Princeton University Press.

Bielschowsky, Ricardo. 1988. *Pensamento Econômico Brasileiro: O Ciclo Ideológico do Desenvolvimentismo.* Rio de Janeiro: IPEA.

Block, Fred. 1977. "The Ruling Class Does Not Rule: Notes on the Marxist Theory of the State." *Socialist Revolution* 7, no. 3: 6–28.

Boschi, Renato. 1979. *Elites Industriais e Democracia: Hegemonia Burguesa e Mudança Política no Brasil.* Rio de Janeiro: Graal.

Boschi, Renato, and Eli Diniz. 1978. "Empresas, Burocracia e Mediação de Interesses." Relatório de Pesquisa, IUPERJ, Rio de Janeiro.

Braga, Carlos Alberto Primo. 1984. "Steel, Trade, and Development: A Comparative Advantage Analysis with Special Reference to the Case of Brazil." Ph.D. dissertation, Department of Economics, University of Illinois.

Bresser Pereira, Luiz Carlos. 1978. *O Colapso de uma Aliança de Clases.* São Paulo: Brasilense.

————. 1981. *A Sociedade Estatal e a Tecnoburocracia.* São Paulo: Brasilense.

———. 1988. "Experiências de um Governo." IUPERJ, Cadernos de Conjuntura, Rio de Janeiro.

Brown, Martin, and Bruce McKern. 1987. *Aluminium, Copper and Steel in Developing Countries.* Paris: OECD.

Bunker, Stephen G. 1983. "Policy Implementation in an Authoritarian State: A Case from Brazil." *Latin American Research Review* 18, no. 1: 33–58.

———. 1985. *Underdeveloping the Amazon: Extraction, Unequal Exchange, and the Failure of the Modern State.* Urbana: University of Illinois Press.

Cammack, Paul. 1982. "Clientelism and Military Government in Brazil." In Christopher Clapham, ed., *Private Patronage and Public Power.* New York: St. Martins Press.

Cardoso, Fernando Henrique. 1972. *Empresário Industrial e Desenvolvimento Econômico no Brasil.* São Paulo: Difusão Européia do Livro.

———. 1973. "Associated-Dependent Development: Theoretical and Practical Implications." In Alfred Stepan, ed., *Authoritarian Brazil.* New Haven: Yale University Press.

———. 1975. *Autoritarismo e Democratização.* Rio de Janeiro: Paz e Terra.

Cardoso, Fernando Henrique, and Enzo Faletto. 1979. *Dependency and Development in Latin America.* Berkeley & Los Angeles: University of California Press.

Carvalho, Getúlio. 1977. *Petrobrás: Do Monopólio aos Contratos de Risco.* Rio de Janeiro: Forense-Universitária.

Carvalho, José Murilo de. 1978. *A Escola de Minas de Ouro Preto: O Peso da Glória.* Rio de Janeiro: FINEP.

Castro, Antônio Barros de, and Francisco Eduardo Pires de Souza. 1985. *A Economia Brasileira em Marcha Forçada.* Rio de Janeiro: Paz e Terra.

Chagas, Carlos. 1985. *A Guerra das Estrelas (1964/1984): Os Bastidores das Sucesões Presidenciais.* Porto Alegre: L & PM.

Chalmers, Douglas A. 1977. "The Politicized State in Latin America." In James M. Malloy, ed., *Authoritarianism and Corporatism in Latin America.* Pittsburgh: University of Pittsburgh Press.

Cleaves, Peter S. 1974. *Bureaucratic Politics and Administration in Chile.* Berkeley & Los Angeles: University of California Press.

Coelho, Edmundo Campos. 1976. *Em Busca de Identidade: O Exército na*

Sociedade Brasileira. Rio de Janeiro: Forense-Universitária.

———. 1977. "Administradores Públicos: Atitudes e Percepções." Relatório de Pesquisa, IUPERJ. Rio de Janeiro (July).

Cohen, Youssef. 1989. *The Manipulation of Consent: The State and Working-Class Consciousness in Brazil*. Pittsburgh: University of Pittsburgh Press.

Collier, David, ed. 1979. *The New Authoritarianism in Latin America*. Princeton, N.J.: Princeton University Press.

Collier, Ruth Berins. 1982. "Popular Sector Incorporation and Political Supremacy: Regime Evolution in Brazil and Mexico." In Sylvia Ann Hewlett and Richard S. Weinert, eds., *Brazil and Mexico*. Philadelphia: Institute for the Study of Human Issues.

Collier, Ruth Berins, and David Collier. 1979. "Inducements versus Constraints: Disaggregating Corporatism." *American Political Science Review* 73, no. 4 (December): 967–86.

CONSIDER (Conselho Nacional da Indústria Siderúrgica). 1984–85. *Anuário Estatístico: Setor Metalúrgico*. Brasília.

Coutinho, Luciano G., and Henri Philippe Reichstul. 1981. "Investimento Estatal 1974–1980: Ciclo e Crise." *IX Encontro Nacional de Economia*. Volume 4. Brasília: ANPEC.

CPDOC (Centro de Pesquisa e Documentação de História Contemporânea do Brasil, Fundação Getúlio Vargas). 1984. *Dicionário Histórico-Biográfico Brasileiro: 1930–1983*. Rio de Janeiro: Forense-Universitária, FGV/CPDOC, and FINEP.

CRVD (Companhia Vale do Rio Doce). 1981. *Projeto Ferro Carajás (Carajás Iron Project)*. Rio de Janeiro.

———. 1982. *Companhia Vale do Rio Doce: 40 Anos*. Rio de Janeiro.

———. *Relatório Anual*. Various years.

Crozier, Michel. 1964. *The Bureaucratic Phenomenon*. Chicago: University of Chicago Press.

Cruz, Paulo Davidoff. 1983. "Notas Sobre o Endividamento Externo Brasileiro nos Anos Setenta." In Luiz Gonzaga Belluzo and Renata Coutinho, ed., *Desenvolvimento Capitalista no Brasil*. São Paulo: Brasiliense.

Cruz, Sebastião Carlos Velasco e. 1984. "Empresários e o Regime no Brasil: A Campanha contra a Estatização." Tese de doutorado, Universidade de São Paulo.

Daland, Robert T. 1967. *Brazilian Planning: Development Politics and Ad-*

ministration. Chapel Hill: University of North Carolina Press.

———. 1981. *Exploring Brazilian Bureaucracy: Performance and Pathology.* Washington, D.C.: University Press of America.

Dantas, Marcos. 1980. "A Questão do Alumínio—O Presente e o Futuro da Indústria do Alumínio no Brasil." Tese preparada para o I Congresso de Defesa da Amazônia (Novembro).

Dias Leite, Jr., Antônio. 1966. *Caminhos do Desenvolvimento: Contribuição para um Projeto Brasileiro.* Rio de Janeiro: Zahar.

———. 1984. *Caminhos da Reconstrução.* São Paulo: Pioneira.

Diniz, Clélio Campolina. 1981. *Estado e Capital Estrangeiro na Industrialização Mineira.* Belo Horizonte: Universidade Federal de Minas Gerais (PROED).

Diniz, Eli, and Renato Raul Boschi. 1978. *Empresariado Nacional e Estado no Brasil.* Rio de Janeiro: Forense-Universitária.

———. 1987. "Burocracia, Clientelismo e Oligopólio: O Conselho Interministerial de Preços." In Olavo Brasil de Lima, Jr., and Sérgio Henrique Abranches, eds., *As Origens da Crise.* Rio de Janeiro: IUPERJ e Vértice.

Doig, Jameson W., and Erwin C. Hargrove, eds. 1987. *Leadership and Innovation: A Biographical Perspective on Entrepreneurs in Government.* Baltimore, Md.: Johns Hopkins University Press.

Downs, Anthony. 1967. *Inside Bureaucracy.* Boston: Little, Brown & Co.

Dreifuss, René Armand. 1981. *1964: A Conquista do Estado. Ação Política, Poder e Golpe de Classe.* Petrópolis: Vozes.

Dresang, Dennis L. 1973. "Entrepreneuralism and Development Administration." *Administrative Science Quarterly* 18, no. 1 (March): 76–85.

Dutra, Wilson, and Vittoria Salles. 1975. "Padrão de Financiamento de Empresas Estatais." Centro de Estudos e Pesquisas/FINEP, Rio de Janeiro.

Duvall, Raymond D., and John R. Freeman. 1983. "The Techno-Bureaucratic Elite and the Entrepreneurial State in Dependent Industrialization." *American Political Science Review* 77 no. 3 (September): 569–87.

Eisenstadt, S. N. 1963. "Bureaucracy and Political Development." In Joseph LaPalombara, ed., *Bureaucracy and Political Development.* Princeton, N.J.: Princeton University Press.

EPEA (Escritório de Pesquisa Econômica Aplicada). 1966. "Siderúrgica e Metais Nao-Ferrosos." Plano Decenal de Desenvolvimento Econômico e Social. Ministério de Planejamento. April.

Erickson, Kenneth P. 1977. *The Brazilian Corporative State and Working-Class Politics.* Berkeley & Los Angeles: University of California Press.

Etzioni-Halevy, Eva. 1983. *Bureaucracy and Democracy: A Political Dilemma.* London: Routledge & Kegan Paul.

Evans, Peter. 1979. *Dependent Development: The Alliance of Multinational, State, and Local Capital in Brazil.* Princeton, N.J.: Princeton University Press.

————. 1982. "Reinventing the Bourgeoisie: State Entrepreneurship and Class Formation in Dependent Capitalist Development." *American Journal of Sociology* 88, Special Supplement, 210–47.

Faoro, Raymundo. 1984. *Os Donos do Poder: Formação do Patronato Político Brasileiro.* 6th ed. 2 vols. Rio de Janeiro: Globo.

Faucher, Philippe. 1979. *Le Brésil des Militaires.* Montreal: University of Montreal Press.

————. 1989. "The New Industrial Policy: A Test for Policy Change in Brazil." Paper presented at the meeting of the Latin American Studies Association, Miami (December).

Fernandes, Francisco Rego Chaves, coord. 1982. *Os Maiores Mineradores do Brasil: Perfil Empresarial do Setor Mineral Brasileiro.* 3 vols. Brasília: Conselho Nacional de Pesquisa, Coordenação Editorial.

Fishlow, Albert. 1972. "On the Emerging Problems of Development Policy: Brazilian Size Distribution of Income." *American Economic Review* 62, no. 2 (May): 391–402.

————. 1973. "Some Reflections on Post-1964 Brazilian Economic Policy." In Alfred Stepan, ed., *Authoritarian Brazil: Origins, Policies, and Future.* New Haven, Conn.: Yale University Press.

————. 1989. "A Tale of Two Presidents: The Political Economy of Crisis Management." In Alfred Stepan, ed., *Democratizing Brazil.* New York: Oxford University Press.

Flynn, Peter. 1974. "Class, Clientelism, and Coercion: Some Mechanisms of Internal Dependency and Control." *Journal of Commonwealth and Comparative Politics* 12, no. 2 (July): 133–56.

————. 1978. *Brazil: A Political Analysis.* Boulder, Colo.: Westview Press.

Franz, Juergen, Bo Stenberg, and John Strongman. 1986. *Iron Ore:*

Global Prospects for the Industry, 1985–1995. Washington, D.C.: World Bank.

Frieden, Jeffry A. 1987. "The Brazilian Borrowing Experience: From Miracle to Debacle and Back." *Latin American Research Review* 22, no. 1: 95–131.

Furtado, Celso. 1971. *The Economic Growth of Brazil: A Survey from Colonial to Modern Times.* Berkeley & Los Angeles: University of California Press.

Gazeta Mercantil. 1984. *Balanço Anual 1984.* São Paulo (September).

GCIS (Grupo Consultativo da Indústria Siderúrgica). 1967. *Plano Siderúrgico Nacional* (December).

Geddes, Barbara. 1986. "Economic Development as a Collective Action Problem: Individual Interests and Innovation in Brazil." Ph.D. dissertation, Department of Political Science, University of California, Berkeley.

Gerth, H. H., and C. Wright Mills, eds. 1946. *From Max Weber: Essays in Sociology.* New York: Oxford University Press.

Gistelink, Frans. 1988? *Carajás: Usinas e Favelas.* São Luis, Maranhão.

Góes, Walder de. 1978. *O Brasil do General Geisel.* Rio de Janeiro: Nova Fronteira.

———. 1983. "O Novo Papel Político das Forças Armadas do Brasil." Paper presented at VII Encontro Anual da ANPOCS, Aguas de São Pedro (October).

Góes, Walder de, and Aspásia Camargo. 1985. *O Drama da Sucessão e a Crise do Regime.* Rio de Janeiro: Nova Fronteira.

Graham, Lawrence S. 1968. *Civil Service Reform in Brazil.* Austin: University of Texas Press.

Grindle, Merilee Serrill. 1977. *Bureaucrats, Politicians, and Peasants in Mexico: A Case Study in Public Policy.* Berkeley & Los Angeles: University of California.

GTI Alumínio (Grupo de Trabalho Interministerial). 1986. "Alumínio e Energia Elétrica no Brasil." Brasília.

Guimarães, César. 1977. "Empresariado, Tipos de Capitalismo e Ordem Política." *Dados* 14: 34–47.

Guimarães, César, and Maria Lúcia Teixeria Werneck Vianna. 1987. "Planejamento e Centralização Decisória: O Conselho Monetário Nacional e o Conselho de Desenvolvimento Econômico." In Olavo Brasil de Lima, Jr., and Sérgio Henrique Abranches, eds., *As Origens da Crise.* Rio de Janeiro: IUPERJ e Vértice.

Hagopian, Frances. 1986. "The Politics of Oligarchy: The Persistence of Traditional Elites in Contemporary Brazil." Ph.D. dissertation, Department of Political Science, Massachusetts Institute of Technology.

Hartlyn, Jonathan, and Samuel A. Morley. 1986. "Political Regimes and Economic Performance in Latin America." In Jonathan Hartlyn and Samuel A. Morley, eds. *Latin American Political Economy.* Boulder, Colo.: Westview Press.

Heclo, Hugh. 1977. *Government of Strangers: Executive Politics in Washington.* Washington, D.C.: Brookings Institution.

Hirschman, Albert. 1967. *Development Projects Observed.* Washington, D.C.: Brookings Institution.

Huneeus, Carlos. 1988. "El Ejército y la Política en el Chile de Pinochet; Su Magnitud y Alcances." *Opciones,* no. 14: 89–136.

Huntington, Samuel P. 1968. *Political Order in Changing Societies.* New Haven, Conn.: Yale University Press.

Ianni, Octávio. 1971. *Estado e Planejamento Econômico no Brasil (1930–1970).* Rio de Janeiro: Civilização Brasileira.

IBASE (Instituto Brasileiro de Análises Sociais e Econômicas). 1983. *Carajás: O Brasil Hipoteca seu Futuro.* Rio de Janeiro: Achiamé.

IBS (Instituto Brasileiro de Siderurgia). 1974. *Anuário Estatístico da Indústria Siderúrgica Brasileira.* Rio de Janeiro.

———. 1985. "A Siderurgia em Números."

Johnson, Chalmers. 1982. *MITI and the Japanese Miracle: The Growth of Industrial Policy, 1925–1975.* Stanford, Calif.: Stanford University Press.

Kaufman, Herbert. 1956. "Emerging Conflicts in the Doctrines of Public Administration." *American Political Science Review* 50, no. 4 (December): 1057–73.

———. 1960. *The Forest Ranger: A Study in Administrative Behavior.* Baltimore, Md.: Johns Hopkins Press.

Kelly de Escobar, Janet. 1982. "Comparing State Enterprises across International Boundaries: The Corporación Venezolana de Guayana and the Companhia Vale do Rio Doce." In Leroy P. Jones, ed., *Public Enterprise in Less-Developed Countries.* Cambridge: Cambridge University Press.

Kim, Byung-Kook. 1987. "Bringing and Managing Socioeconomic Change: The State in Korea and Mexico." Ph.D. dissertation, Harvard University.

Kinzo, Maria D'Alva Gil. 1988. *Legal Opposition Politics under Authoritarian Rule in Brazil: The Case of the MDB, 1966–79.* London: Macmillan.

Klein, Lúcia. 1980. "A Implantação dos Grandes Projetos Governamentais nos Setores Siderúrigicos e Hidroelétricos, 1974–79." FINEP, (June–December).

Krasner, Stephen D. 1978. *Defending the National Interest: Raw Materials Investments and U.S. Foreign Policy.* Princeton, N.J.: Princeton University Press.

Lafer, Betty Mindlin, ed. 1970. *Planejamento no Brasil.* São Paulo: Perspectiva.

Lafer, Celso. 1970a. "O Planejamento no Brasil: Observações sobre o Plano de Metas (1956–1961)." In Betty M. Lafer, ed., *Planejamento no Brasil.* São Paulo: Perspectiva.

———. 1970b. "The Planning Process and the Political System in Brazil: A Study of Kubitschek's Target Plan, 1956–1961." Ph.D. dissertation, Cornell University.

Leeds, Anthony. 1965. "Brazilian Careers and Social Structure: A Case History and a Model." In Rich N. Adams and Dwight B. Heath, eds., *Contemporary Cultures and Society in Latin America.* New York: Random House.

Leff, Nathaniel H. 1968. *Economic Policy-Making and Development in Brazil.* New York: John Wiley & Sons.

Leonard, David K. 1977. *Reaching the Peasant Farmer: Organization Theory and Practice in Kenya.* Chicago: University of Chicago Press.

Lessa, Carlos. 1978. "A Estratégia de Desenvolvimento, 1974/1976: Sonho e Fracasso." Tese para concurso de professor titular, Faculdade de Economia e Administração, Universidade Federal do Rio de Janeiro.

Linz, Juan J. 1964. "An Authoritarian Regime: Spain." In Erik Allardt and Yrjo Littunen, eds., *Cleavages, Ideologies, and Party Systems.* Helsinki: Academic Bookstore.

Lowi, Theodore J. 1964a. *At the Pleasure of the Mayor.* New York: Free Press.

———. 1964b. "American Business, Public Policy, Case-Studies, and Political Theory." *World Politics* 16, no. 4 (July): 677–715.

Lynn, Laurence E., Jr. 1987. *Managing Public Policy.* Boston: Little, Brown & Co.

McDonough, Peter. 1981a. "Developmental Priorities Among Brazilian Elites." *Economic Development and Cultural Change* 29, no. 3 (April): 535–60.

——. 1981b. "Mapping an Authoritarian Power Structure: Brazilian Elites During the Medici Regime." *Latin American Research Review* 16, no. 1: 79–106.

——. 1981c. *Power and Ideology in Brazil.* Princeton, N.J.: Princeton University Press.

Macedo, Roberto Brás Matos. 1985. *Os Salários nas Empresas Estatais.* São Paulo: Nobel.

McGregor, Eugene B., Jr. 1974. "Politics and the Career Mobility of Bureaucrats." *American Political Science Review* 68, no. 1 (March): 18–26.

Machado, Raymundo de Campos. 1983. *Alumínio Primário no Brasil.* Ouro Preto: Fundação Gorceix.

——. 1985. *Apontamentos da História do Alumínio Primário no Brasil.* Ouro Preto: Fundação Gorceix.

——. 1988. *A Indústria do Alumínio neste Final de Século.* Ouro Preto: Fundação Gorceix.

Mackenzie, G. Calvin. 1987. *The Politics of Presidential Appointments.* New York: Free Press.

Mann, Dean E. 1965. *The Assistant Secretaries: Problems and Processes of Appointment.* Washington, D.C.: Brookings Institution.

Martins, Carlos Estevam. 1974. *Tecnocracia e Capitalismo: A Política dos Técnicos no Brasil.* São Paulo: Brasilense.

Martins, Luciano. 1968. *Industralização, Burgesia Nacional e Desenvolvimento (Introdução à Crise Brasileira).* Rio de Janeiro: Saga.

——. 1976. *Pouvoir et Développement Economique: Formation et Evolution des Structures Politiques au Brésil.* Paris: Anthropos.

——. 1985. *Estado Capitalista e Burocracia no Brasil Pós 64.* Rio de Janeiro: Paz e Terra.

May, Peter J. 1986. "Politics and Policy Analysis." *Political Science Quarterly* 101, no. 1: 109–25.

Meltsner, Arnold J. 1972. "Political Feasibility and Policy Analysis." *Public Administration Review* 32, no. 6 (November/December): 859–67.

Mendes, Cândido. 1966. "Sistema Político e Modelos de Poder no Brasil." *Dados* 1: 7–41.

Mendes, Moacélio. 1978. "Açominas Project." Açominas (May).

————. 1979. "Açominas: Um Estilo de Administração." Açominas (March).

————. 1981. "Projeto Açominas: Evolução e Tendências." Açominas (August).

Mericle, Kenneth S. 1977. "Corporatist Control of the Working Class: The Case of Post-1964 Authoritarian Brazil." In James M. Malloy, ed., *Authoritarianism and Corporatism in Latin America*. Pittsburgh: University of Pittsburgh Press.

Moe, Terry M. 1985. "The Politicized Presidency." In John E. Chubb and Paul E. Peterson, eds., *The New Direction in American Politics*. Washington, D.C.: Brookings Institution.

Monteiro, Jorge Vianna, and Luiz Roberto Azevedo Cunha. 1973. "A Organização do Planejamento Econômico: O Caso Brasileiro." *Pesquisa e Planejamento Econômico* 3, no. 4 (December): 1045–64.

Motta, Paulo Roberto. 1972. "The Brazilian Bureaucratic Elite: Social Background and Organizational Attitudes." Ph.D. dissertation, University of North Carolina, Chapel Hill.

Museu da Fazenda. 1983. *Ministros da Fazenda, 1808–1983*. Rio de Janeiro.

Naves, Sidônio Cardoso. 1977. "O Planejamento Siderúrgico Nacional." *IBS Revista*, no. 18 (May-June): 15–20.

Nechemias, Carol. 1986. "Gaus Lecturer Kaufman Predicts Struggle within Public Administration." *PS* 19, no. 4 (Fall): 875–76.

Needler, Martin C. 1982. *Mexican Politics: The Containment of Conflict*. New York: Praeger.

Niskanen, William A., Jr. 1971. *Bureaucracy and Representative Government*. Chicago: Aldine.

Nordlinger, Eric A. 1981. *On the Autonomy of the Democratic State*. Cambridge, Mass.: Harvard University Press.

Nunberg, Barbara. 1978. "State Intervention in the Sugar Sector in Brazil: A Study of the Institute of Sugar and Alcohol." Ph.D. dissertation, Department of Political Science, Stanford University.

Nunes, Edson de Oliveira. 1978. "Legislativo, Política e Recrutamento de Elites no Brasil." *Dados* 17: 53–78.

————. 1984. "Bureaucratic Insulation and Clientelism in Contemporary Brazil: Uneven State-Building and the Taming of Modernity." Ph.D. dissertation, Department of Political Science, University of California, Berkeley.

Nunes, Edson de Oliveira, and Barbara Geddes. 1987. "Dilemmas of

State-Led Modernization in Brazil." In John D. Wirth, Edson de Oliveira Nunes, and Thomas E. Bogenschild, eds., *State and Society in Brazil*. Boulder, Colo.: Westview.

O'Donnell, Guillermo A. 1973. *Modernization and Bureaucratic-Authoritarianism*. Berkeley: Institute of International Studies, University of California.

Oszlak, Oscar. 1980. "Políticas Públicas y Régimenes Políticos: Reflexiones a Partir de Algunas Experiencias Latinoamericanas." *Estudios CEDES* 3, no. 2.

———. 1984. "Public Policies and Political Regimes in Latin America." Working Paper 139, Woodrow Wilson Center, Washington, D.C.

———. 1986. "Public Policies and Political Regimes in Latin America." *International Social Science Journal* 38, no. 2 (108): 219–36.

Paine Webber. 1986. "World Steel Dynamics," no. 12 (June).

Payne, Leigh Ann. 1990. "Pragmatic Actors: The Political Attitudes and Behavior of Brazilian Industrial Elites." Ph.D. dissertation, Department of Political Science, Yale University.

Perfil Açominas. Monthly Açominas publication.

Perrow, Charles. 1986. *Complex Organizations: A Critical Essay*. 3d ed. New York: Random House.

Pimenta, Dermeval José. 1981. *A Vale do Rio Doce e Sua História*. Belo Horizonte: Vega.

Polsby, Nelson W., 1968. "The Institutionalization of the U.S. House of Representatives." *American Political Science Review 62*, no. 1 (March): 144–68.

Powell, John Duncan. 1970. "Peasant Societies and Clientelist Politics." *American Political Science Review* 64 (June): 411–25.

Purcell, Susan Kaufman. 1981. "Mexico: Clientilism, Corporatism, and Political Stability." In S. N. Eisenstadt and René Lemarchand, eds., *Political Clientilism, Patronage, and Development*. Beverly Hills: Sage Publications.

Raw, Silvia. 1983. "The CVRD: Goals and Financing Patterns." Paper presented at the conference on Public Enterprises, Caracas, Venezuela (November).

———. 1985. "The Political Economy of Brazilian State-Owned Enterprises: 1964–1980." Ph.D. dissertation, Department of Economics, University of Massachusetts.

Reinarman, Craig. 1987. *American States of Mind: Political Beliefs and Behavior among Private and Public Workers*. New Haven, Conn.: Yale University Press.

Rezende, Fernando. 1983. "O Crescimento (Descontrolado) da Intervenção Governamental na Economia Brasileira." In IPEA (Instituto de Planejamento Econômico e Social), *Seminário sobre Planejamento e Controle do Setor de Empresas Estatais: Casos Nacionais*. Brasília.

Ricci, María Susana, and J. Samuel Fitch. 1990. "Ending Military Regimes in Argentina: 1966–73 and 1976–83." In Louis Goodman, Johanna S. R. Mendelson, and Juan Rial, eds., *The Military and Democracy*. Lexington, Mass.: Lexington Books.

Richardson, James, ed. 1905. *Messages and Papers of the Presidents*. Volume 2. New York: Bureau of National Literature and Art.

Rodrigues, Lélio. 1986. "Alternativas Sócio-econômicas: Abertura Externa, Integração Nacional e Subsistência Comunitária." In José Maria Gonçalves de Almeida, Jr., ed. *Carajás*. São Paulo: Brasilense.

Roett, Riordan. 1978. *Brazil: Politics in a Patrimonial Society*. New York: Praeger.

Rouquié, Alain, ed. 1980. *Les Partis Militaires au Brésil*. Presses de la Fondation Nationale des Sciences Politiques.

Rueschemeyer, Dietrich, and Peter B. Evans. 1985. "The State and Economic Transformation: Toward an Analysis of the Conditions Underlying Effective Intervention." In Peter Evans, Dietrich Rueschemeyer, and Theda Skocpol, eds. *Bringing the State Back In*. New York: Cambridge University Press.

Sá, Paulo, and Isabel Marques. 1987a. "Análise Crítica da Política Mineral." *Brasil Mineral*, no. 48 (November): 70–82.

———. 1987b. "Projeto Albrás/Alunorte: Do Sonho ao Pesadelo." *Brasil Mineral*, nos. 38 and 39 (January and February): 44–48, 49–53, (parts I and II respectively).

Sabel, Charles F. 1982. *The Division of Labor, Its Progress through Politics: Industrial Work and Workers in the Age of Fordism*. Cambridge: Cambridge University Press.

Samuels, Richard J. 1983. "The Industrial Destructuring of the Japanese Aluminum Industry." *Pacific Affairs* 56, no. 3 (Fall): 495–509.

Santos, Breno Augusto dos. 1981. *Amazônia: Potencial Mineral e Perspectivas de Desenvolvimento*. São Paulo: Queiroz/Universidade de São Paulo.

———. 1984. "Carajás: História e Perspectivas." Testimony before Comissão de Minas e Energia, Câmara dos Deputados. Reprinted in "Informe da Secretaria Executiva Especial," no. 4, Instituto Brasileiro de Mineração (May).

Santos, Wanderley Guilherme dos. 1979a. "The Calculus of Conflict: Impasse in Brazilian Politics and the Crisis of 1964." Ph.D. dissertation, Department of Political Science, Stanford University.

———. et al. 1979b. "Centralização Burocrática e Renovação de Elites: Estudo Preliminar sobre a Administração Decentralizada." IUPERJ, Rio de Janeiro.

———. 1982. "A Elite Invisível: Explorações sobre a Tecnocracia Federal Brasileira." *Revista do Serviço Público* Ano 39, vol. 110, no. 1 (January–March): 67–82.

Saraiva, Enrique. 1977. "Aspectos Gerais do Comportamento das Empesas Públicas Brasileiras e sua Ação Internacional." *Revista de Administração Pública* 11, no. 1 (January–March): 65–143.

Sarmento, Cléa. 1978. "Administradores Públicos de Alto Nivel na Burocracia Brasileira: O Caso do Ministério da Agricultura." Relatório de Pesquisa, IUPERJ, Rio de Janeiro.

Sartori, Giovanni. 1970. "Concept Misformation in Comparative Politics."*American Political Science Review* 64, no. 4 (December) 1033–53.

Schmitter, Philippe C. 1971. *Interest Conflict and Political Change in Brazil.* Stanford, Calif.: Stanford University Press.

———. 1973. "The 'Portugalization' of Brazil?" In Alfred Stepan, ed., *Authoritarian Brazil.* New Haven, Conn.: Yale University Press.

Schneider, Ben Ross. 1987a. "Politics within the State: Elite Bureaucrats and Industrial Policy in Authoritarian Brazil." Ph.D. dissertation, Department of Political Science, University of California, Berkeley.

———. 1987b. "Framing the State: Economic Policy and Political Representation in Post-Authoritarian Brazil." In John D. Wirth, Edson de Oliveira Nunes, and Thomas E. Bogenschild, eds. *State and Society in Brazil.* Boulder, Colo.: Westview Press.

———. 1988–89. "Partly for Sale: Privatization and State Strength in Brazil and Mexico." *Journal of Interamerican Studies and World Affairs* 30, no. 4 (Winter): 89–116.

———. 1989. "The Career Connection: Bureaucrats and State Strength in Comparative Perspective." Mimeo.

————. 1991. "Privatization in the Collor Government: Triumph of Liberalism or Collapse of the Developmental State?" Forthcoming in Douglas Chalmers, Maria do Carmo Campello de Souza, and Atílio Borón, eds., *The Right and Democracy in Latin America*. Westport, Conn.: Praeger.

Schneider, Ronald M. 1971. *The Political System of Brazil: Emergence of a "Modernizing" Authoritarian Regime, 1964–1970*. New York: Columbia University Press.

Schott, Richard L., and Dagmar S. Hamilton. 1983. *People, Positions, and Power: The Political Appointments of Lyndon Johnson*. Chicago: University of Chicago Press.

Schumpeter, Joseph A. 1975. *Capitalism, Socialism, and Democracy*. New York: Harper & Row.

Schwartzman, Simon. 1982. *As Bases do Autoritarismo Brasileiro*. Rio de Janeiro: Campus.

Scott, James C. 1977. "Patron-Client Politics and Political Change in Southeast Asia." In Steffen W. Schmidt, et al., eds., *Friends, Followers, and Factions*. Berkeley & Los Angeles: University of California Press.

SDI (Secretaria Especial de Desenvolvimento Industrial). 1989. *Anuário Estatístico: Setor Metalúrgico*. Brasília.

Selznick, Philip. 1957. *Leadership in Administration: A Sociological Interpretation*. New York: Harper & Row.

————. 1980. *TVA and the Grass Roots: A Study of Politics and Organization*. Berkeley & Los Angeles: University of California Press.

Senate (Senado Federal and Câmara dos Deputados). 1981. Comissão de Minas e Energia e Comissão de Economia. *Simpósio: Alternativas para Carajás*. Brasília.

Seplan (Secretaria de Planejamento da Presidência da República). 1981. "Grande Carajás Program." Brasília.

Serra, José. 1979. "Three Mistaken Theses Regarding the Connection between Industrialization and Authoritarian Regimes." In David Collier, ed., *The New Authoritarianism in Latin America*. Princeton, N.J.: Princeton University Press.

SEST (Secretaria de Controle das Empresas Estatais). 1984. *Cadastro das Empresas Estatais*. Brasília.

Shapiro, Helen. 1988. "State Intervention and Industrialization: The Origins of the Brazilian Automotive Industry." Ph.D. dissertation, Department of Economics, Yale University.

Siderbrás. 1983. "Dez Anos de Siderbrás."

―――― . *Relatório da Administração*. Various years.

Sikkink, Kathryn. 1988. "The New Institutionalism and Economic Policy Making in Latin America: State Autonomy and Developmentalist Policy Making in Argentina and Brazil." Paper prepared for the meeting of the Latin American Studies Association, New Orleans (March).

Silva, Hélio. 1984. *O Poder Militar.* Porto Alegre: L & PM.

Skidmore, Thomas E. 1967. *Politics in Brazil, 1930–1964: An Experiment in Democracy.* New York: Oxford University Press.

―――― . 1973. "Politics and Economic Policy-Making in Authoritarian Brazil, 1937–71." In Alfred Stepan, ed., *Authoritarian Brazil.* New Haven, Conn.: Yale University Press.

―――― . 1985. "The Political Economy of Policy-Making in Authoritarian Brazil, 1967–70." In Paul Cammack and Philip O'Brien, eds., *Generals in Retreat.* Manchester: Manchester University Press.

―――― . 1988. *The Politics of Military Rule in Brazil, 1964–85.* New York: Oxford University Press.

―――― . 1989. "Brazil's Slow Road to Redemocratization: 1974–1984." In Alfred Stepan, ed., *Democratizing Brazil.* New York: Oxford University Press.

Sloan, John W. 1982. "Comparative Public Choice and Public Policy in Latin America." *Journal of Developing Areas* 16, no. 3 (April): 421–46.

―――― . 1984. *Public Policy in Latin America: A Comparative Survey.* Pittsburgh: University of Pittsburgh Press.

Smith, Peter H. 1979. *Labyrinths of Power: Political Recruitment in Twentieth-Century Mexico.* Princeton N.J.: Princeton University Press.

Soares, Gláucio Ary Dillon. 1978. "After the Miracle." *Luso-Brazilian Review* 15, no. 2 (Winter): 278–301.

Sorj, Bernado. 1983. "Public Enterprises and the Question of the State Bourgeoisie, 1968–76." In David Booth and Bernard Sorj, eds., *Military Reformism and Social Classes.* London: Macmillan.

Souza, Maria do Carmo Campello de. 1983. *Estado e Partidos Políticos no Brasil (1930 a 1964).* São Paulo: Alfa-Omega.

Souza, Miguel Augusto Gonçalves de. 1985. *Açominas: Aspiração de Várias Gerações de Mineiros.* Belo Horizonte: Açominas.

Stanley, David T., Dean E. Mann, and Jameson W. Doig. 1967. *Men Who Govern: A Biographical Profile of Federal Political Executives.* Washington, D.C.: Brookings Institution.

Stepan, Alfred. 1971. *The Military in Politics: Changing Patterns in Brazil.* Princeton, N.J.: Princeton University Press.

————. 1988. *Rethinking Military Politics: Brazil and the Southern Cone.* Princeton, N.J.: Princeton University Press.

Stepan, Alfred, ed. 1973. *Authoritarian Brazil: Origins, Policies, and Future.* New Haven, Conn.: Yale University Press.

————. 1989. *Democratizing Brazil: Problems of Transition and Consolidation.* New York: Oxford University Press.

Stinchcombe, Arthur. 1968. *Constructing Social Theories.* New York: Harcourt, Brace & World.

————. 1974. *Creating Efficient Industrial Administrations.* New York: Harcourt Brace Jovanovich.

Story, Dale. 1986. *Industry, the State and Public Policy in Mexico.* Austin: University of Texas Press.

Strasser, Richard Frederick. 1981. "The State-Controlled Enterprise in Economic Development: A Brazilian Case Study." B.A. thesis, Department of Economics, Harvard University.

Suleiman, Ezra N. 1974. *Politics, Power and Bureaucracy in France: The Administrative Elite.* Princeton, N.J.: Princeton University Press.

Suzigan, Wilson. 1988. "Estado e Industrialização no Brasil." *Revista de Economia Política* 8, no. 4 (October–December): 5–16.

Suzigan, Wilson, ed. 1979. *Indústria: Política, Instituições e Desenvolvimento.* Rio de Janeiro: IPEA.

Tendler, Judith. 1968. *Electric Power in Brazil: Entrepreneurship in the Public Sector.* Cambridge, Mass.: Harvard University Press.

Thompson, James D. 1967. *Organizations in Action.* New York: McGraw-Hill.

Toffler, Alvin. 1970. *Future Shock.* New York: Random House.

Trebat, Thomas J. 1983. *Brazil's State-Owned Enterprises: A Case Study of the State as Entrepreneur.* Cambridge: Cambridge University Press.

Tullock, Gordon. 1965. *The Politics of Bureaucracy.* Washington, D.C.: Public Affairs Press.

Tyler, William G. 1981. *The Brazilian Industrial Economy.* Lexington, Mass.: D. C. Heath.

Uricoechea, Fernando. 1980. *The Patrimonial Foundations of the Brazilian Bureaucratic State.* Berkeley & Los Angeles: University of California Press.

Van Maanen, John. 1977a. "Introduction: The Promise of Career

Studies." In John Van Maanen, ed., *Organizational Careers: Some New Perspectives*. London: John Wiley & Sons.

———. 1977b. "Experiencing Organization: Notes on the Meaning of Careers and Socialization." In John Van Maanen, ed., *Organizational Careers*. London: John Wiley & Sons.

———. 1977c. "Summary: Towards a Theory of the Career." In John Van Maanen, ed., *Organizational Careers*. London: John Wiley & Sons.

Véliz, Claudio. 1980. *The Centralist Tradition of Latin America*. Princeton, N.J.: Princeton University Press.

Velloso, João Paulo dos Reis. 1977. *Brasil: A Solução Positiva*. São Paulo: Abril-Tec.

Vianna, Maria Lúcia Teixeira Werneck. 1982. "A Administração do 'Milagre': O Conselho Monetário Nacional, 1964/1974." Tese de mestrado, IUPERJ.

———. 1987. *A Administração do Milagre: O Conselho Monetário Nacional, 1964–1974*. Petrópolis: Vozes.

Villela, Anníbal Villanova. 1984. *Empresas do Governo como Instrumento de Política Econômica: Os Sistemas Siderbrás, Eletrobrás, Petrobrás e Telebrás*. Rio de Janeiro: IPEA.

Viola, Eduardo, and Scott Mainwaring. 1984. "New Social Movements, Political Culture, and Democracy: Brazil and Argentina in the 1980s." *Telos*, no. 61 (Fall).

Warner, W. Lloyd, and James C. Abegglen. 1955. *Occupational Mobility in American Business and Industry*. Minneapolis: University of Minnesota Press.

Warner, W. Lloyd, Paul P. Van Riper, Norman H. Martin, and Orvis F. Collins. 1963. *The American Federal Executive: A Study of the Social and Personal Characteristics of the Civilian and Military Leaders of the United States Federal Government*. New Haven, Conn.: Yale University Press.

Weber, Max. 1958. *The Protestant Ethic and the Spirit of Capitalism*. New York: Charles Scribner's Sons.

White, Lynn T., III. 1978. *Careers in Shanghai: The Social Guidance of Personal Energies in a Developing Chinese City, 1949–1966*. Berkeley & Los Angeles: University of California Press.

Wiarda, Howard J., ed. 1974. *Politics and Social Change in Latin America: The Distinct Tradition*. Amherst: University of Massachusetts Press.

Wildavsky, Aaron. 1966. "The Political Economy of Efficiency: Cost-

Benefit Analysis, Systems Analysis, and Program Budgeting." *Public Administration Review* 26, no. 4 (December): 292–310.

Willis, Eliza J. 1986. "The State as Banker: The Expansion of the Public Sector in Brazil." Ph.D. dissertation, Department of Political Science, University of Texas, Austin.

———. 1988. "Investing in the Poor: State Autonomy and Social Distribution in Brazil." Paper prepared for the meeting of the Latin American Studies Association, New Orleans (March).

Wirth, John. 1970. *The Politics of Brazilian Development, 1930–1954.* Stanford, Calif.: Stanford University Press.

World Bank. 1972. "Brazilian Steel Expansion Program. Part I: Appraisal of the Expansion Program."

———. 1982a. "Carajás Iron Ore Project." Staff Appraisal Report (July).

———. 1982b. "Report and Recommendation on Proposed Loan to Companhia Vale do Rio Doce for the Carajás Iron Ore Project."

Wormald, Avison. 1972. "Growth Promotion: The Creation of a Modern Steel Industry." In Stuart Holland, ed., *The State as Entrepreneur.* London: Weidenfeld & Nicolson.

Zartman, I. William. 1974. "The Study of Elite Circulation: Who's on First and What's He Doing There?" *Comparative Politics* 6, no. 3 (April): 465–88.

Index

331

PITT LATIN AMERICAN SERIES
Cole Blasier, Editor

OTHER NATIONAL STUDIES

Black Labor on a White Canal: Panama, 1904–1981
Michael L. Conniff

The Catholic Church and Politics in Nicaragua and Costa Rica
Philip J. Williams

The Origins of the Peruvian Labor Movement, 1883–1919
Peter Blanchard

The Overthrow of Allende and the Politics of Chile, 1964–1976
Paul E. Sigmund

Peru and the International Monetary Fund
Thomas Scheetz

Primary Medical Care in Chile: Accessibility Under Military Rule
Joseph L. Scarpaci

Rebirth of the Paraguayan Republic: The First Colorado Era, 1878–1904
Harris G. Warren

Restructuring Domination: Industrialists and the State in Ecuador
Catherine M. Conaghan

A Revolution Aborted: The Lessons of Grenada
Jorge Heine, Editor

SOCIAL SECURITY

Ascent to Bankruptcy: Financing Social Security in Latin America
Carmelo Mesa-Lago

The Politics of Social Security in Brazil
James M. Malloy

Social Security in Latin America: Pressure Groups, Stratification, and Inequality
Carmelo Mesa-Lago

OTHER STUDIES

Adventurers and Proletarians: The Story of Migrants in Latin America
Magnus Mörner, with the collaboration of Harold Sims

Authoritarianism and Corporatism in Latin America
James M. Malloy, Editor

Authoritarians and Democrats: Regime Transition in Latin America
James M. Malloy and Mitchell A. Seligson, Editors

The Catholic Church and Politics in Nicaragua and Costa Rica
Philip J. Williams

Female and Male in Latin America: Essays
Ann Pescatello, Editor

Latin American Debt and the Adjustment Crisis
Rosemary Thorp and Laurence Whitehead, Editors

Perspectives on the Agro-Export Economy in Central America
Wim Pelupessy, Editor

Public Policy in Latin America: A Comparative Survey
John W. Sloan

Selected Latin American One-Act Plays
Francesca Collecchia and Julio Matas, Editors and Translators

PITT SERIES IN POLICY AND INSTITUTIONAL STUDIES
Bert A. Rockman, Editor